McCOWN'S LAW
THE 100 GREATEST HOCKEY ARGUMENTS

BOB McCOWN

WITH DAVID NAYLOR

ANCHOR CANADA

Library and Archives Canada Cataloguing in Publication

McCown, Bob, 1952–
McCown's law : the 100 greatest hockey arguments / Bob McCown
with David Naylor.—Anchor Canada ed.

ISBN 978-0-385-66676-3

1. Hockey—Miscellanea. 2. National Hockey League—Miscellanea.
I. Naylor, David, 1967– II. Title.

GV847.M25 2008   796.962   C2008-902802-3

Cover photo: The Fan
Cover design: Terri Nimmo
Printed and bound in the USA

Published in Canada by
Anchor Canada, a division of
Random House of Canada Limited

Visit Random House of Canada Limited's website:
www.randomhouse.ca

BVG   10   9   8   7   6   5   4   3   2   1

To my family, who are the centre about which I revolve.
—Bob McCown

To my parents, whose support pursuing my dream is why
I can make a living writing and talking about sports.
—David Naylor

CONTENTS

FOREWORD

ANYONE WHO HAS HAD the privilege of playing the sidekick's role on "Prime Time Sports,"—Canada's longest running sports talk presentation—knows the scene all too well. Just seconds before air time, with the theme music already piping over the speakers, the host, Bob McCown, saunters his way into the studio, arriving not a moment earlier than necessary. He plunks down in his chair, pops on his sunglasses, puts on his head set, turns on the mike, and then spins out an argument on some issue of the day, a talking point that will keep the phones busy and keep the show humming until sign-off three hours later.

The more you work with Bob, the more you come to understand his particular genius. There are all kinds of loud-mouths in the talk show racket, all kinds of on-air bullies, but contrary to what some have suggested, Bob McCown isn't one of them. His long-lasting appeal isn't based only on his ability to hit the hot buttons, to entertain and occasionally enrage his listeners and viewers across Canada. It comes out of the fact that there's just about always compelling logic in what he's saying, a coherent, clearly presented position that at the very least makes you think. The fact that a day or a week or a month later, he might argue exactly the opposite point of view, that occasionally you can detect a wink and a smile behind the bombast, doesn't detract one lick from an art form he has mastered better than anyone else in North America.

Bob may have missed his calling in life. He would have made one heck of a lawyer. (Of course, he also tried to be a professional bowler for awhile—no kidding—so maybe that's two missed callings.) But as he would be only too happy to point out, he couldn't afford the pay cut, and the world of sport—always a little bit the same, but also always a little bit different day to day—offers him the perfect palette.

He's not a jock, bowling aside, and he doesn't think like a fan. He'd much rather talk to commissioners and general managers and coaches than athletes, and he's more intrigued by the big picture than who scored when and how and why. And always, there's something in the day's events that he can distill into a one sentence thesis—"This is true because of this and this, and if you don't understand that, you're a bonehead." Watch the phones lines light up. Listen to the great debate begin anew.

The truth is, though I like Bob very much (as I'm sure comes across on the show), he and I honestly disagree about a wide variety of topics in sports, and in the larger universe. We have had some terrific verbal brawls over the years, many of which kept right on going even while the audience was listening to commercials. I know he's dead wrong about all kinds of stuff (Listen, the NFL really is coming to Canada. . . .) But, as Bob happily noted the other day, several times in the recent past I have begun sentences with the phrase, "I can't believe I'm saying this, but I agree with you. . . ."

Perhaps like an old married couple, we are simply growing to resemble each other more and more, though the day I start wearing shades on air, please shoot me.

Bob is partnered here with David Naylor, a colleague from *The Globe and Mail* who I consider the best pure sports reporter in Canada. Dave's greatest professional joy is to come up with the counter-intuitive truth, to upset assumptions about how things work that turn out to be based on habit and faulty conventional wisdom and pure thin air. It's a perfect pairing—Bob the conspiracy theorist, the sceptic who is forever "arching a Spock-ian eyebrow," and Dave, the great debunker.

You're not going to like the answers to all of the big questions that follow. Some will surprise, some will anger, some you might simply dismiss. But just try and do any of the above without imagining the bar-room conversation, without wondering what they'd say about this or that on the Prime Time Roundtable.

See . . . he's got you hooked again.

Stephen Brunt
June 2007

1. Looking for an argument? Then let's talk hockey. Bob explains why hockey is the ultimate sport to disagree over.

TRY THIS EXPERIMENT the next time you watch a National Hockey League game.

Afterwards, listen to what they say about it on sports talk radio, to the opinions of your co-workers in the office the next day and to the views of the pundits on television or in the newspapers.

Chances are you're going to encounter more opinions than you can count. And you're going to think a good number of them are nonsense.

I mean, is there another sport where two fans can sit side by side, watching the exact same game, and then completely disagree about who played well, who didn't and why one team won and the other didn't?

No, there's not. Only in hockey is so much of what occurs in the eye of the beholder.

It's the same thing when fans talk about a particular team or a problem in the game and how they think it should be addressed. Everyone has a different solution, because everyone sees something different.

Heck, even the stakeholders in the National Hockey League can't agree about what goes on in the game. One week late in the 2006–07 season, you had the league's general managers voting to recommend an increase in the number of instigator penalties required for a suspension from three to five because the fighters need more room to do their jobs. Then, a few weeks later, the league's director of hockey operations, Colin Campbell, says it's time to look at taking fighting out of the game entirely.

And then the commissioner, Gary Bettman, comes out and disagrees with him!

Is it any wonder there is so little consensus in this sport?

Fans can't even agree on how hockey should be played. Just think for a moment how much time and energy is spent discussing ways to improve hockey. Sometimes it's the rules that must change, sometimes the officiating and at other times it's the equipment or something else. It makes you wonder how in the world a sport can have any fans when it's so imperfect that people are always trying to turn it into something else.

Football fans don't sit around debating whether a field goal should be worth three points or four. You won't hear baseball fans discussing whether a walk should be awarded after five balls or whether tie games should be settled with a home run contest. And the height of the rim in basketball is just fine where it is, thank you.

But in hockey, about the only thing everyone can agree on is that the game should be played on ice.

Part of hockey's charm is that so little of it can be captured in a boxscore.

In baseball, basketball or football you can look at a boxscore and get a pretty good idea of what happened. Get a more detailed summary of a game in any one of those sports and it becomes hard to argue over what took place.

But in hockey, there's no such thing. You hear coaches talk about chances, but what's a "chance"? Shots on goal are only one small measure of a team's effectiveness. And as for hits and some of the other garbage statistics the NHL has come up with, they're completely useless.

Sure, power-play and penalty-killing stats are helpful. And so are blocked shots. But beyond that, how do you statistically measure a hockey game?

Which is why you can pretty much argue anything you want in hockey. Who's to say you're wrong? The only thing you can be sure of is that someone is going to agree with you and someone is going to disagree.

And yet, hockey is enveloped by a culture that demands that everything be rationalized or explained.

Just consider what gets said to the media after a game. After a loss, players usually mumble something about "not skating" or "forgetting to keep their feet moving" or not "playing as a team" or "working hard"—which, frankly, could mean anything. And when they win, it's because they "got pucks on net" or "moved the puck real well" or "got some big saves" from the goaltender.

All of those things could pretty much describe any hockey game at any time, anywhere, at any level from peewee to the pros.

And it's hilarious the way fans react when their team loses a close game. You'd swear the players couldn't do anything right. And yet, when the same team wins a game by a one-goal margin, it's showered in platitudes.

So here's an experiment I'd love to perform sometime.

Let's take the tape of a five-year-old NHL game—any game—in which the score ended 3–1. Now, let's edit out the goals and leave all the rest, so that about 59 of the 60 minutes are there to watch.

Now show it to an audience of hockey fans and see if they can guess who won.

I bet they couldn't, because aside from the moments in which the goals are scored, an awful lot of hockey games are nothing but back-and-forth flow, the trading of chances and puck luck.

To have some fun, let's try the same experiment with a bunch of reporters. Then let's show them the stories they wrote about that exact game.

Most nights in hockey, both teams skate hard, check hard and go to the net. They both create traffic in front, are tough on the penalty kill and forecheck like mad. And one of them has a puck hit the post and bounce into the net. And the other hits a post and watches it bounce wide. On more nights than you'd believe, the difference is as simple as that.

You'd be hard pressed to find that analysis in the newspapers the next day or expressed by the many pundits who cover the sport. But it is the truth in far more hockey games than is ever acknowledged.

In fact, I would say that puck luck, as it is often called, decides roughly half of the close games in the National Hockey League. That's right: a bounce here, a deflection there, a puck that skids off a post and away from the net at one end of the rink, then catches the corner of the top shelf a few moments later.

Look, hockey isn't football. It's not the coaches who win individual hockey games—it's the players. Hockey is a game of flow, of action and reaction, far more than it is of programmed plays and tactics like post patterns and wheel routes. In hockey, nearly every play is a broken play. In fact, the game is kind of like one long broken play during which players must constantly adapt.

But we rarely acknowledge that, among all the skill and decision making, a good portion of what occurs isn't anyone's fault or the result of anyone's genius. It's just the spontaneous bounces of a frozen rubber disc on ice.

But that kind of analysis doesn't make for good copy. And if writers wrote the truth every time a game came down to dumb luck, we'd all tune out.

I know that the next time the Stanley Cup final is on, someone will be able to explain that the team emerging with a 2–1 win in Game 7 did so because of a speech the coach made back in September. Or because an assistant coach whispered an inspirational message to the goaltender after the second period, or because of a hit a defenceman made that sent a message to his teammates back in the first period.

Those types of things make for wonderful storylines. And, from my point of view, they're mostly a bunch of crap. No doubt someone reading this will disagree with me.

2.

For years, hockey persistently avoided assessing penalties with a game on the line. The league didn't want the officials to decide the outcome. Now the pendulum has swung to the other extreme. Bob weighs in on who's right and who's wrong.

HOCKEY IS THE ONLY SPORT in which, for years, officials had to keep more in mind than just what they saw happen in front of them when deciding whether to call a penalty.

They had to be aware of which team was winning and by what margin, and how much time was left to play. They also had to consider at what time of year the game was being played and how important it was to each team. And if it happened to be a playoff game . . . well, *then* there was a whole different set of standards.

Only by weighing all of those factors was it possible for a National Hockey League referee to make the right call.

All of which made the NHL pretty unique in the world

of professional sports. It may be inherently more difficult for an official in any sport to make a tough call in the dying seconds of a close game. But only in hockey were officials encouraged to alter the standards used to call a game, depending on the circumstances.

In football, the definition of holding or clipping has always been the same in the first quarter as the fourth. In basketball, a foul or goaltending is the same from tip-off to countdown. And no, the strike zone in baseball doesn't change when you get to extra innings. And a player is either called out or safe without the umpire glancing at the scoreboard.

But for some reason, in hockey, the expectation had always been that the referees should back off when a game was on the line and "let the players decide it."

Television commentators, led by Don Cherry, were the worst offenders when it came to encouraging this. When a penalty occurs late in a football game, you'll never hear the broadcasters criticize the official. You'll hear them come down on the player who committed the foul. It's "How could that guy block from behind on the runback?" Not, "How could the official call him for blocking from behind on the runback?" Same thing in basketball. Yet in hockey, when a player made a flagrant hook or slash with only a minute to play, somehow it was the official's fault if that guy gets sent to the box.

Thankfully, the National Hockey League has lately gotten off this archaic horse and, for once, is actually backing its officials for showing some balls. But it's pretty incredible to watch the league brag about its new, more consistent officiating standards when for years it was complicit in allowing officials to make themselves nearly invisible with a game on the line.

Of course, there are still those who don't like to see penalties called late in close games. There are those who insist that the game is only pure when you "let them play."

I've never understood exactly what "let them play" means.

I mean, it's an incomplete thought. What comes next? Let them play . . . and kill each other? Let them play . . . and do whatever they want? Let them play . . . until no one is standing? How far are you willing to go with this argument?

If letting the players decide a game is such a good idea, then why have any officials at all?

But the thing is, in addition to being stupid, the argument that when the refs put away their whistles late in the game the players decide the outcome is simply wrong anyway.

That way of thinking assumes that when a referee calls a hooking penalty early in scoreless game it doesn't affect the final result. But think about it. Let's say an official makes a call that leads to a power-play goal early on in a game that ends 1–0. How is that different than making the same call in a 4–4 game with three minutes remaining? Among the many flaws in the NHL's old way of thinking is the notion that only those penalties called during the late stages of the third period or overtime affect the outcome of a game.

In fact, *all* penalties, no matter when they are called, have the same potential to affect the final result.

I'm not sure what it was that finally made the NHL decide that enough was enough and to get in line with the way the rest of the sports world is officiated. But thank God it did. And here's hoping the whiners are never able to turn the clock back.

3. ■ It's the oldest hockey argument there is: does fighting belong in the National Hockey League? Bob says to find out, just look at what happens when the games matter most.

THE LONG-STANDING DEBATE about fighting in the National Hockey League is really two arguments. The first pertains to whether the NHL needs fighting to attract audiences in places where hockey isn't part of the culture. The second involves deciding whether fighting actually has a role in the game—that is, does it help teams win, and is having enforcers on the ice necessary to protect the so-called stars?

First, in terms of marketing, I think you have to recognize that fighting in hockey has shrunk to the point where, on many nights, there aren't any fights at all. In fact, you can sometimes go through an entire week of games for some teams without seeing a fight.

It's not like the old days of the Broad Street Bullies, when Philadelphia Flyer fans could go to the Spectrum knowing they were almost assured of seeing blood.

Nowadays, it would be pretty hard for an NHL team to market something—even subtly—that doesn't happen on a consitent basis for most teams. It's not like baseball, where, while there's no guarantee you'll see a home run, the chances are still pretty good.

I find it hard to believe that fans in non-traditional hockey markets these days are shelling out $70 or $80 a ticket on the off chance that someone might drop the gloves. I'm not saying the old-fashioned line brawls, the kind that had coaches sending players over the boards à la *Slap Shot*, didn't attract a certain element of the population. Of course they did. But those free-for-alls are almost extinct, to the degree that going to a game in the hope of seeing the benches clear makes about as much sense as buying a lottery ticket.

Which brings us to the part of the debate where logic can be hardest to come by.

The loudest argument for keeping fights in the game has to do with protecting the stars. There's this idea that if a player takes a liberty with the other team's star player, he'll have to deal with the fists of that team's toughest player. The thing is, that almost never happens. What you see is enforcers squaring off with other enforcers. How that actually acts as a deterrent to any player who's thinking of taking a cheap shot at a star player, I've never understood.

Late in the 2006–07 season, the Pittsburgh Penguins traded for Georges Laraque from Phoenix, supposedly to get some protection for Sidney Crosby. But how in the world does Laraque protect Crosby when he's hardly ever on the ice at the same time as the young star? He's never going to face the opposing players who are matched up against Crosby.

But all that aside, let's agree that any element of a sport that is fundamentally important—no matter what sport we're talking about—should be critical when the games matter most. By that logic, enforcers should certainly be out there protecting the stars when the playoffs roll around.

But that's simply not the case. In fact, the exact opposite seems to be true.

In 2005–06, Ottawa's Brian McGrattan led all NHL players with 19 fighting majors. The Senators were a team perceived to be in need of toughness at playoff time. And yet McGrattan never put on a jersey for any of Ottawa's 10 playoff games that year. Steve Ott of Dallas had 16 fights in 2005–06, but didn't perform that vitally important role in any of Dallas's playoff games that season. Anaheim's Todd Fedoruk, who had 15 fights during the regular season, did actually have two in the playoffs. But, predictably, they both involved going up against his mirror image on the Edmonton Oilers, Georges Laraque.

During the 82 playoff games played in 2005–06, there were just 14 fights. Once the first round was over, there were only five. And there were none in the Stanley Cup final.

In 2006–07, there were no fights in the second round of playoffs, one in the third and none in the Stanley Cup finals. That's right—one fight in seven series after the first round! Or expressed another way, one fight between April 21 and the final game of the Stanley Cup finals on June 6.

It's often argued that hockey fights are the natural outlet for aggression in an emotionally intense game. So tell me why, when the sport is at its peak of emotional intensity, are there almost no fights?

Now, I'm not saying that any of this is good or bad for hockey. I'm just asking: If fighting is such a critical part of hockey, if enforcers are needed to protect the stars and make space, what happens to all this logic at playoff time?

Maybe, just maybe, there is so little fighting in the playoffs because fighting *doesn't* help teams win. For example, of the teams that ranked in top half of the NHL in fighting majors during the 2005–06 season, just five made the playoffs. Of the teams that ranked in the bottom 15 for fights, 11 were playoff teams.

Much was made of the fact that Anaheim led the NHL in fights in 2006–07 and then went on to win the Stanley Cup. But the one thing the Ducks did during the regular season, but hardly at all during the playoffs, was fight. And which teams ranked behind the Ducks in this all-important category during the regular season? How about, in order, Phoenix, Edmonton, Los Angeles, St. Louis, Chicago, Nashville, Philadelphia, Washington and Columbus. That's right: of the nine teams that ranked second through 10th in fighting that season, eight of them didn't make the playoffs.

I know some fans think a fight is critical in an important game because it can lift a team emotionally. And that example is trotted out whenever a team goes on to win after one of its skill players drops the gloves, especially if it's someone like Calgary's Jarome Iginla.

The fact is that fans love to use this argument whenever their team goes on to win following a fight, but they ignore it whenever they lose. Take, for example, the first round of the 2007 playoffs, when Ottawa's Mike Comrie, not usually a fighter, fought Pittsburgh's Colby Armstrong in the second period of Game 2. Had Ottawa gone on to win that game, Comrie's fight would have been heralded as a turning point in the Senators' playoff history. But because they lost, it was never discussed.

If you want to suggest that a fight gives a team a necessary lift, you've got to recognize all the times it doesn't change anything. Which is most of the time.

All of which brings us to the simple question of how to minimize fights and eliminate goon tactics from hockey. The answer is to look at every other major sport. If you fight, you automatically get a game misconduct. Do it repeatedly and you will be suspended. And habitual offenders will be told to seek alternative employment.

Such measures would merely bring hockey into line with accepted behaviour in every other sport.

Fighting doesn't sell tickets. It doesn't win games. And it nearly vanishes from the National Hockey League each spring when the games matter most. So remind me again why we can't live without it?

4. Mark Messier has been knighted in hockey circles as the greatest leader in the history of hockey. Some say the greatest in all of sports. Bob says Messier's leadership skills are as overrated as they are legendary.

IN HIS PRIME, Mark Messier was a tremendous all-around hockey player.

He was fast. He could score. He was tough and he could intimidate teammates and foes alike with just a stare.

And he was a key part of an Edmonton Oiler dynasty that won five Stanley Cups in seven years.

But along the way, Messier also earned a different label, one that has stuck to him like glue: greatest leader in hockey history.

So accepted is the legend of Mark Messier's leadership that you rarely hear his name mentioned without a tribute to it being made in the same breath. It has become so engrained in the hockey psyche that you'd think this guy transformed losing teams into winners merely by stepping into the dressing room and giving them his patented stare. So I can't say I was surprised when the NHL announced during the 2006–07 season that it had come up with the Mark Messier Leadership Award, bestowed monthly and at season's end on the player who displays the greatest leadership skills. None other than Messier himself is among those who pick the winners.

It's almost as if people who wanted to mention Gretzky and Messier in the same sentence needed something to pull Messier up to Gretzky's level. And so the answer became his supposedly awesome leadership skills.

But let's examine this legend more closely.

The Messier leadership myth was really born during the 1994 Stanley Cup playoffs, when he helped lead the New York Rangers to their first championship in 54 years.

Heading into Game 6 of the Eastern Conference final that season, with the Rangers down 3–2 in the series, Messier "guaranteed" a series victory over the New Jersey Devils.

He then went out and seized the moment by scoring a natural hat trick during the third period to lead New York to a 3–2 win. The Rangers went on to win Game 7 against the Devils and then take out the Vancouver Canucks in seven games during the Stanley Cup final, with Messier scoring the Cup-clinching goal. And the image of Messier holding the Cup at the end of that run has come to define his career more than any other.

Now, I have to admit, that's a pretty dramatic series of events. But let's put Messier's guarantee during those playoffs into a bit of perspective.

It was not Joe Willie Namath guaranteeing a victory over

the Baltimore Colts, the 18-point favourites, leading up to Super Bowl III.

It was nothing like Muhammad Ali guaranteeing he would defeat Sonny Liston.

It was a case of the captain of a team that had finished the season with the NHL's best record guaranteeing a win over a team that had finished six points behind it in the standings.

And since Game 6 was being played in New Jersey, there was plenty of support in the stands for the "visiting" team that night. So it's not as if the Rangers were in completely hostile territory for this supposedly historic comeback.

Guarantees in sports should be revered only when they predict an upset. The fact that the Rangers won that series hardly came as a shocker, despite their being down 3–2 in the series. And frankly, had New York not won that series, it would have gone down as a huge disappointment for Ranger fans.

But from that moment onward, it didn't seem to matter what Mark Messier did. In fact, given the aura that surrounds him, you'd think he put the Cup down and retired that night in 1994. But he didn't. He kept playing. And during the next 10 years of his career, his supposedly magical leadership abilities added up to zilch.

So let's look at the legend of Mark Messier this way: Was there a hockey player who played on more underachieving teams from 1994 until the lockout than Number 11 did? If there was, I can't think of him.

Messier played three seasons with New York after the Stanley Cup year. The Rangers got past the first round of the playoffs just once.

Then he left via free agency for Vancouver, where he replaced Trevor Linden as the Canucks' captain.

The year before Messier got there, Vancouver had reached the playoffs with 79 points. In the three seasons he was there, they finished with 77, 64 and 58 points, moving backwards each season and missing the playoffs in all three.

Messier then returned to New York to reunite with Wayne Gretzky, where he made another guarantee, one that seems to have been buried by history.

At the news conference announcing his return to the team, Messier guaranteed the Rangers would return to the playoffs that season.

Alas, they didn't. Not that season, or the next one or the next one or the one after that.

Seems like a pretty disappointing performance for a team that spent more money on players than any other in the National Hockey League, adding such players as Eric Lindros, Jaromir Jagr, Pavel Bure and Alexei Kovalev along the way.

In my book, leadership in hockey is defined as the ability of a player to help a team become more than the sum of its parts.

And yet, Messier's Rangers were the ultimate example of a team that functioned as far less than the sum of its parts during that span.

The Rangers unloaded coaches, general managers and lots of players amid all the losing. But no one ever seemed to point a finger at the greatest leader in the history of sports. Ever. Even though, in leading Vancouver to finish out of the playoffs three years in a row and the Rangers for four more, Messier earned roughly $36 million.

Messier is a surefire Hall of Famer who deserves recognition for the things he accomplished. But let's all agree that the list of great leaders who went seven consecutive years without reaching the playoffs on teams packed with talent is a pretty short one.

5. ■ **The captain of a hockey team is supposed to be a shining example of character, experience and leadership. Bob says teams should remember that when it's time to pin the "C" on a guy's sweater.**

NO SPORT REVERES its captains the way hockey does.

In sports like baseball or football, fans don't even know who the captain or captains of a particular team are. But step on the ice with a "C" on your sweater and all the world knows it's your team.

Now, while captains are often the most talented players on their teams, that shouldn't be why they get the job.

Legitimate captains are guys who symbolize the character and heart of a hockey team. Captains are players who've been around, seen it all and lived to tell about it. They're the ones who can stand up in the dressing room, say what has to be said and be believed because they've been there. And they can lead by example, either by what they do on the ice or off it.

And most importantly, they're players who bring a team-first attitude to the rink with them every day.

When I think of great captains, I think of Jean Beliveau. Beliveau was an exceptional talent, sure, but he was also the consummate team player, both in the way he played the game and in how he carried himself around it. By the time he was made Montreal's captain, he was entering his ninth NHL season and had already played on five Stanley Cup–winning teams.

Similarly, Gordie Howe was in his 13th NHL season before Detroit made him captain.

But there are too many instances of teams selling out the captaincy by handing it to young players with a lot of skill but not much life experience. It's almost as if teams are counting down the days until they can make their young star the poster boy for the franchise by handing him the "C."

You look at the Canadiens of the 1970s and '80s. Their captains were Henri Richard, Yvan Cournoyer, Serge Savard and Bob Gainey. If those Canadiens were around today, there'd be a race to stick the "C" on Guy Lafleur's jersey halfway through his first good season.

This scenario was played out by the Tampa Bay Lightning and Vincent Lecavalier. Back in 1999–2000, the Lightning was a horrible team. And so, with his team floundering that year, what did head coach Steve Ludzik do? He made 19-year-old Lecavalier—a player halfway through his second NHL season, a guy whose peers were still playing junior hockey—the captain. Not only was Lecavalier not ready to be a leader at the NHL level, but being captain turned him into a whiner who was actually benched for entire periods of some games. How's that for leadership?

It may have been John Tortorella's most courageous act as head coach when, in October of 2001, he took the "C" off Lecavalier's sweater.

"You don't name a player captain based on the talent they possess," Tortorella said, explaining the move. "That's not what [being the] captain is about. [The "C"] was taken away so Vinny could see what leadership is all about. There are plenty of guys around here to show him."

One of those proved to be Dave Andreychuk, who replaced Lecavalier as captain and led the team to its Stanley Cup win in 2004.

But the most ridiculous example of NHL captaincy isn't Lecavalier. It's Alexei Yashin, one of hockey's most selfish, aloof players of all time. Incredibly, he has been captain of not one, but *two* NHL teams.

The Ottawa Senators were the first to commit this blunder, in the hope of appeasing a player whom teammates didn't like and whose personality is as sweet as an unripe grapefruit. The New York Islanders traded for him, handed him a $90 million contract and then sat back in disappointment while Yashin loafed through the next three seasons as his production fell steadily each year. So what did they do? They made him their captain.

In most cases, however, it's simply a case of teams mistaking talent for experience.

Paul Kariya was a great young player during his first two years with Anaheim. But the Ducks knew they needed to keep him happy for upcoming contract negotiations. So at the start of his third season, he was the captain.

There have been plenty of debates about Eric Lindros, about what he is and what he isn't. But there was nothing in Lindros's career or the way he handled himself to suggest he was a team-first kind of guy. Eric Lindros was a great hockey player who has always been in the business of Eric Lindros. That's okay. But don't make him the captain, which is exactly what Philadelphia did in Lindros's third season. Several years later, that mistake was repeated when Philadelphia general manager Bob Clarke, acting on behalf of the Canadian Olympic team, made Lindros captain for the 1998 Games in Japan. That team finished fourth.

Pittsburgh's Sidney Crosby played exactly half an NHL season, at age 18, before Penguins coach Michel Therrien stuck an "A" on his jersey. At the time, Crosby was already losing favour in his dressing room for his crybaby antics with the referees. Given that he'd been coddled as a hockey prodigy since the age of 10, given that adversity or failure were things he'd never experienced, what exactly did Sidney Crosby know about life?

Therrien resisted the temptation to make Crosby the captain leading up to the 2006–07 season, deciding to go with three alternate captains instead. Then reporters rushed out and asked Crosby if he was okay with *that*.

By having no official captain, the Penguins found a way to put Crosby into that role without having to take the criticism for it. And then at the end of the 2006–07 season, with Crosby still just 19, they went ahead and did it.

The situation was similar in Washington, where the Capitals were sizing up 20-year-old Alexander Ovechkin for the captaincy before the 2006–07 season. Never mind that Ovechkin still has a lot of trouble with the English language. This was a guy with exactly one year of experience on an awful NHL team. What was he going to teach his teammates?

But let's give Ovechkin some credit—the kid had the good sense to take himself out of the running for the "C" before the Caps could give it to him. They ended up doing the sensible thing, handing it to Chris Clark, a 30-year-old veteran who'd hit the 20-goal mark only once in his career.

Now, there are exceptions to the rule that making young stars into captains is a bad idea. Sometimes it works out. The Red Wings gave the "C" to Steve Yzerman when he was 21, and while that was probably eight years too early, he certainly grew into the role. But on too many teams, the captain isn't the guy the players can rally around. He's the guy the team wants to keep happy for when the time comes to negotiate his next contract.

6. **The Memorial Cup features some of the most entertaining hockey played each spring. But hardly anyone outside of the rink sees it or remembers who played. Bob says there has to be a better way to showcase the Canadian hockey league's premier event.**

JUNIOR HOCKEY IS ONE of the truly great entertainment bargains out there. Walk into any rink across this country and you're sure to see two teams giving it their all, no matter what time of year it happens to be and no matter what the score is.

And since the Canadian Hockey League continues to be the biggest supply chain of National Hockey League players, major junior hockey has more than its share of star power as well.

So, given all of that, and given that this is Canada, where we're supposed to be mad about all things hockey, how come no one watches junior hockey's championship, the Memorial Cup?

Now, I guess lots of people watch it in whatever city it happens to be held in. But to the average hockey fan in Canada it's a non-event. In fact, try this experiment the next time you're out with a bunch of friends talking hockey: ask them who won the last Memorial Cup. Chances are you'll be faced with a lot of blank stares.

So why is major junior hockey's premier event such a dud?

Well, the first reason is the format, which features the winners of the Ontario, Quebec and Western leagues, plus a host team, in a round-robin format. Two things stink here. The first is the concept of a host team, which suggests to everyone concerned that this event is Mickey Mouse. If you can't earn your way into a championship event, you shouldn't be there at all.

And the host-team concept has led to some ridiculous circumstances. In 1999, the Ottawa 67's lost in the Ontario Hockey League playoffs to the Belleville Bulls, who then went on to earn a berth in the Memorial Cup by winning the OHL title. But because the 67's were the host team, they got to go on to the Memorial Cup after having six weeks off. Refreshed and healthy, they defeated the Bulls at the Memorial Cup tournament en route to winning it all. How stupid is *that*? About as stupid as what happened the next year, when another host team, the Halifax Mooseheads, lost out in the Quebec league playoffs, then fired its coach and came back to the Memorial Cup with a new one. Thankfully, they still didn't win anything.

Junior hockey should find a way—any way—to have four teams earn their way into the tournament and get rid of the free pass for the host team.

Then they should dump the round-robin format, which draws the event out over nine days. Right now the tournament starts on a Saturday in late May but doesn't finish until the following Sunday, all the while going up against the Stanley Cup playoffs. Is it really any wonder that no one watches this thing?

Of course, all the Canadian Hockey League cares about is selling tickets in the host city for nine dates. But by doing so, it sells this championship short of ever becoming a true marquee hockey event.

The best idea I've heard for revamping the Memorial Cup comes from Bobby Brett, the owner of the Western Hockey League's Spokane Chiefs, who also happens to be the brother of a Hall-of-Fame third baseman for the Kansas City Royals.

Brett suggests getting rid of the host team and dumping the round-robin tournament. Instead, he suggests scheduling two semifinal games on one night, followed by a championship game on another, much like NCAA basketball's Final Four. And that's it. No more fuss.

This way, fans would have a chance to take in the entire championship by investing just a couple of nights. And people from around the country could actually attend it without having to use up a week's vacation.

And here's where the NHL could take a lesson from the way the National Football League and college football work together when it comes to scheduling. The NHL should give its playoff schedule a rest for one Friday night and one Monday night at the end of May, when the Memorial Cup plays its semifinals and final. That way the Memorial Cup could have the stage to itself, with the eyes of all the hockey world watching.

You get a sense of what the Memorial Cup could be when you consider the disparity between the television audience for the tournament in 2004 and the number of viewers in 2005. In '04, the Memorial Cup final drew an audience of 238,000, which was actually up significantly from the year before. But in '05, when the NHL was shut down because of the lockout, the final drew 825,000 viewers. Part of that was because of Sidney Crosby's presence. And part of it was the lack of hockey on television elsewhere all year. But with an audience that peaked at over a million viewers, it should be easy to see the potential this event would have with a different format, a better schedule and some cross-promotion and co-operation from the NHL.

Of course, this idea would entail the Canadian Hockey League taking a hit in the pocketbook over the short term in order to build something more valuable for the future. Which is why the league will never go for it.

But if it did, within a few years the tournament would be incredible. And the Stanley Cup wouldn't be the only trophy people actually remember being handed out each spring.

7

The National Hockey League season is akin to a marathon, not just for players, but for fans as well. Bob says that in a perfect world, the Stanley Cup final wouldn't be played in June.

ONE OF THE PROBLEMS with all professional team sports is that seasons keep getting longer.

The Super Bowl is now played each year in February. The Grey Cup is still in November, but Canadian Football League training camps open in May. Baseball plays its World Series when the snow is already flying in much of the Northeast. And even the NBA has resorted to four rounds of seven-game series to determine a champion in mid-June.

But no sport strings out its season like the National Hockey League, with training camps that open just after Labour Day and a Stanley Cup final that pushes into mid-June.

Granted, 2006 was an Olympic year, which pushed the Stanley Cup final back to one of the latest dates ever. But it's still ridiculous for there to be only 87 days between the handing out of the Stanley Cup and the official opening of training camp for the 2006–07 season.

I think most fans would agree that by the middle of March, they're ready for the regular season to end. Just as they'd be happy to see the Stanley Cup hoisted before the end of May.

Which is what used to happen before the NHL trod into June for the first time in 1992. Here's a historical reminder of when the Stanley Cup used to be hoisted:

1991	May 25
1984	May 19
1977	May 14
1970	May 10
1967	May 2

Of course, once the NHL's economics got out of control during the 1990s, there was no way owners were going to give up short-term revenue gains for the long-term good of the game. They couldn't. But I believe the league missed an opportunity during the lockout to sit down with the players and say, "Look, none of this is good for the game. We're playing too much damn hockey."

Reducing the schedule by 10 games per team would

knock about three weeks off the regular season. In a normal year, that would allow the regular season to end around the 20th of March and have the Stanley Cup final over with by mid- to late May. Or, if the league simply wanted to give its players more down time during the season, it could shorten the schedule by just two weeks and still avoid the June swoon.

Granted, cutting nearly 12 percent off the schedule would not have been an easy sell during the lockout negotiations. But there would have been multiple benefits to such a move, and maybe not as much downside as people think.

First of all, cutting back the schedule by 12 percent wouldn't mean cutting revenues by the same margin. In the first place, not all revenues are derived from tickets sold. And secondly, in a lot of cities where NHL attendance is weak (which is a lot these days), cutting the five worst home dates off the schedule wouldn't hurt much at the turnstiles anyway. Fans in a city like Atlanta, who are going to go to three or four games a year, will do so no matter how many there are. Whether you add 10 games to the schedule or cut 10 games, it's not as if that fan is going to go to any more games or any fewer.

On the plus side, a shorter schedule would reduce the enormous wear and tear the players are subjected to. Between international tournaments and long playoff runs, the best players in the game are being worn into the ground. Which can't be good for the lengths of careers.

So, while there may be some short-term economic pain for the players, you'd hope they could see that there was something in it for them as well. Not to mention that the product would benefit from players being better rested. Fewer games overall would also mean more games that matter.

The most powerful and successful sports league in the world plays a 16-game schedule in a season that lasts six months from the start of training camp to the Super Bowl.

Meanwhile, even in Canada, the length of the hockey season creates a fatigue factor among fans each spring. Which is why hockey is the one sport with more buzz around the opening round of the playoffs than the finals.

It shouldn't be that way.

The NHL needs to learn that sometimes less means more.

8 ■ **The NHL All-Star Game has used every format imaginable over the past 60 years to try to give it some legitimacy. Bob wonders if there's a way to make the midseason game a classic.**

NOPE. NEXT CHAPTER.

(I mean, since nothing has worked to motivate the NHL all-stars to try to win this game, why not get a sponsor to put up $5 million in cash for the victorious team. Have the money sitting right there in the penalty box—then watch what happens when there's a loose puck in the corner. You got a better idea?)

9 ■ **Goaltending is supposed to be the most important ingredient to a Stanley Cup contender. Bob explains why teams are so hesitant to spend their top draft picks trying to find the next Patrick Roy.**

IN 1997, the New York Islanders made Roberto Luongo the highest pick ever for a goaltender in the National Hockey League entry draft. Selecting fourth overall, the Islanders took the talented Montreal native, who displayed all the attributes you'd want in a future NHL netminder. And he turned out to be exactly what the scouts projected him to be. But if Islander general manager Mike Milbury was smart enough to spend his first pick on the NHL's next great puck stopper (that is, until he later traded him to Florida), how come other general managers are so hesitant to do so?

Think about it. Quarterbacks are the most important position in football, so every year a handful are taken near the top the National Football League draft. But in hockey, most teams don't want to spend their top pick on the game's most important position.

So, how come? Well, because while the NHL entry draft may be a crapshoot at any position, it's especially so in goal. Between 1992 and 2001, twenty-four goaltenders were selected as first-round picks. Of those, only nine had managed to play at least 100 National Hockey League games by the end of the 2005–06 season. Meanwhile, 11 of them had played fewer than 20 NHL games. Which is to say, they didn't make it.

While there's no guarantee that any first-round pick will play in the NHL, for barely 50 percent of the goalies to attain semi-regular playing time at any point in their careers—that's a pretty lousy batting average.

Of the nine who managed to play in more than 100 NHL games, only Luongo could be considered a star. At the start of the 2006–07 season, just five—Rick DiPietro, Dan Cloutier, Pascal Leclaire, Marc Denis and Luongo—had No. 1 jobs.

Considering that we're talking about 24 first-round picks, players whom scouts would have deemed to be surefire NHL goaltenders, you'd think that more than one of them would be able to crack the NHL's elite. DiPietro may be on his way to that level, but he's not there yet.

As a study of NHL goaltenders demonstrates, some of the best netminders come from well back in the draft, including Ryan Miller (fifth round), Henrik Lundqvist (seventh round), Miikka Kiprusoff (fifth round), Marty Turco (fifth round), Tomas Vokoun (ninth round) and Nikolai Khabibulin (ninth round). In fact, at the start of the 2006–07 season, there were more No. 1 goaltenders who were picked in the fifth round or later (14) than there were in the first (11).

And consider that by the end of that season, the NHL's leader in goals-against average and save percentage was Niklas Backstrom, a 29-year-old rookie who'd never even been drafted.

The challenge with goalies is that even some of the best still take four or five years to develop into NHL players. So when you're looking at an 18-year-old kid, you've got to try and project what he's going to be like when he's 22 or 23. With most forwards or defencemen, you've only got to project what a player will be like by 20 or 21, because that's when you realistically expect them to be in the NHL.

Most general managers I know are in the business of trying to keep their jobs. Using a top pick to select a player who may be years away from having an impact isn't a very good way to achieve that goal. You may make the right pick, but by the time it bears fruit, there's someone else in your chair reaping the rewards.

So, if I'm a GM and my turn comes in the first round, I'm taking a forward or defenceman every time. Because the draft is like gambling. And in gambling, you always want to play the percentages.

10. Hockey players have the means to protect themselves from most eye injuries. But too many players still won't wear visors. Bob says this is one area where the players need some parenting.

DURING THE FIRST ROUND of the 2005–06 Stanley Cup playoffs between Montreal and Carolina, Canadiens defenceman Sheldon Souray opened up on why he and a lot of other National Hockey League players still refuse to wear visors.

It has nothing to do with comfort. And it isn't a matter of players not being able to see properly when they go out on the ice. Souray conceded that the reason players like him don't wear visors is that it would raise too many questions about their toughness. Souray, considered by many to be one of the most candid and honest hockey players out there, went on to say he would welcome the introduction of mandatory visors in the NHL, in part because it would take the pressure off of players not to wear them.

"If they imposed the rule, I wouldn't be against it," Souray said. "It's still primarily a macho thing. I think any guy who plays a physical style would say the same thing. It doesn't really make sense."

Hockey has always been a sport where establishing one's toughness is important. For example, you have to believe that a lot of NHL players would love to see fighting abolished from the sport. But try to find one who'll say that on the record.

The same is true of visors. Even though many players believe that protecting their eyes is more important than looking tough, there are others who feel it's still too much of a hit to their reputation.

Sean Avery, as a member of the Los Angeles Kings in 2005–06, reminded us that visors are still closely associated with sissies when he referred to "French guys in our league with a visor on, running around and playing tough and not backing anything up."

All the same, more players than ever have come around on the visor issue. In 2005–06, a *Hockey News* survey found that 38 percent of players wore visors, up from 24 percent five years earlier.

Some of that has to be attributable to the fact that many high-profile NHL players, including Steve Yzerman, Bryan Berard, Al MacInnis and Mats Sundin, have suffered eye injuries.

But what's most amazing is that this generation of players who still rebel against visors all grew up wearing facial protection. There hasn't been a player entering the NHL in years who didn't grow up looking through a shield or cage of some kind. At the next tier, U.S. college hockey introduced full face shields during the late 1970s. In major junior hockey, visors have been required since the mid-1980s. And during the 2006–07 season, the American Hockey League introduced the mandatory wearing of visors for the very first time.

So, how is it possible that a player who has played his entire life with facial protection suddenly can't deal with it when he reaches the NHL? Look, Steve Yzerman never wore a visor during his first 21 years in the NHL before suffering a close call with his eye during the 2004 playoffs.

From that point onward, Yzerman wore a visor and claimed to have no trouble adjusting. So if Steve Yzerman, at age 39, can adjust to a visor, how is it that some 20-year-old kid who's worn one all his life can't play with one in the NHL?

Hockey is the only sport I'm aware of where, when players reach the highest level, when the speed and the dangers make the risks more serious, they remove equipment. Which makes about as much sense as stepping into the batter's box against a pitcher throwing 100 miles per hour and deciding it's time to shed the batting helmet.

"In any other situation, employers are obligated by law to protect their workers," Toronto Maple Leaf ophthalmologist Robert Devenyi told *The Globe and Mail* in the spring of 2006. "What's the difference between a guy on an assembly line whacking a piece of metal and a hockey player?"

None, really. Except that the guy whacking the piece of metal isn't given the choice of putting himself at risk. And if hockey players weren't so afraid of what their peers would think, they'd stop making that choice.

11. **Want to get your kid to the NHL? Better not let him slip behind the neighbour's kid. If little Billy next door is spending his summers in a rink, then your kid had better do the same. Bob puts the heat on the summer hockey craze.**

DURING HIS YEARS as president of the Canadian Hockey Association, Murray Costello would often be prodded by journalists reminding him that hockey was no longer the most popular participation sport for Canadian youth. That distinction, he was told, belonged to soccer.

Costello's reaction provided a bit of insight into the breadth of the man. Instead of trying to rationalize this trend, or defend what some might perceive as a negative for minor hockey, Murray Costello had a different take.

"Good," he'd say. "And I hope that as many of those young soccer players as possible are hockey players getting away from the game for a while."

Costello was getting at what he considered to be a disturbing trend. The 12-month hockey season, he believed, was leading parents to take their kids out of sports such as soccer, baseball and lacrosse in favour of more time in the rink.

There were lots of things Costello didn't like about summer hockey. One of them is the fact that it's not officially recognized by Hockey Canada, and therefore not regulated.

But his biggest problem was his suspicion that kids aren't being enrolled in summer hockey so much for fun as to ensure that they don't lose ground in the competition to become a National Hockey League player.

And I think he had a point.

First of all, if a kid can't reach his potential playing hockey from mid-September until May, I have my doubts that filling in what little off-season still exists will make the difference.

And then there's the danger of burnout. Part of being a kid is that you get to experience as much of kid life as you can. We're all going to reach a point in our lives when it's time to focus on one thing, be it athletic, academic or otherwise. To suggest to a 10-year-old kid that he shouldn't bother with baseball or lacrosse or soccer because of the need to pursue professional hockey is ridiculous. But you know that's exactly what's happening. And yet we wonder why so many youngsters quit the game at 11, 12 or 13 years of age.

What parents need is a little reminder of the odds their children face against making it to the National Hockey League. Which is why the study called "Straight Facts about Making It in Pro Hockey" by Jim Percels should be required reading for all of them.

Percels studied players in the birth year of 1975 to try to get a handle on what percentage of young players who lace on the skates will actually play in the NHL—and how many will make a living at it. Parcels found that there were approximately 30,000 young boys born in 1975 who entered Ontario's minor hockey system. Of those 30,000, just 232 were eventually drafted by an Ontario Hockey League team in their mid-teens, the first major cutoff for players hoping to stream towards the NHL. Less than half of those players, 105, actually played in an OHL game. Another 42 played in the top tier of U.S. college, which is another viable route to the NHL.

Overall, just 47 wound up with NHL contracts after being drafted in 1993 or 1994, or signing later as free agents.

By April of 2002, only 32 had actually played in an NHL game, and only 15 had more than one NHL season under their belts. At that time, only 21 were still on active NHL rosters and just six had met the NHL's minimum standard of 400 league games for inclusion in the pension program. Of those, only two—Jason Allison and Todd Bertuzzi—could be considered household names.

The point is not to diminish a child's dreams. But let's let kids be kids. Let them be out in the sunshine on a summer's day. Let them learn to hit a line drive in baseball or kick a winning soccer goal or learn what it's like to score with a bounce shot in lacrosse.

Hockey is a great game for kids. But the overwhelming number will never make a living at it. And what is surely best for all of them is to get away from it for at least part of the year.

12. Picking early in the entry draft is easy. The real skill comes on day two, when no one is watching and late rounds are being filled out with longshots. Bob has an all-star team of players who were never supposed to make it.

NHL DRAFT DAY is as much about crushing dreams as it is about fulfilling them. Sure, on television we get to see the next generation of household names hit the stage, pull on the jersey and sport the hat, all with Mom and Dad standing by, beaming wide smiles.

What we don't see are the dashed hopes of those whose names are called long after the party has died down and the signing bonuses have been trimmed to nothing. Later still, there are those who never hear their names at all.

There are plenty of examples, however, of players who've proven the scouts wrong and come from the back of the pack to have tremendous National Hockey League careers.

So, what would an all-star team of low-drafted NHL players look like? Here's one that takes into consideration how far off the radar a player came from and how great a career he wound up having.

FIRST LINE

Brett Hull, RW. Not drafted when eligible in 1982 or '83, Hull was the 117th player taken in the '84 draft as a 20-year-old, coming off a 105-goal season in the British Columbia Junior Hockey League. This afterthought finished his NHL career with 741 goals, good enough for third all-time.

Doug Gilmour, C. Not drafted when eligible in 1981, Gilmour was the 134th player taken in the 1982 draft. A game-breaker who could carry a team on his back, Gilmour played in 1,474 games and scored 450 goals.

Luc Robitaille, LW. Selected 171st in 1984, Robitaille retired as the highest-scoring left winger in history with 668 goals.

SECOND LINE

Daniel Alfredsson, RW. Mr. Everything for the Ottawa Senators was picked 133rd in 1994 at age 21. Calder Trophy winner in 1995–96 has hit at least 20 goals in eight seasons.

Steve Larmer, C. The 120th pick of the 1980 draft, he scored 40 or more goals five times. Scored the Canada Cup tournament winner versus the U.S. in 1991, while leading Team Canada with six goals.

Kevin Stevens, LW. Picked 108th in 1983, Stevens won two Cups with Pittsburgh and twice hit the 50-goal mark.

THIRD LINE

Petr Bondra, RW. Selected 156th by Washington in 1990. A member of the 500-goal club, he twice hit 50 during the mid-1990s.

Igor Larionov, C. Selected 214th by Vancouver in 1985, he played 941 NHL games and won three Cups with Detroit. Centred the famous KLM Line between Vladimir Krutov and Sergei Markarov with Moscow Central Red Army, where he was a five-time all-star. A good gamble by the Canucks in the days before Russians were free to join NHL clubs.

Brian Savage, LW. Four-time 20-goal scorer was picked 171st in 1991. Would have been even better had injuries not hampered him throughout his entire career.

FOURTH LINE

Theoren Fleury, RW. Undrafted in 1986, Fleury was taken by Calgary 166th overall in the 1987 draft. Standing just five-foot-six didn't stop him from scoring 455 goals.

Ray Ferraro, C. Selected 88th in 1982, Ferraro played 18 NHL seasons, scoring at least 20 goals in 12 of them en route to the 400-goal club.

Miroslav Satan, LW. A natural scorer taken 111th by Edmonton in 1993, Satan had 18 goals as an Oiler rookie before breaking the 20-goal barrier in 10 consecutive seasons with Buffalo and the New York Islanders.

DEFENCE

Tommy Albelin. The 152nd pick of 1983 played on two Stanley Cup winners with New Jersey.

Gary Suter. The 180th pick in 1984 played 1,145 games. Easily the American defenceman most loathed by fans in Canada, he beat out Wendel Clark for the Calder, knocked Wayne Gretzky out of the Canada Cup with a hit from behind and kept Paul Kariya out of the 1998 Olympics with a cross-check to the face.

Don Sweeney. Sixteen NHL seasons for the 166th pick of 1984.

Bret Hedican. Picked 198th in 1988; played in three Stanley Cup finals.

Igor Ulanov. Stay-at-home defenceman was the 203rd pick of 1991.

Tomas Kaberle. Fantastic puck skills are the calling card of the 204th pick of 1996. The only Leaf invited to the 2007 All-Star Game.

GOALTENDERS

Dominik Hasek. Six Vezina Trophies for the 199th pick of 1983.

Nikolai Khabibulin. The 204th pick in 1992 led Tampa to the 2004 Stanley Cup.

ALL-TIME UNDRAFTED TEAM

Adam Oates, C: 19-year NHL career; 1,079 assists.

Dino Ciccarelli, RW: 1,200 points.

Geoff Courtnall, LW: 1,049 NHL games.

Bryan Rafalski, D: mainstay of two Stanley Cup teams in New Jersey.

Dan Boyle, D: top defenceman on Tampa's Cup winner in 2004.

Ed Belfour, G: won Calder Trophy and two Vezinas.

13.

What's the value of a first-round pick in the National Hockey League? Not much if you don't pick the right player. Bob says the draft—and the game—would be much better off if it didn't involve 18-year-olds.

I LOVE THE DRAMA of the first few picks in the National Hockey League draft.

Usually, you know who the first four or five picks are going to be. It's just the order that's a mystery. And because most of the top half-dozen selections will play in the National Hockey League within a year or two, you can often project where they're going to fit in on the team that takes them.

But *after* the first few picks, the draft loses me very quickly. Once you get past the first handful of prospects, it's hard to say when—or if—you'll see any of these players again. Which is probably unavoidable when teams are drafting players who are still in the late stages of adolescence and whose potential as pros is extremely tough to project.

Here's a list of the number of first-round picks, for each draft of the 1990s, who played fewer than 150 NHL games:

1990	4
1991	5
1992	10
1993	4
1994	10
1995	8
1996	11
1997	12
1998	7
1999	16

Remember, these were first-round picks—the cream of the crop. These players were evaluated and measured and scouted by dozens of professional hockey men. And yet 87 of them failed to become NHL regulars for any length of time. Among those 87, there were 23 who played fewer than 25 NHL games, and 21 who never played at all.

At the same time, you have all kinds of good players, who come from way down in the draft, whom the scouts seemed to miss completely. Players such as Doug Gilmour, who scored 450 goals in 1,474 NHL games, but was the 134th player taken in the 1982 draft. That year, 45 players who never played a game in the NHL were taken before Gilmour. It makes you wonder how all of those scouts and GMs could have been so ridiculously wrong.

Well, here's one reason: it's tough to know how most teenage hockey players are going to turn out, either physically or mentally. Which is why it would make complete sense to move the NHL draft age up to at least 19 instead of the current 18 (so long as the kid's birthday is before mid-September).

The junior teams would love it, since they'd get an extra year to market and build around their best players. And really, what would the NHL lose? In most years, there are one or two 18-year-old players good enough to play in the NHL in some capacity right away. There are, of course, the exceptions, like Sidney Crosby or even Jordan Staal, who proved remarkably adept at 18 during the 2006–07 season. But how many players are there who are too good for junior at age 18? Out of the last 20 years I can think of only two: Crosby and Eric Lindros, who wound up sitting out that season anyway, waiting for his trade from Quebec to Philadelphia.

The fact is that the overwhelming majority of even the best 18-year-old players are better off playing junior. And yet teams can't help themselves, so they promote so many of the top prospects before they're ready.

Did Joe Thornton or Vincent Lecavalier absolutely have to be in the NHL at age 18? Of course not. And certainly players like Manny Malhotra or Alexandre Daigle had no business being in the NHL at that age.

The problem is that teams are seduced by what players do during training camp, or during the first 10 games of a regular season. But that's not a realistic way to make an assessment of whether a guy is ready for the NHL. Most 18-year-olds lack the physical and mental maturity needed to endure the grind of an NHL season. Think back for a moment to what you were like at 18. Were you ready to live and work in an adult environment, handle the kinds of pressures that go with making a lot of money and being in the public eye, sustain the ups and downs of trying to make it in an ultra-competitive field? Probably not. Well, hockey players are no different.

Instituting a 19-year-old draft would save teams from the pressure to keep 18-year-olds in the NHL when they shouldn't be there. And, as a bonus, delaying entry into the NHL also postpones the onset of unrestricted free agency. That means teams would get one more year of a player in his prime in exchange for forgoing one while he's still developing.

No player is going to be ruined by having to wait to play in the NHL until he's 19. But you sure can ruin a player by allowing him to play at 18 because, beyond talent and hard work, success in professional sports is mostly about confidence. And when you rush a prospect to the NHL, you're putting his confidence at risk more than anything. And once that's gone, there's no magic formula to get it back.

Conversely, players can build confidence by being allowed to dominate at the junior level. Tampa Bay's Brad Richards played not one, but two full seasons of junior after his draft year. In that second year, he was almost too good for the league. He won a scoring title and led his Rimouski team to a Memorial Cup. But he also spoke about how he developed his game by being able to experiment and try things he couldn't when he was just trying to survive.

Now, I suppose, as a compromise, you could come up with a rule that allowed teams to select 18-year-olds only in the first round of the draft. And, with so many good 19-year-olds available each year, you can be sure the first 30 picks wouldn't be dominated by 18-year-olds.

One thing that National Basketball Association commissioner David Stern proved is that 18-year-old athletes do not have an inherent right to play professional sports. So, if the NBA can keep high school seniors out of the draft, why can't the NHL?

About the only ones who would be dead set against raising the draft age in hockey would be a lot of agents. Agents want their clients to turn pro as quickly as possible, because that's when they get paid. And the sooner a player signs his first contract, the sooner he gets to his second, which is where the really big money starts to roll in.

But I've got an idea. Under the latest collective bargaining agreement, the NHL managed to put a much tighter lid on the salaries and signing bonuses that can be paid to draft picks. What if the league raised those limits in exchange for a 19-year-old draft? I've got to believe teams would be happy to pay out more in bonuses to players who were more likely to play in the NHL, and put less money into signing bonuses for players who end up never playing for them.

And we'd have fewer trivia questions about which first-round picks made the biggest headlines of their careers on draft day.

14. Almost everything the National Hockey League has done in the past 25 years has been with the goal of selling the game to Americans. Bob says forget it: Americans have seen hockey, and most of them just don't care for it.

THE NATIONAL HOCKEY LEAGUE is not new to Americans.

Dating back to the days of the Original Six, two-thirds of the NHL was based in the United States. And NHL hockey has been on national television in the U.S. since 1960.

So this notion that NHL hockey is Canada's game is simply preposterous. Since 1926, it has been a league with a greater presence in the U.S. than Canada. And since then, it has always been a league that has mattered far more in Canada than in the U.S.

Those things have not changed in 80 years.

So you'd think that, if Americans as a whole were going to fall in love with hockey, it would have happened by now. Obviously, they haven't. The NHL remains peripheral to the culture in all but a few places. And with a professional sports landscape more crowded than ever, hockey is losing ground, not just to traditional sports such as the NFL and the NBA. It's also slipping against what were once dismissed as niche sports like NASCAR and arena football. That's right: arena football.

And while professional hockey has always been a difficult proposition in non-traditional markets, now we're seeing interest dwindling in such places as St. Louis, Chicago and even Boston. So whatever momentum exists around professional hockey in the U.S. right now seems to be in reverse.

Somehow, amazingly, the NHL has become less relevant with 24 teams in the U.S. than it was back in the early 1970s, when there were just 11. You can listen to national sports radio programs in the U.S. for weeks and never hear a mention of hockey. Because unless some player clubs an opponent over the head with his stick, the sport is completely ignored. In a lot of non-NHL markets, the daily newspapers don't even print NHL standings. And there is no reason to believe any of this is going to change.

The bottom line is that, unlike Canadians, most Americans have never picked up a hockey stick. I don't care how much marketing is directed at sports fans; if they've never lived and breathed the sport, if they didn't grow up with it in some sort of organic way, it's never going to matter the way sports like football and baseball and basketball do, sports that are woven into the fabric of their lives.

There are actually only about 100,000 fewer hockey players in the U.S. than Canada. But when you spread them across a population of 300 million, it hardly makes a dent. And whatever dent it does make tends to be confined to a few areas—New York, Minnesota, Massachusetts and Michigan, mostly. All of which just happen to be places where NHL teams traditionally do very well. But in most U.S. cities where kids have easy access to basketball courts and baseball fields, hockey rinks are hard to come by.

You'll often hear people talk about the NHL reaching out to the casual hockey fan in the United States. Well, I don't believe casual hockey fans exist. You either love the game or you don't. Which explains why it's possible to have NHL arenas sold out to the rafters in many American cities, while just a few blocks away people don't even know a game was played. Everyone who cares is in the building.

And yet the NHL never stops making inane and insulting decisions in the name of attracting that casual American viewer who does not exist. Consider April of 2007, when the league insisted on scheduling the second game of an opening-round series between Ottawa and Pittsburgh on a Saturday afternoon instead of a Saturday night. Why? Because the NHL wanted the game on NBC, to expose Sidney Crosby to its American fans—thus denying the CBC, the league's most valuable broadcast partner, the opportunity to air the game on Saturday night, when most Canadian fans are watching. This, despite the fact that NBC pays no money for NHL rights, while the CBC had recently committed roughly half a billion dollars to a new agreement.

Yes, it's all about that new frontier of fans, a frontier that seems to be getting further and further away, not closer.

The other problem with hockey for Americans right now is that the game just seems too foreign. While there are more Americans playing NHL hockey than ever, there's also a tonne of players with first names such as Marian, Zdeno, Evgeni and Sergei. Let's be honest: Americans like things that seem American. And while the NBA has its share of foreigners, there's no doubt that basketball is their game. All these foreigners in hockey, however, are just one more reason for Americans to give the sport a pass.

Coming out of the lockout, the reaction to the return of the NHL on both sides of the border was predictable. In Canada, where the sport is like a drug, the addicts rushed back to get their fix like never before. And in the U.S., where hockey is like an occasional habit, most people went on, happy to live without it.

Traditional hockey fans have always arrogantly suggested that anyone who doesn't love their game must not have seen it, or given it enough time, or whatever.

Well, sorry, folks. Most Americans *have* seen professional hockey. They've experienced the marketing campaigns and they've even sat down to watch a time or two. And most of them simply don't like it—and never, *ever*, will.

15. It seems everyone has an idea of how to improve the Natonal Hockey League. But some things about the sport are just fine the way they are. Bob lists the six worst hockey ideas of all time.

THERE HAS ALWAYS been a battle in hockey between traditionalists and innovators, those who want to change the game and those who like it just the way it is. Usually the traditionalists win, which is why there are still goal judges in the National Hockey League, even though no one ever uses them anymore. But a few good ideas have been welcomed into the sport over the years. Things such as curved sticks, the elimination of the red line for offsides, goalie masks and video review have worked out just fine. Others, however, have been less successful. Here are the dumbest of the dumb ideas to make it into hockey.

6. THE PRESIDENTS' TROPHY

At the start of the 1985–86 season, the NHL introduced the Presidents' Trophy to recognize the team that finishes with the best record during the regular season. Why the NHL would want to honour an achievement that is completely meaningless, I have no idea. In fact, winning the Presidents' Trophy is the last thing you want to have happen if you're a general manager or a coach. Because if you don't win the Stanley Cup, that Presidents' Trophy banner hanging from the rafters serves as a reminder to everyone that you screwed up by failing to win the Cup despite having the best team in hockey.

5. THE FOXTRAX GLOWING PUCK

In 1996, Fox Sports went to ridiculous lengths to make televised hockey more appealing to Americans. By using a computer-generated coloured blob to indicate the location of the puck (complete with a red comet tail each time the puck travelled faster than 70 miles an hour), Fox made NHL hockey look like a video game. Now, I'm not arguing that hockey was easy to watch for Americans in the age before Fox came up with the glowing puck. But how anyone thought this made it more understandable, let alone watchable, I can't imagine. And to viewers who did understand the game, it was simply embarrassing. Fortunately, the glowing puck had a short life.

4. COOPERALLS

It was the equipment revolution that was supposed to change the look of hockey. And by the early 1980s, major junior hockey teams had dropped the traditional pants and socks for the one-piece trousers that made players look as though they were out for a skate on the pond. The Philadelphia Flyers and Hartford Whalers both sported them for the 1982–83 season, before hockey's fashion police moved in and said enough was enough. Not only did the outfits look ridiculous, but players who went down in them were prone to sliding uncontrollably along the ice.

3. SEAMLESS GLASS ON THE END BOARDS

The folks who pay $200 a ticket to sit down in the lower bowl behind the net don't much like having their view obstructed by bars separating the panes of glass. So seamless glass was invented to give high-paying patrons a clearer view. The only problem is that seamless glass has virtually no give to it, meaning that players thrown up against it often have their brains rattled. Since throwing your opponent into the boards is a big part of the game, someone should have known this was a stupid idea. By the 2006–07 season, many NHL rinks were removing seamless glass and reinstalling the bars to give the glass some bend. But the league still hasn't banned this dangerous innovation.

2. SKATE IN THE CREASE

In an effort to protect goaltenders, the National Hockey League decided in 1991–92 to enforce a rule that said goals would be waved off if any part of an attacking player enters the crease before the puck does. It's unfathomable that no one could envision the potential problems with this one. In addition to giving goaltenders room to do their job, which is fine, the rule had the unintended effect of eliminating all kinds of goals when there was no goaltender interference whatsoever. And gosh, what a mess there would be if officials were forced to make that kind of call in the deciding game of a Stanley Cup final. Whoops! The NHL changed the rule just months after the Dallas Stars scored the Stanley Cup–winning goal in 1999 against Buffalo while Brett Hull's skate was clearly in the crease before the puck.

1. OPTIONAL HELMETS

Thirteen years after making helmets mandatory for new players, the NHL decided to make them optional before the 1992–93 season. All a player had to do was sign a waiver and he could go helmet-free. This one was a stunner, coming at a time when only a handful of players from the bygone days before helmets were mandatory were still playing lidless. It was largely believed that the NHL thought players without helmets would be more recognizable for television, which would make it easier to market the game in the United States (an always-familiar theme in NHL decision-making). The players didn't bite. "Kind of high risk," said Boston defenceman Glen Wesley at the time. "Like risking your life." The rule making helmets mandatory was reinstated before the 1997–98 season.

16. The Toronto Maple Leafs haven't won a Stanley Cup in 40 years. Big deal, says Bob. It's far more amazing that the team at the centre of the hockey universe has employed so few great players over that span.

TORONTO MAPLE LEAF fans believe their team has been cheated during the past four decades. They think that somehow the

Leafs' true destiny has been denied—somewhere along the way, they think, the Leafs deserved to win the Stanley Cup. Fate, they would suggest, has turned against them. But there is no reason to blame fate when there is a perfectly logical reason why the Leafs haven't even been to a Stanley Cup final since Canada's centennial year. They've simply had teams full of consistently crappy players.

Granted, there are exceptions—Darryl Sittler, Borje Salming and Mats Sundin, to name a few. But it's shocking how few great NHLers have come through Toronto at any point in their careers.

Dumb luck alone would suggest that, at some point since 1967, some of the very best hockey players in the game should have been Toronto Maple Leafs. After all, until the mid-1970s, the National Hockey League was only a 12-team league. And even into the late 1980s, there were just 21 teams wading in the NHL's talent pool.

Yet I have to struggle to name the greatest NHL player of the past 40 years who wore a Leafs uniform at any point in his career. I guess it would be Eric Lindros, who for a while during the 1990s was considered the best player in hockey. But by the time Lindros suited up for his one and only year as a Leaf in 2005–06, he was a shell of his former self. *This* is the high-water mark for a team with such pride, whose fans are loyal beyond those of any others in hockey?

How poor have the Leafs been when it comes to individual greatness? Since Dave Keon was awarded the Conn Smythe Trophy as most valuable player in the playoffs during the spring of 1967, just two Maple Leafs have captured one of the NHL's annual awards: Doug Gilmour, who won the Selke for being the game's top defensive forward in 1993, and Alexander Mogilny, who won the Lady Byng in 2003 for sportsmanship and gentlemanly play. As for the Art Ross Trophy, Calder Trophy, Conn Smythe Trophy, Hart Trophy, Norris and Vezina

Trophies, the Leafs have been completely shut out. Same for the Rocket Richard Trophy, which was added in 1998–99 for the league's top goal scorer.

By comparison, consider that the Montreal Canadiens have had 37 winners of individual awards during that span: eleven Vezinas, seven Selkes, three Norrises, three Harts, eight Conn Smythes, one Calder, three Art Rosses and one Lady Byng. In other words, the talent gap is not even close.

The Leafs have the same pathetic record when it comes to career achievements. Of the top 20 goal scorers in NHL history at the end of the 2006–07 season, only one played at any point for the Maple Leafs: Dave Andeychuk. And of the 640 goals Andreychuk scored, only 120 came in a Toronto uniform. Of the top 30 in career assists, only Doug Gilmour and Larry Murphy, who between them played eight seasons for Toronto, are listed. And among the top 30 point-getters, only Andreychuk is there as a one-time Leaf.

Mats Sundin will likely crack the top 20 of all time in both goals and assists, making him instantly the most individually accomplished Leaf player in history, if he is not already.

So, the question is: Why has a team in the media capital of Canada, the supposed home of hockey, produced or attracted so few great players? Part of it has to do with the culture around the Maple Leafs. Since their games are guaranteed sell-outs, the Leafs have simply had no bottom-line reason to seek out greatness, no need to cultivate the next great star player in order to sell tickets, and no need to match the highest salaries in the sport.

It was that way under Harold Ballard in the 1970s and '80s, and it's that way today.

Another problem has been scouting and player development. Since the Leafs drafted Lanny McDonald fourth overall in 1973, there have been precious few Toronto draft picks who rose to great heights in the NHL. In fact, over the ensuing 30 years there were only four Leaf draft picks one could fairly say became top-tier NHLers during their career, and none who were bona fide stars. Wendel Clark was certainly a decent NHL player who will live on in highlight reels, but his legend is much greater than his career, thanks to his battles with injuries and being surrounded by lousy players during his Toronto years. Meanwhile, the other three—Russ Courtnall, Doug Jarvis and Vincent Damphousse—all spent their best years wearing Montreal Canadien colours. The next tier of successful draft picks includes such names as Luke Richardson, Randy Carlyle, Al Iafrate, Gary Leeman, Drake Berehowsky, Joel Quenneville, John Anderson, Felix Potvin, Yanic Perreault and Kenny Jonsson. Those are some half-decent players, but hardly the makings of an all-star team.

How poorly have the Leafs drafted? A short list of players the Leafs have decided not to take since '73 includes Mike Bossy, Al MacInnis, Scott Stevens, Cam Neely, Brian Leetch, Joe Sakic, Rod Brind'Amour, Martin Brodeur, Todd Bertuzzi and Cam Ward. Pretty stunning when you consider the mediocrity of the players who've worn the blue-and-white amid all the fanfare of the modern game in Toronto.

Now, to be fair, there are a couple of names I've omitted when it comes to all-time NHL achievement among Maple Leafs, players who certainly racked up stats in a way few others have in the National Hockey League. But if Tiger Williams and Tie Domi ranking first and third, respectively, in all-time penalty minutes is the proudest Leaf accomplishment of the past four decades, that certainly speaks volumes about why this franchise has been swimming in mediocrity for so long.

17.

Wayne Gretzky was the greatest offensive player in hockey history. His career earned him

61 officially recognized records, and dozens more that aren't. Bob says his name will still be etched all over the record book long after he and the rest of us are gone from this world.

EVER SINCE THE Great One began inscribing his name in the National Hockey League record book, hockey fans have been awaiting the "Next One," someone to come along and rewrite the record book the way Gretzky did.

First, it was supposed to be Mario Lemieux, then Eric Lindros—and put up your hand if you said it was going to be Alexandre Daigle. Now Sidney Crosby carries that torch, having been anointed by the Great One himself while still in his mid-teens.

There may someday be an offensive talent in hockey as great as Gretzky. You can never say never. But I will say this: No one will ever threaten his place in the record book.

Here's why. By the start of the 2006–07 season, Gretzky had been gone from the game for six full seasons. During that time, two of his records had fallen, while he'd actually achieved another one in retirement. Nicklas Lidstrom (16), Adam Oates (17) and Mark Messier (18) have all passed Gretzky's previous record of 15 overtime assists. But Gretzky would surely still own this record had there been regular-season overtime throughout his 21-year career and not just in the final 16. During Gretzky's first five seasons, in which he averaged more than 100 assists per season, there was no regular-season overtime, and therefore no Gretzky overtime assists.

Gretzky's only other record to fall since his retirement is for assists in an All-Star Game, which both Ray Bourque and Mark Messier surpassed. But the All-Star Game isn't real hockey, so I don't consider this a real record.

Meanwhile, Mario Lemieux's semi-successful comeback from retirement from 2000–01 to 2005–06 cost him the record for highest points-per-game average in a career, dropping him down to 1.883 and leaving Gretzky in first place at 1.921.

As for active veteran players who might have a shot at Gretzky's significant career milestones, no one even comes close. To put this in perspective, consider that Joe Sakic began 2006–07 at age 37 with the NHL's highest active points total at 1,489. Yet Sakic has barely achieved half of Gretzky's career mark of 2,857 points. If he plays for another 20 years, he *might* have a shot.

Besides Gretzky's pure ability, there are all kinds of other factors that will keep his records safe.

Number 99 had the good fortune to play his prime years with an Edmonton Oiler dynasty that was among the greatest collections of players ever. From the time he broke into the league in the fall of 1979 until his departure from Edmonton nine years later, Gretzky played with such talents as Jari Kurri, Glenn Anderson, Mark Messier and Paul Coffey, all of whom hit the 40-goal mark at least once during those years. All but Coffey, who had 48 in 1985–86, hit 50 at least once. In today's NHL of salary-cap parity, that kind of team will almost surely never exist again.

Gretzky's Oilers of the 1980s managed the five highest single-season goal totals in NHL history. During Gretzky's time in Edmonton, the Oilers averaged 386.4 goals per year in an 80-game schedule. By comparison, amid all the hype of the new, higher-scoring, post-lockout NHL game, the Ottawa Senators led the league in 2005–06 with 314 goals in an 82-game season. So, even in the "new NHL," no team is anywhere close to achieving in a single season what Gretzky's Oilers *averaged* during the 1980s.

And even if a team managed to score that many goals in one season, there's no way that they'd be able to keep that team together year after year under the NHL's current economic model. So, even if Sidney Crosby does manage to match Wayne

Gretzky's talent level, he'll never be surrounded by the kind of cast Gretzky played with all those years in Edmonton.

The same applies to Gretzky's astonishing playoff stats. The Oiler dynasty occurred during a time when the NHL allowed 16 of its 21 teams into the postseason. As a result, Gretzky never missed the playoffs the way a lot of good players do today, in a league that eliminates 14 of 30 teams from participating in the playoffs.

Gretzky's teams in Los Angeles weren't of the Oilers' calibre. But he still went to the playoffs in each of his first five seasons with the Kings, playing alongside such players as Bernie Nicholls, John Tonelli and Luc Robitaille.

Gretzky also had the good fortune to play during an era when NHL goal scoring was at an all-time high. From 1979–80 until 1992–93, the NHL averaged better than seven goals per game in all but just two seasons (6.91 in 1990–91 and 6.96 in 1991–92). There's nothing saying the league couldn't go that way again. However, given the emphasis coaches put on defence, and the skill of today's goaltenders, I think it's unlikely we'll ever see those levels again, barring something like making the nets bigger. (By comparison, the NHL in 2006–07 averaged 5.89 goals per game.)

And then there is Gretzky's remarkable physical health. For a guy who didn't look all that durable, he had just two seasons during which he played fewer than 70 regular-season games out of an 80- or 82-game schedule. In a sport as punishing as professional hockey, given all those playoff games, international tournaments and the fact that Gretzky played every game of his career with a bull's-eye on his back, his ability to stay healthy was amazing.

You could argue that Mario Lemieux would have reached many of Gretzky's records if he'd remained healthy throughout his career. But the fact is that he didn't.

So, here's what a player would need to approach Wayne

Gretzky's status in the NHL record book: an otherworldly talent, an equally uncanny ability to avoid getting hurt, and the good fortune to play on great teams through the prime of his career—during an era of high-scoring hockey. If all those elements fall into place, I guess you might need to take an eraser to Gretzky's name in the record book. But don't count on it happening.

Here are, in my opinion, the five Gretzky records, official or unofficial, that will be the hardest to break:

5. Fastest to 50 goals: 39 games in 1981–82. Fifty goals remains an extremely high standard for an entire season, let alone a half season.

4. Most career playoff points: 382. There are only about 100 active NHL players with that many *regular-season* points in their careers.

3. Most assists, one season: 163 in 1985–86. Consider that the top seven performances in this category all belong to Gretzky. Mario Lemieux comes in eighth, with 114—which he shares with Gretzky. That's right: the Magnificent One's best season ties the Great One's eighth best.

2. Most three-or-more-goal games: 50. Lemieux is closest at 40, one of only four players who have ever had at least 32 such games, and none of them are active.

1. Most points in a career: 2,856. The player behind Gretzky on this list (Mark Messier) played 25 years in the NHL until age 43, was part of the same point-scoring dynasty as Gretzky in Edmonton, and still ended up 1,001 points behind him when all was said and done.

18. **Remember the French Connection, the Triple Crown Line and the Production Line? Hockey used to be full of great line combinations, players**

who seemed to know what the other two were thinking before the play unfolded. Bob explains what happened to one hockey's great characteristics.

THERE WAS A TIME when every team in hockey had at least one superior line you could count on seeing, night in and night out. Sometimes they had cute nicknames, and sometimes they didn't. But great lines were part of what gave teams their flavour, along with goaltenders and individual stars.

And at the end of every season you could debate which line was the best and why, who made it tick, and which lines were more than the sum of their parts.

But these days, lines are constructed and deconstructed before anyone can stick a nickname on a trio of players. Every once in a while you'll see a newspaper ask its readers to name a line combination that has had some success over a short period of time. And, invariably, the line's been broken up before the contest is over.

It can seem as if coaches have attention deficit disorder—if a line doesn't produce for two or three games, it no longer exists. Heck, a lot of times lines are broken up if they can't produce for one or two *periods*.

So why don't lines stay together anymore?

There are lots of reasons, many of them having to with the emphasis on scouting in today's game. Thanks largely to video, teams these days know far more about their opposition than their counterparts of a generation ago. They know their tendencies, their strengths and weaknesses, all of which are used to find ways to neutralize the opposition attack.

So, one thing teams do to counter the scouting reports and video is to shuffle their deck to keep the opposing coaches guessing.

Specialization in hockey is another factor. Most teams have a shutdown forward line as well as a defence pair which they try and match up against the opposition's strongest line. When a team has all its best offensive players on one line, it becomes easy to throw a blanket over them. So coaches try to spread out their offensive talent to keep teams from matching up. But if they happen to face a team where the shutdown line or defence pair doesn't scare them, they're tempted to stack one line in the hope it will have a big night.

They'll often do the same thing in mid-game if they're down a goal or two in the second or third period and need to mount a comeback.

A lot of teams have dumped line combinations in favour of forward pairs. When they find two players who work well together (usually a passing centre and winger with a great shot), they'll leave them alone and then tinker with the third position as matchups warrant.

I only wish coaches would show a little more patience when a line starts clicking. It's only natural that your best players aren't going to score every night. Heck, look at baseball, where even the best hitters go through 0-for-20 slumps. In a long NHL season made worse by horrific travel, it only makes sense that not every player is going to be at his peak throughout.

But because of the competitiveness of the regular season, hockey coaches aren't willing to be as patient as they used to be. Even good teams can't just assume they'll make the playoffs every year. Back when teams had playoff spots sewn up by midseason, a coach didn't have to panic if his team lost three in a row in January. But with the parity in hockey today, and the knowledge that14 teams miss the playoffs every year, even the coaches of good teams feel the need to do something—anything—when their players struggle. And the easiest thing to reach for is a line change. At least it looks like they're doing something.

Line juggling is also a way for coaches to exert control

over players in a subtle way. It's not that long ago that hockey players were modestly paid professionals who all believed they were lucky to be playing a game for a living. But nowadays, with the money and the agents, coaches have to be far more creative when it comes to keeping their players motivated throughout an 82-game regular season. And since offensive players are paid mostly according to their stats, there's no better way to get a player's attention than sticking him on the third or fourth line for a couple of nights.

I wish I could say I thought that long-standing line combinations would come back in hockey, but I think they're gone for good. Hockey's salary cap means that no team is going to have enough scoring depth to load up one line and stick with it for an entire season. And that, unfortunately, robs the sport of a little richness.

19.

He's known to most fans as a pariah and a crook, a man who took far more than he gave to hockey and its players. But Bob says Alan Eagleson's contributions to hockey shouldn't be dismissed.

ALAN EAGLESON WAS the czar of the hockey world, a man respected and often feared by owners, general managers and players at the game's highest levels.

Yet today, you can't mention Alan Eagleson's name among hockey fans without it being scorned.

Look, Alan Eagleson wasn't perfect. Far from it. He was a my-way-or-the-highway kind of operator who could be a bully when he wanted to get his way.

But there's this attempt these days to pretend he didn't exist, to whitewash him from hockey history and deny him credit for any of the many things he did during his 25 years in the sport. So much so, that even discussing his contributions to hockey is, quite frankly, intolerable to a lot of fans.

When I've had Eagleson on *Prime Time Sports*—not to defend himself but to talk hockey—the hate mail that follows comes fast and furious from fans who have come to believe that he corrupted everything he touched and that he set hockey back into the Dark Ages.

Let's put this into perspective. The Dark Ages were, in fact, what Eagleson discovered when he came along and successfully formed the National Hockey League Players' Association in 1967.

That was an accomplishment in itself, since earlier attempts to organize hockey players had failed miserably. We're talking about a group of players comprised largely of small-town Canadians who felt lucky every single day they put on a hockey sweater, no doubt well aware of how much worse life could be.

Quite literally, they would have played for nothing in those days.

And so, getting them to challenge the people who paid them, to demand more than just the gift of playing a game for a living, scared the heck out of them. It was Eagleson who understood that getting the stars on each and every team to buy in meant getting the others to follow. Eagleson had the will, he had a plan and he had the connections to do what others couldn't. That's how Eagleson did everything.

It's easy to forget what the hockey world looked like when Eagleson first encountered it in the 1960s. Here was a league controlled by six owners. The average NHL salary at that time was about $7,500. Players didn't have the right to own a copy of their contracts. Besides the fact that they were being paid, they were slaves.

Among the very first things Eagleson did was go to the players and ask what was important to them. Do you know what they said? They wanted Christmas Eve and Christmas Day to spend with their families. So Eagleson got that for them. He also got them guaranteed contracts, medical benefits, disability insurance and a pension plan. Before Alan Eagleson, players had no rights to endorsement money. Every penny went to the owners.

Under Eagleson, average salaries grew at an annual rate of 12 percent from 1967 to 1986, enough that they doubled every six seasons. From 1986 to 1991, that annual rate rose to 17 percent, and the average salary neared $300,000 by the end of his tenure. That's roughly the same rate at which salaries increased under Eagleson's successor, Bob Goodenow, during his 15 years running the union, except that under Goodenow, the players lost a season and a half in pay from the lockout years of 1994–95 and 2004–05, money they were never able to get back.

Now, you can look at where hockey salaries had got to by the time the lockout began and say, "Wow. After Eagleson left, the average salary went up more than $1.5 million in 13 years." But to look solely at the dollar value and say that Eagleson increased the average salary by only a quarter of a million dollars while Goodenow drove it up by about a million and a half is misleading.

It's true that hockey players weren't paid as well as professional athletes in some other sports during Eagleson's time. But that's still true today, more than 15 years after Eagleson departed, because guess what? Hockey isn't as popular as basketball, football or baseball, and it doesn't have the same revenue streams.

And yet Eagleson is plagued by this notion that he somehow conspired with owners to keep salaries artificially low. That makes no sense at all when you think about it, because Eagleson's income came mostly from the players he represented in contract negotiations. (Eagleson's top salary as

NHLPA executive director was $275,000. By comparison, Bob Goodenow was earning $2.5 million when he left the job in 2005.) Since Eagleson represented about 20 percent of the league's players during the 1970s (roughly 120 players), and 50 or so of its top players during the 1980s, conspiring to keep salaries artificially low would have taken money out of his own pocket.

Much is made of the way Eagleson supposedly hid from Bobby Orr an offer that included an 18 percent stake in the Boston Bruins in 1976, urging him instead to take a less lucrative offer from his friend Bill Wirtz, owner of the Chicago Blackhawks. The fact is that while Orr claimed to know nothing of the Bruins' offer, it was hardly a secret in hockey circles and was actually reported in the pages of the *Toronto Star*. It's hard to keep a secret from a client when he can read about it in the papers.

But Eagleson's greatest contributions may have come in the arena of international hockey.

Eagleson understood the frustration of Canadian hockey fans who watched their country go to the world championships every year during the 1960s and lose. He knew the idea of a best-on-best tournament would hold tremendous appeal and that the players, the owners and the game in Canada could benefit.

And while credit for the 1972 series doesn't belong to him alone, it was Eagleson who pushed forward the notion of a series between the best players in Canada and the best of the Soviet Union. More than 25 years later, baseball is just now beginning to enter the world of international competition involving its best players. Eagleson got that ball rolling in hockey long before any other sport.

The 1972 Summit Series was a 50/50 partnership between Hockey Canada and the NHL Pension Society. It led to Eagleson's Canada Cup tournaments, which once again put money straight into the pockets of Hockey Canada as well as a joint venture between the NHL and NHLPA.

Eagleson was also instrumental in creating the World Junior Championship, believing that a mini–Canada Cup could evolve into something big. In Vancouver in 2006, that tournament netted $9 million, of which Hockey Canada received half.

It was Eagleson who pushed to get Canada back into the World Championship in 1976 by using NHL players to end the country's seven-year absence. And by seeing the best from Europe compete against NHL players each spring, NHL teams were inspired to recruit overseas, which helped create the great wave of European talent.

Look, for many years, the business of hockey was the business of Alan Eagleson. The sport was an immature business in which Eagleson saw opportunity where others saw none. That's not his fault.

And the fact that he may have personally profited from some of those opportunities shouldn't mean he doesn't deserve credit for his vision and his leadership in a sport that was in the Stone Age before he came along.

Did he wear too many hats? If he'd concentrated solely on leading his union, would the NHL owners have got away with unfairly withholding pension surplus money from retired players?

Should he have been negotiating television deals, representing players, running the union and brokering international hockey tournaments? Today, we'd certainly say no. But in those days there were no rules, nothing against conflict of interest in the sport, so long as everyone kept making money. And let's keep this in mind: the players, the owners, Eagleson—everyone was happy.

It's easy to say in hindsight that hockey players should have been more militant. But most hockey players in those days didn't have the stomach to go to war with the hockey establishment. Eagleson in retirement remains friendly with a large part of the hockey world, many of whom wrote letters of support for him at the time of his sentencing—a list that includes Paul Henderson, Bob Clarke, Darryl Sittler, Bryan Trottier and Bob Gainey.

The fact is that those players and many, many others understood the challenges, understood the times and the things he did for players and the game, even if he wasn't perfect.

And the fans? Most of them can't even tell you what Eagleson went to jail for.

In the U.S., he pleaded guilty to three counts of fraud involving players' disability insurance premiums. And in Canada he was charged for skimming 1991 Canada Cup tournament money into his own pocket.

And that was it.

The FBI spent millions pursuing Eagleson, but that's all that stuck to him. And when the players later tried to file suit that he had conspired with owners to keep salaries artificially low, a judge threw it out, saying the claim was "patently lacking in merit."

You can criticize Alan Eagleson for the things he did wrong. I'm not going to try to stop you. You can second-guess his overinvolvement in some deals. And, yes, there appear to be some things he did which were both illegal and immoral. But pretending he didn't exist, trying to erase his name from history and forgetting his contributions to hockey—that, in itself, is a crime.

20. Thirty-five years after he scored the most meaningful goal in hockey history, Paul Henderson's name still makes Canadians stir. But

does he belong in the Hockey Hall of Fame? Not a chance, says Bob.

IF THE HOCKEY HALL OF FAME were truly the Hockey Hall of the Famous, then Paul Henderson would surely belong. Without a doubt, Henderson has a name that has stood the test of time in hockey circles, especially in Canada.

But let's be clear about what the Hockey Hall of Fame really is. It's the Hockey Hall of Career Achievement. It's for players and builders who, over a large number of years, have made significant contributions to or had an impact on the game of hockey. Which certainly can't be said about Paul Henderson.

Henderson was a very good junior hockey player who helped Hamilton capture a Memorial Cup title in 1962–63. He went on to a career in the National Hockey League, over the course of which he eclipsed the 20-goal mark seven times and had a career best of 38 goals in 1971–72. When he was added to Team Canada for the Summit Series, it was as a role player—a checker on a line with Ron Ellis and Bobby Clarke.

The rest, as they say, is history. Henderson scored the winning goal in each of the last three games of the Summit Series, including the winner in the final and deciding game with just 34 seconds to play.

Henderson played two more seasons in the NHL before moving to the World Hockey Association, where he scored 140 goals over five seasons. Those are all decent accomplishments in a more than decent hockey career.

But let's be realistic about what gets players into the Hockey Hall of Fame and consider where Henderson stands in each category.

From my point of view there are three main reasons for a player to be given a place in the Hockey Hall of Fame:

1. Outstanding career statistics. You can certainly

argue about how much longevity should matter when it comes to measuring greatness. But there are certain milestones that will guarantee that a player gets into the Hall of Fame. In 1,067 professional games, Henderson scored 376 goals and added 384 assists. But 360 of those games were in the World Hockey Association. Compare Henderson's numbers with Hall of Fame forwards from the same era—Jean Ratelle, Phil Esposito, Rod Gilbert, Stan Mikita, Bobby Hull, John Bucyk. He just doesn't compare.

2. Outstanding individual greatness during his career. Paul Henderson never led the NHL in any offensive category. He played in two NHL All-Star Games. Enough said.

3. Association with great teams and championships. There are some players in the Hockey Hall of Fame who got there mostly because they happened to be in the right place at the right time and wound up getting their names carved on the Stanley Cup repeatedly. Henderson played in two Stanley Cup finals, both of which occurred during his first three NHL seasons with Detroit. After a trade to Toronto in 1968, Henderson played in just 19 Stanley Cup playoff games in seven seasons with the Leafs and four more as an Atlanta Flame. Had he been a member of the Montreal Canadiens, would he be in the Hall of Fame? Sure. But so would a lot of other players who aren't in.

You could certainly argue that Henderson's stats are comparable to those of someone like Dick Duff, who was inducted in 2006 with 1,030 games, 283 goals and 572 career points. But Duff played in seven All-Star Games and had his name carved on the Stanley Cup six times. Or Bob Gainey, who played in 1,160 games with 239 goals and 502 points. But Gainey was the pre-eminent defensive forward of his era, a four-time Selke Trophy winner and a key ingredient in five Montreal Stanley Cup championships.

Most of what made Henderson great comes down to a

short period in September of 1972, during which he helped win three of the most important hockey games Canada will ever play. And that's it.

There's one other point worth remembering when it comes to this argument. The Hockey Hall of Fame is not the Canadian Hockey Hall of Fame. And so, while Henderson's goals during the '72 Series may have mattered a lot to the people of Canada and the Soviet Union, they didn't mean near as much to the rest of the hockey-playing world at the time, and still don't matter much today. It's true that Canada and the USSR represented the two greatest hockey-playing nations on Earth at the time. But let's remember that this was a series played between two countries, and two countries only.

Paul Henderson belongs in Canada's Sports Hall of Fame, which he was inducted into in 1995. And on any list of great Canadian sporting accomplishments, his name has to be there. But honouring him as one of the all-time greats ever to have laced up the skates is simply laughable.

21. **Coaching in the National Hockey League looks easy. I could do it. You could do it. Or so a lot of ex-players conclude once they've hung up the skates for good. Bob looks at where the game's greatest coaches come from.**

IT'S TOO EARLY to tell whether Wayne Gretzky will ever approach the level of greatness as a coach that he achieved as a player. But I'm betting against it.

It seems pretty clear that the qualities that made Gretzky such a great player—his ability to anticipate the play, his uncanny vision, and that instinct to know where to be on the ice and what to do with the puck—don't add up to a hill of beans when it comes to coaching.

Greatness as a player rarely if ever translates into greatness as a coach. You only need to look at the name of the National Hockey League's all-time leader in coaching victories, winning percentage and Stanley Cups to find a guy who never had a cup of coffee in the NHL as a player. And Scotty Bowman isn't the only one among the league's most successful coaches who never played at any significant level of professional hockey. The same is true of Mike Keenan, Bryan Murray, Roger Neilson, Pat Burns, Ken Hitchcock, Punch Imlach and Jacques Martin. And we might as well add Don Cherry and his one career NHL game to this list.

The sum total of NHL games played by Peter Laviolette, John Tortorella, Pat Burns, Scotty Bowman and Bob Hartley—the five head coaches to win the Stanley Cup from 2001 to 2006? How about zero.

There are lots of football coaches who weren't great players and successful baseball managers who didn't achieve much in their sport. But in hockey it seems especially irrelevant to have played the game at its highest level in order to be a good coach.

Which isn't to suggest that it's impossible to go from a distinguished playing career to a great coaching career, or that there aren't players who've been able to do that. But it's interesting that the vast majority of those who have successfully made that transition come from a defensive stream. They're almost always defencemen, goalies or forwards who spent their years as checkers or grinders rather than as guys who filled the net.

Take Al Arbour and Pat Quinn—who sit at numbers two and five in all-time NHL coaching victories. As players they both had decent careers, each of them playing more than 600 games as NHL defencemen. And yet they combined for just 30 career goals, Quinn scoring 18 and Arbour 12.

When you go through the list of former players who've

made a successful transition to coaching, it's dotted with defensive-oriented guys, but the list of ex-players who've had marginal or unsuccessful NHL coaching careers is full of scorers.

Consider that Craig MacTavish, Bob Gainey, Larry Robinson, Lindy Ruff and Ron Low have all been pretty successful going from the ice to behind the bench.

Conversely, Bill Barber, Dirk Graham, Phil Esposito, Tony Granato, Butch Goring, Ted Lindsay, Bernie Geoffrion and Maurice Richard were not.

There are exceptions to every rule, of course. And I guess the biggest of these would be Jacques Lemaire, who scored 366 goals in 12 seasons with the Montreal Canadiens. In fact, Lemaire is the only guy on the NHL's list of top 100 goal scorers who's ever had any degree of success as a head coach. But it's interesting that the most successful offensive player ever to become a successful coach in the National Hockey League has done so by being one of the most defensive-minded coaches in history.

It makes sense, because NHL coaches spend a lot more time trying to get their players to prevent goals than they do teaching them how to score. Think about it: every time a young scorer comes into the NHL, his coach will always talk about how he needs to learn to play defence in order to earn his ice time. When was the last time you heard a coach say that a player who isn't a natural scorer has to learn to score goals if he wants to play? The offensive part of the game is more innate. By the time a player reaches the NHL, he either has a knack for it or he doesn't. And if he doesn't, there's not much a coach can say to a player or show him to turn him into a goal scorer. That's just not a coach's job.

Defence is where coaches do their work—teaching systems, tactics to get the puck out of the zone safely and to neutralize the other team's best players.

Who knows? Maybe Gretzky will be the exception to the

rule, the one who figures it all out despite spending most of his playing days thinking of ways to score goals. But if I were picking a former NHL player who was destined to become a great coach, I'd certainly lean more towards Guy Carbonneau than Gretzky.

22.
It has become Canada's Christmas ritual: open some presents, eat some turkey and take in Team Canada playing at the World Junior hockey tournament. Bob explains why the World Junior Championship has become more meaningful to Canadians than the Stanley Cup Final.

BACK IN THE 1970S, it was hard to find anyone who even knew when the World Junior Championship was being played.

In fact, when the tournament was played in Canada for the first time, back in 1977, there were barely 1,000 fans at some of Team Canada's games. And that was with a 16-year-old named Wayne Gretzky in the lineup. Canada lost the semifinal that year to Sweden by a score of 6–5, and all of 2,200 people were at the Montreal Forum to see it.

What has occurred since then is nothing short of miraculous. Now Canadians rally around the WJC unlike anything else in hockey, including the Stanley Cup.

Don't believe me? Take a look at the numbers. In 2003, the gold-medal game involving Canada at the World Junior Championship in Halifax drew a television audience of 3.4 million. That was an all-time record for programming of any description on the The Sports Network. It also dwarfed the number the CBC pulled in several months later for the Stanley Cup final, when 2.589 million tuned in for Game 7 between

Anaheim and New Jersey.

And that's not adjusting for the fact that the CBC reaches roughly 50 percent more homes than TSN does across the country.

The Stanley Cup final numbers are higher when a Canadian team is involved. But even when 4.73 million tuned in to watch Game 7 between Edmonton and Carolina in the spring of 2006, I'm guessing there wasn't the same level of passion from coast to coast as there is for a WJC final involving Canada.

In fact, if you had asked most fans outside Edmonton whether they'd rather have seen the Oilers win the Cup or Canada grab the World Junior gold, it wouldn't even be close.

So how did a tournament that no one even knew about 30 years ago get to be bigger than the Stanley Cup final?

Canadians have always loved to see players wearing the red and white show off their skill and passion in international hockey. That's why, to this day, the Canada–Russia Summit Series is up held up as the country's greatest sporting moment.

But since then there has been very little that can equal the way Canadians felt in '72. The Canada Cup tournaments that followed certainly provided their share of great moments, but they couldn't quite match level of energy and passion Canadians experienced in 1972. And by the 1980s, international hockey was losing that sense of worlds colliding, since many of the best players from overseas were in the NHL. That became especially true with the fall of the Iron Curtain, after which international hockey has felt like a bunch of professional players switching jerseys.

The same is true of the recent Olympic experiences, notwithstanding the surge of patriotism triggered by Canada's gold medal win in 2002.

The World Junior Championship flew under the radar for a long time, but there were two years that really put it on the map for good. The first was the 1986 tournament in Hamilton,

Ontario, just the second to be held in Canada. Having the tournament so close to the nation's media capital gave it tremendous exposure. Organizers got the hoped-for Canada-versus-Russia matchup in the gold-medal game. And even though the Canadians had to settle for silver, the closeness of the game and the fact that everyone could smell that gold medal created a buzz that didn't go away.

A year later, a different kind of buzz swept the country when the Canadians and Russians went toe to toe in one of the biggest hockey brawls of any kind, anywhere. Both countries were kicked out of the tournament, which was being held in Piestany, Czechoslovakia. But the media attention created by the fight made it impossible for anyone not to be aware of what was going on and engage in the debate about it, particularly since Canada had a shot at the gold (while the Soviets didn't) and were guaranteed a medal when the game was called.

By 1991, when the tournament moved back to Canada (in Saskatoon), it was clear the event was feeding Canada's hunger for international hockey like no other. And it has been that way ever since.

There are some things the World Junior Championship can deliver that the pros just can't. Unlike the pros, the juniors still live and play hockey in small towns and cities across this country, giving them close associations to the places where they play the game and where they grew up. So whether fans are watching the tournament from Swift Current, Vancouver, Cape Breton or Winnipeg, they feel a closeness to the team unlike any other. It's almost an organic experience to cheer for Team Canada.

When Canada's best pros go international, I think fans sometimes wonder if the boys in red and white always care as much as they do. Are guys who drive expensive sports cars—and in some cases haven't even lived in Canada for 10 or 15 years—really putting it all on the line for the Maple Leaf?

A lot of Team Canada's juniors go on to become millionaires. But for that couple of weeks in December and January, it seems like it's the most important time of their lives. And I think the fans feel that passion.

So, combine those elements with a tournament that includes most of the future stars of the National Hockey League from around the world, and you've got quite a package.

Unlike the Stanley Cup final, which takes place in June when most people are thinking about summer, the World Junior Championship actually happens at a point when most people feel like watching hockey. And so the WJC has become to Canadians what the college bowls are to Americans during the holiday season.

But while Canadians celebrate this event, the rest of the world barely knows it exists.

Which raises the question of why the International Ice Hockey Federation bothers to hold this thing anywhere but Canada. I have yet to witness a WJC played in Canada that wasn't an overwhelming success. And I've got to scratch my head to think of one played outside of Canada that was.

There's nothing more deflating than watching a supposedly important sporting event being played in an empty facility. It doesn't matter what sport we're talking about. If there's nobody there, if there's not a packed house reacting to everything that happens, it's tough to get drawn into it on television.

In Canada, even the games between two non-contenders draw big crowds. Yet outside of Canada, some of the best games of the week draw a yawn.

At the 2007 WJC in Sweden, Canada and the United States played one of the most riveting games in recent tournament history, a 1–1 semifinal tie that went to a shootout before Canada emerged with the win to move on to the gold-medal game.

But there was nobody there watching it. Here was a game

between two teams packed with future NHL players, playing for the right to compete for a gold medal. And the locals took a pass.

About the only ones who appeared to care were the several hundred Canadians in attendance. And while I hate to say it, there's something just a little bit pathetic about one country getting excited about an event that none of the others—including the United States—seemed to know was going on.

If you handed this event to a marketing company, the first thing they would tell you is to hold it in Canada each and every year. I mean, it's not like there's any shortage of Canadian markets to host it. It's not as if you'd have to go to the same three or four cities all the time.

I'll bet there are at least two dozen markets in Canada capable of hosting the WJC and beating the pants off anyplace in Europe or the United States.

And if you're going to hold it in the U.S., just make sure it's somewhere close to the border. That seemed to work in Grand Forks, North Dakota, in 2005, when Manitobans made their way south to fill the joint.

But when it was held in Boston in 1996, it was an absolute disaster. And Boston, while it has eroded into a crappy NHL town, is very supportive of amateur hockey at the high school and college levels. But they were offered the best high school and college-age players in the world and they couldn't have been less interested.

The WJC's appeal in Canada has been built on three things: our love of hockey, Canada's success in the tournament and TSN's ability to turn the event into a centrepiece of its programming at Christmastime.

No other country has that synergy, and no other country is going to develop it.

If Europe or the United States wants this thing, then let

them bid against Canadian cities for it. Let them prove that there's going to be legitimate interest before they earn the right to play host.

If you did that, the IIHF would solve its problem, and the WJC would be held in Canada every year.

23. Phone in sick. Tell your boss you're in bed. It's NHL Trade Deadline Day. Bob explores how an otherwise ordinary day in February became a national holiday, and why it's mostly meaningless.

IT HAS BECOME one of the three biggest days on the hockey calendar. For some, in fact, NHL Trade Deadline Day might be a bigger deal than the entry draft or the last game of the Stanley Cup final.

In terms of talking points, rumours and general buzz for hockey fans, nothing comes close. Which is why I'm sure you can walk into the offices of many businesses on Trade Deadline Day and find more people staring at television sets or clicking on websites than actually getting work done.

How in the world did a day that used to be about nothing more than filling a few depth roles for a handful of teams turn into such a circus?

Back on Trade Deadline Day 1980—which was long before anybody called it Trade Deadline Day—there were just three trades involving five players. Or how about 1983, when the only Trade Deadline Day deal saw Edmonton send Laurie Boschman to Winnipeg for Willy Lindstrom? Pretty hard to fill eight hours of network programming with that one.

Even as late as 1993, there were just nine deals involving 14 players. Nothing like the orgy of action that saw 24 deals involving 46 players in 2003, or the 25 trades that moved 40

70

players in 2006.

What's changed more than anything is simple: good old supply-and-demand economics. Back when the NHL allowed nearly all its teams to make the playoffs, all but the very worst clubs had a mathematical shot at the Stanley Cup when the deadline came around in early March. (It's only recently been moved back to February.) When the NHL awarded playoff spots to 16 out of 21 teams, only two or three teams had given up thinking about the playoffs by the time the trade deadline rolled around.

Meanwhile, you had 18 or 19 teams that were either in the playoff picture or aiming for it. In a market that included two or three sellers and 18 or 19 buyers, the relationship between supply and demand was out of whack.

But as the NHL began expanding towards 30 teams, that all changed. All of a sudden the number of sellers started to increase to the point where in an average year there are roughly 10 teams that have written off the playoffs by the time the deadline rolls around. With roughly twice as many buyers as sellers, it's a nice environment for teams that want to cash in by putting their players on the open trade market.

But in order for Trade Deadline Day to reach its current status, there needed to be a catalyst. And that catalyst was television. The all-sports networks in Canada have made a feast out of Trade Deadline Day, promoting it for days and weeks in advance, then celebrating it like a bunch of kids opening presents under the tree at Christmas.

Of course, with hours upon hours to fill, a lot of insignificant deals get more than their share of attention. Like the year the networks spent a good part of their afternoon analyzing Edmonton's trade of Dan LaCouture to Pittsburgh for Sven Butenschon, since for several hours that was the only deal that had taken place.

When news does break, it usually breaks furiously late in

the day. Trades are analyzed—and analyzed and analyzed. And then they're analyzed. And now even the analysts are analyzed. It all makes for pretty compelling television, as well as a real buzz around the sport at a time that used to be dull and boring.

I think that to some extent Trade Deadline Day has become a self-fulfilling prophecy. So much attention is devoted to it each year that general managers feel pressured to make a deal—any deal—just to say they did something. Somehow it seems as if you're not willing to mortgage some of your future for the present, you're not doing your job. God forbid that a general manager should feel his team is fine just the way it is, thank you very much—or even worse, is hesitant to trade away the team's best prospects because he doesn't think this year's team has much hope of winning the Cup no matter whom it acquires at the deadline.

It's become like fishing. And no GM wants to be left standing there at the end of the day explaining why he doesn't have any catch to show.

Just ask Maple Leaf general manager John Ferguson, who was hammered for not making a deal on Deadline Day 2006, even though he'd made a couple of minor deals leading up to it. But did anybody really think the 2005–06 Maple Leafs were going to win the Stanley Cup?

You hear a lot of evaluations of general managers based largely on what they've been able to do on Trade Deadline Days. What gets overlooked is the fact that most trade deadline deals have little or no effect on who wins the Stanley Cup. In fact, the formula for success in the playoffs in most instances seems to be to do nothing at all on Trade Deadline Day.

Here's what the last several Stanley Cup champions have done on Trade Deadline Day:

2007   Anaheim Ducks trade minor league goaltender Mike Wall for forward Brad May.

| 2006 | Carolina Hurricanes trade forwards Niklas Nordgren and Krystofer Kolanos and a second-round pick in 2007 for forward Mark Recchi. |

| 2004 | Tampa Bay trades a sixth-round pick in 2004 to Nashville for defenceman Stan Neckar. |

| 2003 | New Jersey makes no trades. |

| 2002 | Detroit makes no trades. |

| 2001 | Colorado makes no trades. |

| 2000 | New Jersey trades forwards Brendan Morrison and Denis Pederson to Vancouver for forward Alexander Mogilny. |

| 1999 | Dallas makes no trades. |

| 1998 | Detroit trades a fourth-round pick in 1998 to Toronto for defenceman Jamie Macoun. The Red Wings also deal defenceman Jamie Pushor and a fourth-round pick to Anaheim for defenceman Dmitri Mironov. |

| 1997 | Detroit trades future considerations to Toronto for defenceman Larry Murphy. |

| 1996 | Colorado trades a sixth-round pick in 1996 to Buffalo for forward Dave Hannan. |

| 1995 | New Jersey makes no trades. |

Of those players, Recchi, Mogilny and Murphy all proved useful, although even Mogilny only ranked 10th on the Devils in playoff scoring in 2000.

All of which suggests that the best move on Trade Deadline Day is to do nothing. That's right, unplug the phone, turn off the Blackberry and wait for the deadline to pass.

Hockey is a true team sport in which consistency and familiarity among players are critical. And so when you drop a player into a lineup with six weeks to go in the regular season, there's not enough time to make that work. Adding a role player might be different. But landing the big fish on draft day almost never works because he's stepping into a team that wasn't built around him.

Also—under the current economic framework of the NHL, nothing is as valuable as draft picks and young, cheap, up-and-coming talent. And what do teams trade away on Trade Deadline Day? Draft picks and young, cheap, up-and-coming talent. Which is crazy because since only one team can win the Stanley Cup, the odds are you're selling out the future to be disappointed. And there's nothing to suggest that the difference between winning a Cup or not, or even making the playoffs or not, can be solved with a late-season trade. Don't the Maple Leafs look pretty silly for trading young defenceman Brendan Bell and a second round pick for six weeks of Yanic Perreault at the end of the 2006–07 season?

Consider the Trade Deadline moves of the final four teams from the 2006-07 Stanley Cup playoffs. The Ottawa Senators picked up Oleg Saprykin, who played on their fourth line and was often a health scratch in the playoffs. The Anaheim Ducks got Brad May who played on their fourth line where he had one assist in 18 playoff games. The Buffalo Sabres added forward Dainius Zubrus who collected eight assists during the playoffs but failed to score a goal. Detroit, meanwhile, picked up Todd Bertuzzi who played okay while scoring three goals and collecting four assists during Detroit's playoff run.

Were any of these players difference makers? No.

Unless it's an absolute steal, or a minor deal to add some depth, the best Trade Deadline Day strategy is—do nothing.

24. You can argue all you want about which is the most exciting professional sport. But when you're talking about live entertainment, hockey is the one sport you must see in person.

A LOT OF PROFESSIONAL sports are actually better on television. Baseball and football come to mind, since so much of the play occurs far from where most people sit and watch. Television can bring you the angles, the close-ups and facial expressions you'd never see from the crowd.

And basketball, played on a relatively small floor space compared to the crowds that watch a game, is far better when seen on television—unless you're sitting at courtside. Since basketball, football and baseball all have lots of breaks in play, there's all kinds of time for replays and analysis on TV. You miss out on the atmosphere when you're at home; but if you're talking about the pure pleasure of watching the game, TV is the better option for almost every sport there is.

Except hockey. Hockey is one the professional sport that television just can't do justice to. I don't care whether we're talking about big-screen or high-definition or whatever. TV simply can't capture the *speed* of hockey, the one element that sets it apart from all other sports.

No football player runs as fast as Alexander Ovechkin skates when he's coming down the wing. And no play in any sport develops as quickly as a smart pass from the blue line that finds the open guy and ends up in the back of the net.

And because hockey moves so quickly, television cameras can't keep up. In an arena, you can see the play develop in a way you can't on television because television is a slave to the puck. But by following the puck, the camera can't show you which forwards have been caught up ice, which defenceman cheated a little too much, or who has just got himself open. You don't see these things on TV until the puck gets there.

Sometimes, television directors can use alternate camera angles to capture these things and show them on replay. But hockey is a sport that sometimes goes three or four minutes without a whistle, so there are all kinds of critical plays that fans watching on television never really get to understand—they just haven't seen enough to put it all together. It's like trying to put together a puzzle without all the pieces.

Wider angles can show us more, but they also make it hard to identify players on the ice, which is frustrating for any viewer. When I watch a team I'm familiar with, the wide angle doesn't bug me that much because I can still tell who's who. But show me a team I don't often watch and the players might as well all be silhouettes when the camera pulls back.

Watching on television, you also miss out on the *sound* of hockey. When skates cut through fresh ice, bodies bang against the boards or a puck ricochets off a crossbar, you can sense it in an arena, even when the place is rocking.

It's interesting that traditional hockey fans rarely complain about the coverage of their sport on television. That's because they have watched so much of the game throughout their lives that they've developed an ability to make inferences about what's going on beyond the camera lens and use their imaginations to fill in what they can't see.

But newer hockey fans who haven't grown up with the sport can't do that. They can't imagine what they can't see. Which is why a lot of them complain about not being able to find the puck. The puck does disappear from view on television more often than most hockey fans think it does. But longtime fans don't mind because they understand where it's going at any given time, partly because of the way players on the ice react.

Baseball and football are so static and routinized that even casual fans can follow the action. The same goes for basketball, which tends to be an exchange of scoring opportunities through one possession after another.

But hockey has no such predictability. That's great for those of us who know the game, but not so great for those to whom it can look a lot like bees buzzing around a nest.

So it should come as no real surprise when you hear someone who's just attended their first hockey game marvel about a sport they've ignored all their lives on television. It's a different game, a different experience, and one you have to catch in person to really appreciate.

25. Parity has been praised as a panacea for hockey—the ultimate instrument of fairness. But Bob says that, in achieving competive balance, the National Hockey League has lost something far more valuable.

WHEN THE NATIONAL HOCKEY LEAGUE delivered a salary cap to its teams at the end of the 2004–05 lockout, you could almost hear the hallelujahs across the land. The sport has been saved! Competitive balance is back! Every team can win the Stanley Cup!

Yes, hockey had succeeded in achieving the loftiest of lofty goals for any professional sport: parity. No more dynasties! A different Stanley Cup winner every year! Every team gets a turn!

And sure enough, by the start of the 2006–07 season, 26

of the NHL's 30 teams had payrolls roughly within the same range, between $40 million and $44 million (U.S.). Great teams had been broken up and talent was spread far and wide across the league.

All of which may sound great. Except that parity is the last thing any professional sports league should be striving for. It's dull, it's colourless and it's just another way of saying that none of the teams is all that much better than any other.

Take a walk through the history of professional sports, and without exception the greatest eras of any sport are defined either by dynasties or by individual greatness. While fans may complain about seeing the same team or individual on top for long periods of time, the fact is that nothing compels us to pay attention more than greatness and dominance.

Think about it. What's the greatest era in NFL history? How about when the Packers, Cowboys, Steelers, 49ers or Patriots were on top? Has there been a more compelling CFL era than the one in which the Edmonton Eskimos won five consecutive Grey Cups with Warren Moon at quarterback? In baseball, just about every golden era has been built on the success of the New York Yankees. And in basketball, take your pick: Magic's Lakers or Michael's Bulls?

It's the same in individual sports. There was a time when the PGA Tour was boring because every week there seemed to be a different winner. And with no dominant favourite, no player that everyone was trying to knock off, the sport lacked appeal for a lot of sports fans. Then along came a guy named Woods. Did fans turn away? No, they did not. They tuned in like never before to see the greatness of Tiger Woods and to find out whether anyone could beat him.

And what about boxing? There's a sport that's fallen off the map in large part because its most prestigious division—the heavyweight class—hasn't had a dominant champion since Mike Tyson last had his head screwed on correctly.

The same is true in hockey. If you were to trying to sell someone on hockey, you would show them the Canadiens of the 1950s or 1970s, or the Oilers of the 1980s. Or maybe even Steve Yzerman's Detroit Red Wings.

You wouldn't, I'm guessing, show them the Carolina Huricanes from 2005–06, a team that couldn't hold a candle to any of the great teams in NHL history.

In fact, Carolina is a great example of everything that is wrong with parity in hockey. The Hurricanes were a good regular-season team without a particularly compelling identity. Then they got on a roll during the playoffs to win the first Stanley Cup of the NHL's parity-ridden post-lockout era.

They had a no-name defence, a rookie goaltender and some good forwards—but none you could say were at the peaks of their careers, not even Rod Brind'Amour or Eric Staal. Staal may be a superstar someday, but it's fair to suggest his best years in the NHL are still years away.

I'm sure that the Hurricanes were a very compelling story to people in the hockey Mecca known as Raleigh. But to the rest of the hockey world, they were a bore.

And once they'd won the Cup they were gone before we got to know them. Roughly a third of their roster turned over before the start of the 2006–07 season. That's the new NHL in a nutshell right there: a nondescript Stanley Cup champion dismantled almost before the parade is over.

At the start of every season, fans should be buzzing with a debate over whether any team is good enough to defeat the previous year's Stanley Cup winner. It was certainly that way in the 1970s, when the Philadelphia Flyers and Montreal Canadiens were winning Cups. And it was that way right through the 1980s and 1990s. Even though Detroit, Colorado or New Jersey never strung Cups together like teams did in the 1970s or '80s, each of their Stanley Cups was accompanied by the sense that the Red Wings, Avalanche or Devils might repeat.

But there was no such buzz about Carolina in the fall of 2006. Anaheim was competitive enough a year after winning the Cup, in 2006–7, but was far from being the Stanley Cup favourite when eliminated in the first round in April, 2008.

The NFL and NBA have been lucky because they've had it both ways. They've brought in salary caps and still managed to produce dynasties. In the NBA it's because two or three great players can sustain such a run. In the NFL, the same can be true because of the importance of certain positions, and because coaching alone can go a long way towards sustaining success year after year.

But hockey is a player's game. And without a concentration of great players, there can be no great teams. If you want your sport to have wider appeal—which seems to be the NHL's never-ending quest—then you'd better be able to show fans something they might never see again. And in a hockey world paved over with parity, that's never going to happen.

26.

When the National Hockey League came back from its one-year hiatus, fans couldn't wait to applaud the new game. From the elimination of the two-line offside, to the new officiating standards, to all those pretty goals, it was all good news. But Bob says the biggest change in the new game was putting something old back in it.

FROM THE MID-1990S until the lockout began in the fall of 2004, there was no shortage of critics of the on-ice product in the National Hockey League.

They criticized the neutral-zone trap, the hooking, holding and interference and the stickwork that routinely saw players head to their benches with gashes carved into their faces.

There were complaints about a dearth of pretty goals and the fact that goal-scoring itself was becoming a lost art.

But almost everyone missed the sum total of all these facts, the thing that, more than anything else, had transformed hockey from an exciting sport to one that left us disappointed most nights. The fact of the matter is that the comeback, the surprise ending, had virtually disappeared from hockey.

In fact, most nights you could safely predict which team was going to win by the middle stages of the second period. And if the lead by that point happened to be two or three goals . . . well, there was little reason not to pack it in.

Which is critical, because the uncertainty of the outcome is what sets professional sports apart from all other forms of entertainment. When you go to movies, the theatre, the circus or a concert, you may not know how it's going to end. But the people providing that entertainment certainly do. It's scripted, like most things in life. No one bets on the symphony.

Which is why sports has always been unique. The promise of sports is that when you buy a ticket, you never know what you're going to see. There's no guarantee that you'll see a great game, or that your favourite team is going to win. The only thing certain is that what you'll see can't be predicted, because it depends on a great deal of skill and determination and no small amount of luck.

But in hockey, that was no longer true most nights, because the rules allowed teams with a lead to simply clutch and grab their way to the final buzzer while barely allowing a scoring chance.

Back in the 2003–04 season, *The Globe and Mail* tracked the first 142 games of the season to measure this phenomenon. It found that teams that scored first had an accumulated record of 92–24–26 in regulation time. (Overtime results were not included.) A team trailing 1–0 at any point in a game had only a 16.9 percent chance of winning in regulation. If you spotted a team a 2–0 lead, their record was 56–6–10.

That is, a team that gave up the first two goals had only an 8.3 percent chance of winning within regulation time.

But what was most startling was the manner in which teams could hold onto leads after two periods of play. The *Globe* found that any team leading by any margin heading into the third period of an NHL game had a cumulative record of 87–7–19.

In other words, in the majority of instances, hockey games were over long before over the final horn. And I really think that's part of what killed the sport for new fans, particularly in the United States. People who don't love hockey for its own sake want to see excitement. But so often hockey games ended with one team sitting on a lead while the other team tried against the odds to chip the puck over the offensive blue line.

Can you imagine what it would have been like to get to your seat a little late, only to learn it was 2–0 after only five minutes of play? Why bother sitting through the slow asphyxiation of a hockey team in the grip of the left-wing lock?

Thankfully, the NHL reversed this trend after the lockout. Now it's not uncommon to see teams come back from two- or even three-goal deficits. You can actually see several lead changes within the course of a game. And teams can't just sit on a lead for 30 minutes to cash in the two points.

I mean, was there a better example of this point than the final game of the 2006–07 season between Montreal and Toronto, the epic showdown between two teams with a potential playoff spot at stake? The Leafs led 3–1 early in the second period. But less than 13 minutes later it was 5–3 for Montreal. Then the Leafs came back with three unanswered goals in the second and third periods to win 6–5.

I can say with absolute certainty that there is no way this would have occurred in the years leading up to the lockout. Not a chance. The Leafs would have gotten their 3–1 lead and then used every tactic possible, and whatever the officials would allow, to sit on it the rest of the way.

Look, I love all the speed in the new game—the passing, the playmaking and all the goals. But the biggest difference for me is knowing that when a game is 3–1 in the middle of the second period, it's worth sticking around to see who wins.

27.

Nothing fuels the imagination of fans and general managers like a trade. It's often said that every trade looks good from both sides on the day it is made. But that's not always true. Bob looks at the five most lopsided trades of the post-expansion era.

GENERAL MANAGERS IN the National Hockey League love to make trades. They trade at the draft, during the summer, during training camp and right through the season. About the only time they don't trade is during the playoffs, and they'd make trades then, too, if the league would let them.

Evaluating trades involves more than determining which ones turned out to be the most lopsided. They've also got to be graded for what they were on the day they were made. For example, I wouldn't say the Vancouver Canucks trading Cam Neely to Boston for Barry Pederson was that bad a trade on the day it was made. At the time, Pederson was a 26-year-old who already had more than 160 goals to his credit. And Neely hadn't blown anyone away during his first three years in the NHL. It turned out to be a horrible deal for the Canucks, but in order to make my top five, a deal has to be downright foolish the minute it takes place.

Here are my top five from the post-expansion era.

5. June 24, 2001: The New York Islanders send Zdeno Chara, Bill Muckalt and the second-overall pick in the

2001 draft to the Ottawa Senators for Alexei Yashin.
Everyone in the world knew that the Ottawa Senators had to
trade Alexei Yashin after the 2000–01 season. But that didn't
stop Islander general manager Mike Milbury from overpaying
for one of the most selfish players in the game. The Senators and
Yashin had been to court the previous summer, battling over
whether he owed Ottawa a year of service for sitting out the
entire 1999–2000 season while he still had a contract. When a
judge ruled that he did, Yashin returned for 2000–01, played for
his stats and then promptly quit on his team during the first
round of the playoffs as Ottawa was swept by the Toronto in
four games. Despite the alarm bells about Yashin's character and
the obvious fact that the Senators were desperate sellers, Ottawa
general manager Marshall Johnston managed to pull off a sweet
deal. Yashin went to Long Island, where the dumbest team in
hockey signed him to a 10-year, $90 million contract. Yashin
immediately went to sleep, and the Islanders bought him out of
his contract after the 2006–07 season. Muckalt was a bust in
Ottawa, but Chara quickly evolved into one of the game's premier defencemen. He was the Senators' shutdown defenceman
for four seasons before cashing in as a free agent, signing with
Boston after the 2005–06 season. Meanwhile, Ottawa used the
second pick of the 2001 draft to take Jason Spezza, who became
their number one centre and finished second in the league in
assists to Joe Thornton during the 2005–06 season. Not a bad
return for someone they had to get rid of anyway.

**4. March 20, 1996: The Pittsburgh Penguins trade
Markus Naslund to the Vancouver Canucks in exchange
for Alek Stojanov.** Markus Naslund's slow start to his NHL
career caused the Penguins to write him off too early. The
16th pick of the 1991 draft, Naslund scored just six goals in his
first 85 NHL games. But general manager Craig Patrick should
have seen his potential when he scored 19 goals and 33 assists
in 66 games in 1995–96 before the trade. Instead, Pittsburgh

dumped him for Stojanov, a forward who'd been drafted nine places ahead of Naslund because teams saw him as a future Bob Probert. Besides sharing a hometown with the former Detroit tough guy (Windsor, Ontario), scouts thought Stojanov had that same combination of skill and toughness. Well, they were half right. In 59 games leading up to the trade, Stojanov had just one assist and 123 penalty minutes. By then it was widely recognized that his skating skills needed considerable work to make him an effective NHL player. The rest is history. Naslund developed into one of the NHL's premier scorers, approaching 350 career goals by the end of the 2006–07 season at age 33. Stojanov scored just two goals as a Penguin and none as a Canuck before embarking on a journey through the minor leagues that ended with the Central Hockey League's New Mexico Scorpions in 2001–02.

3. November 7, 1988: Toronto trades Russ Courtnall to Montreal for John Kordic. In another classically flawed trade involving a tough guy for a talented forward, the Canadiens came out laughing in this one. Courtall, a former seventh-overall pick, already had three 20-goal seasons on his resume by age 23, when the 1988–89 season began. And yet, 30-year-old Leaf general manager Gord Stellick, the youngest person ever to occupy such a job in the NHL, dealt him to Montreal for Kordic just nine games in. It would be easy to blame the trade on poor judgment of the young GM. But Stellick said at the time that coach John Brophy and the Leafs' full scouting staff were behind the move. Kordic's game was no mystery—the guy had accumulated almost 700 penalty minutes in three seasons in the Western Hockey League. Kordic could certainly fight, but he had limited skills otherwise, as his seven goals in 115 NHL games with Montreal suggested. After the trade, Courtnall scored 75 goals in his first three seasons with Montreal, and later hit 36 in a season with the Minnesota North Stars. He played 11 seasons after the trade, finishing his career with 297 goals. John Kordic scored 10 goals over parts of three seasons with the Leafs, managing 252 penalty minutes in 1989–90, a year cut short when the Leafs suspended him indefinitely after he failed to show up for a game. He played just 38 more NHL games over the next two seasons, finishing his NHL career in 1992 with the Quebec Nordiques. His life of drug use and excess away from the rink ended that summer, when he suffered a heart malfunction after a struggle with police at a Quebec City motel.

2. August 7, 1992: Chicago trades Dominik Hasek to Buffalo for Stephane Beauregard and a fourth-round draft pick in 1993. The Blackhawks had one of the National Hockey League's all-time great goaltenders and apparently didn't know it. Hasek had come to the NHL as a 27-year-old, having amassed a resume in his native Czechoslovakia that included goaltender-of-the-year honours five years running and three player-of-the-year awards. Hawks general manager Mike Keenan wasn't enamoured of Hasek's off-ice behaviour, which included spending the entire off-season in Europe and acquainting himself only marginally with his teammates, his community and the English language. Hasek played 20 games during the 1991–92 season and was understandably eager to get out of Ed Belfour's shadow in Chicago. The Sabres obviously knew what they were getting, because general manager Gerry Meehan said Buffalo had spent five months trying to get Hasek. Beauregard, meanwhile, was dealt three days later to Winnipeg for Christian Ruuttu in a prearranged trade. The Hawks used the draft pick from Buffalo (90th overall) to take Eric Daze. Not bad, especially for a fourth-round pick, but hardly fair compensation for a goaltender who went on to win six Vezina and two Hart Trophies.

1. December 6, 1995: Montreal trades Patrick Roy and team captain Mike Keane to Colorado for goaltender Jocelyn Thibault, forward Martin Rucinsky and

forward Andrei Kovalenko. This one is the all-time winner, because no one should ever trade the best goaltender of his era at the peak of his career. Look, even if Patrick Roy and head coach Mario Tremblay were at loggerheads, sometimes you just have to let a superstar have his way. At least you do when he's Patrick Roy. And besides, what was Roy going to do? Never play again? The Canadiens held all the cards, and they panicked. So they got just what they deserved. Rucinsky hit the 25-goal mark for Montreal three times, but battled injuries and inconsistency during his time with the Habs. Thibault never developed into a dependable number-one goaltender in Montreal (or in Chicago, for that matter). And Kovalenko played exactly 51 games for Montreal. Roy went on to lead Colorado to Stanley Cup wins in 1996 and 2001, and won a Conn Smythe Trophy (you never want the guy you trade away to win the Conn Smythe). In six of his first seven seasons with Colorado, he got the Avs to at least the third round of the playoffs. Keane also won two Cups after leaving Montreal, one with the Avalanche in 1996 and another with Dallas in 1999. How have the Habs done since the trade? They haven't advanced past the second round of the playoffs.

P.S. It may be too early to say that this deal definitely belongs among the all-time worst, but Florida's trade in 2006 of goaltender Roberto Luongo, defenceman Lukas Krajicek and a sixth-round pick for defenceman Bryan Allen, goaltender Alex Auld and forward Todd Bertuzzi is certainly a candidate. This deal amounts basically to Luongo, considered by some the best goaltender in all of hockey, for Bertuzzi, who scored one goal in seven games for Florida before being dealt to Detroit at the 2007 trade deadline.

28. On the eve of the 2007 Stanley Cup playoffs, Ottawa Senators head coach Bryan Murray went ballistic about his team being called "choking dogs." While the Senators shed most of that label with some convincing wins, Bob says their reputation to that point was well earned.

YOU'LL HAVE TO excuse me if I wasn't particularly excited about the Ottawa Senators at the start of the 2007 Stanley Cup playoffs. I mean, can you blame me?

Because the cold, hard truth of the matter is that one of the most talented teams in hockey over the past seven or eight years, a juggernaut during the regular season, hadn't won a thing.

The Senators are the only Canadian team to reach the playoffs in each of the past 10 seasons. And other than Detroit, no National Hockey League team has had more success during the regular season over that span. None.

But while the Red Wings had two Stanley Cups to show for their efforts, what did the Senators have? One appearance the Eastern Conference finals. Four series victories in nine years. Five first-round knockouts.

It wasn't just that that Ottawa lost at playoff time; it's *how* they lost: looking gutless and scared and mentally fragile. It was as if all you had to do to them was say "boo!" during Game 1 of a series and they were yours.

It was as if the minute they knew it was playoff time, something changed in that dressing room. The certainty, the kind of confidence that surrounds all winners in sports, just wasn't there.

Put simply, they became a different team. And though some of the players changed from year to year, it almost seemed like something in the DNA of that franchise was wrong. They just did things at playoff time they never did during the regular season.

In 1998–99, the Senators went an entire season without losing four games in a row. Yet, when the playoffs began, they were swept four straight by Buffalo.

In 2000–01, Ottawa lost four games in a row only twice all season. Then came the playoffs, and they dropped four in a row to the Toronto Maple Leafs, whom they'd beaten in all five meetings that season.

In 2003–04, Ottawa was shut out just twice during the entire regular season. Yet, during the opening round of the playoffs that followed, they failed to score in three of seven games en route to losing to the Leafs for the fourth time in five seasons.

It's popular to suggest that goaltending was the issue in Ottawa all this time. And no, they didn't have a Patrick Roy or a Martin Brodeur or a Dominik Hasek (at least not when they needed him). But it was never goaltending that was Ottawa's downfall during these years.

It was goal *scoring*.

In 71 playoff games leading into the 2007 playoffs, the Senators had averaged just 2.15 goals per game. In 16 of those games they were shut out. In 13 they scored a single goal. In 18 they scored two. That's well over half their playoff games in which the Senators managed two goals or fewer.

This from a team that consistently ranked among the highest-scoring teams in hockey during that span.

"Choke" isn't a word anyone should throw around loosely in sports. But these guys were trying to swallow peach pits.

When you earn home-ice advantage for a series and lose in four games straight, as Ottawa did in 1999 and 2001, that's choking.

When you go 0–4 playing in Game 7 of a playoff series, that's choking.

When you lose four playoff series in five years to the same team, your archrival, the hated and perennially mediocre Toronto Maple Leafs, while absorbing seven shutouts, that's choking.

When your ability to score goals is inversely related to the importance on a game on any given night, that's definitely choking.

And when you lose to inferior teams, teams that everyone knows you should beat, that is the essence of choking.

Losing to a superior team, as Ottawa did to Anaheim in the 2007 Stanley Cup final, is different. There's no shame in that because the Ducks clearly deserved to win the Cup. The fact that they were better than Ottawa shouldn't detract from what the Senators accomplished during the first three rounds of the playoffs.

But given the way the Senators collapsed halfway through the 2007–2008 season, I'd say they still have issues.

29.

Want to win the Stanley Cup? Well, you'd better load up with a bunch of "our" boys. Or at least that's what a lot of fans would tell you. Bob gets to the bottom of whether North Americans are more valuable at playoff time than players from across the pond.

NO DEBATE IN HOCKEY circles is more likely to elicit nods of approval than the notion that European players, no matter how talented and useful during the regular season, are less valuable at playoff time.

If you want to win the Cup, the conventional wisdom goes, you need players who grew up with the Stanley Cup tradition and understand the importance of what it all means.

It's a notion that gets a lot of traction with Don Cherry and his disciples. But it also gets a fair bit of credence from some general managers around the National Hockey League. And while it may be taboo to say so out loud, it's not uncommon to hear a general manager or a scout suggest quietly that such-and-such a team isn't going very far because it's "too European."

This argument has a lot of momentum behind it right now because the last three Stanley Cup champions have been low in European content. In 2004, Tampa Bay had only six players from Europe. In 2006, Carolina had only four players from across the pond. And in 2007 Anaheim had just three.

But consider that from 1994 to 2006, Stanley Cup winning teams were overall an almost exact reflection of the league during that span when it comes to European content.

From 1994 to 2006, the NHL player pool was composed of an average of 26.46 percent non–North American players. Over that same span, Stanley Cup champions were only slightly less European, at 25.46 percent.

Of the 12 teams that won the Stanley Cup during those years, nearly half of them (five) have had a higher percentage of European players than the league average of that season. Six had a lower percentage, and one (Colorado in 1996) had a makeup identical to the league average.

Now, it's a popular misconception that North American players are the ones doing the dirty work of scoring those difficult playoff goals. After all, the Euros get soft when the game gets rough. They can't take the tough going.

Well, not exactly.

In fact, when it comes to carrying the scoring load at playoff time, European players are considerably overrepresented among Stanley Cup champions.

Of the top five scorers on those same Stanley Cup champions, nearly 32 percent have been Europeans. Extend that to the top 10 scorers on each team and the number drops just slightly, to 30 percent.

Both of those figures are considerably higher than the percentage of Europeans, both in the league and on Stanley Cup winners.

So, not only do European players fail to wilt at playoff time, but it appears that they thrive. This notion that they don't perform in the spring, that somehow the North Americans have an inherent edge, is bunk. That's not something you're going to hear from the cheerleaders in this country who believe "our boys" have some innate instinct that gives them an edge when the Cup in sight. But it is the truth.

30.

We all cheer when Canada wins women's hockey gold at the Winter Olympics. And the rise of the women's game is one of the great sports stories of the past 25 years. But Bob says putting this sport on the biggest stage in sports is unfair to everyone.

THE GREATEST ARGUMENT against women's hockey being part of the Winter Olympic Games wasn't made on the ice.

It was advanced in the hallways of the Olympic arena in Turin, in the moments after Canada's women's team had defeated Sweden to win their second consecutive gold medal.

Instead of being able to rejoice in the moment, to talk about the triumph and joy of winning an Olympic gold medal, the Canadian women were forced to defend what they'd just done.

In every other sport, it's common for athletes to find themselves on the defensive when they lose. But the Canadian women were forced into the unique and uncomfortable position of trying to justify a gold medal. That's what happens when you win a championship by outscoring opponents by a margin of 46–2.

You could suggest that the only adversity the Canadian women encountered during their journey to Olympic gold was the constant suggestion that what they were doing didn't mean very much.

Which is why including women's hockey in the Olympic Winter Games isn't just unfair to the Olympic movement and the fans. It's downright unfair to the players as well.

Canada won that final game by a score of 4–1 over Sweden. Earlier, during the round robin, they'd defeated the same team 8–1. My bet is that if the Canadians had spotted the Swedes a dozen goals from the opening face-off of that gold-medal game, they'd have found a way to win it. The players and coaches understood that the wider the margin of victory, the less significant their gold-medal was going to be. Which is why the Canadians ended up winning by just three goals.

I understand why the women want to be there. And the fact that the Canadians cakewalked their way to the gold doesn't diminish one bit the level of commitment they made en route. But in order for a gold medal to have value in the truest sense, there has to be some sense of uncertainty about the outcome.

Well, in Torino, you knew exactly how it was going to end. Just like you do every time Canada plays anyone but the United States. And if the U.S. happens to be off its game a bit, as it was in Torino, then whatever small degree of suspense might have existed is gone.

You could say the same thing about the U.S. Dream Team in men's basketball when it went to the 1992 Olympics and obliterated everything in its path. In fact, many people did. But in that instance there was a slew of countries at that next tier. And you knew that, given the soaring participation levels of basketball around the world, some team—or teams—was going to close that gap quickly. And that's exactly what happened.

American basketball in 1992 was about as good as it's going to get. So the rest of the world was not chasing a moving target. But women's hockey in Canada is still in the early stages of growth. It keeps getting better and better and better thanks to more players, better training and a stronger commitment to excellence.

So, even if the Swedes or the Finns are better by the next Olympics, guess what? The Canadians are going to be better, too.

We may be years—even decades—away from seeing any of these other countries ready to contend for Olympic gold. Until that happens, I say let's leave Olympic hockey to the men, for whom, as we know, gold for any country is never a sure bet.

31. It was Commissioner Gary Bettman's dream to get National Hockey League players into the Olympics. Now Bob wants to know where the payoff is for hockey, and why the Stanley Cup is being awarded in mid June.

GARY BETTMAN WAS groomed for his job as commissioner of the National Hockey League in the sport of basketball. No surprise, then, that Bettman had the NHL follow the National Basketball Association into the Olympics, allowing the best pros to participate on the world's biggest sporting stage.

Sounds great. But while the involvement of NBA pros might make sense at the Summer Games, when the NBA is enjoying its off-season, it's been a terrible idea for the NHL.

The NHL presumably believed it could use the Olympics to market its game to a global audience, just as the NBA had. Now, I can certainly understand the notion of using the Games to turn players into international stars, thus driving broadcast and licensing revenues.

Except that basketball is played throughout the world, while hockey is not. And so, what tends to happen during the Winter Olympic Games is that a lot of people who already like hockey get to watch more of it. And while the Olympic hockey tournament does attract broader interest in some countries, depending on the results, those new viewers seem to tune out as soon as the Games are over and the NHL resumes play.

Of course, the "international" viewers Bettman is most interested in are Americans.

But consider what happened in 2002, when Bettman got his dream matchup on American soil: Canada playing the United States for the gold medal at Salt Lake City. That final drew an audience of 10.7 percent of all U.S. television viewers, the largest to watch a hockey game since the Miracle on Ice in 1980. And yet television ratings for hockey in the U.S. since that time have been nothing short of a disaster. So bad, in fact, that ESPN ultimately walked away from the property three years later, leaving hockey on the Outdoor Life Network (now known as Versus). So I'm asking: Where exactly is the synergy from this great Olympic experience?

One thing that can be said for having NHL players at the Olympics is that it produces very good hockey. But it's ridiculous to interrupt the NHL season and pretend that these teams have been preparing for months or years, just as the other athletes at the Olympics have done. Canada's Christina Groves wins a medal at speed skating in Torino and it's the fulfillment of a journey that began 18 years earlier, when she was 11. Mats Sundin gets his medal with Team Sweden and it's the fulfillment of a journey that began on the previous Tuesday.

And shutting the NHL season down for three weeks in midwinter makes about as much sense as playing the Stanley Cup final in mid-June, which is what the NHL does during Olympic years.

That should be reason enough to put an end to the Olympic experiment. But it gets worse. Another problem is that Olympic participation puts everyone in a potential conflict of interest that is just bad for the NHL.

Players who nurse minor injuries don't know whether to go or not. Now, if I'm an NHL owner, there's no way I want one of my players going to the Olympics if he's got so much as an ingrown toenail, never mind a hamstring injury or sore back. Yet the owners have no say in the matter because they waived their rights during collective bargaining. GMs, too, lie awake at night hoping none of their stars come home with season-ending injuries—ask former Ottawa GM John Muckler about this one after the Dominik Hasek fiasco in Torino.

Olympic coaches who also work behind NHL benches are compromised by their roster decisions. Do you play the guy you've brought along from your NHL team, even though he's not producing? Or do you put the national team first and leave your player on the bench? There is no good answer. Which is why Pat Quinn's relationship with Curtis Joseph went to hell after he opted to sit the goaltender during the 2002 Olympics in favour of Martin Brodeur. And that was with Brodeur leading Canada to the gold!

Then there is the fatigue factor, which is especially damaging to teams that send the largest numbers of players to the Olympics. Do the math on how much hockey is being played between early February and mid-June and it becomes obvious that it would be impossible for a player to go to the Olympics *and* complete a Stanley Cup playoff run without paying some sort of price.

Let's use the Carolina Hurricanes' Stanley Cup season as an example. The Hurricanes were lucky that just three of their players went to the Olympics, because here is the schedule they endured from February to June: they played three games in four days before the Olympic break began on February 13; after the break ended, two and a half weeks later, they played 25 games in 49 nights to close out the regular season. Then they had two days off and began a sum of 25 playoff games in 59 nights.

Now, you can't tell me that if the Hurricanes had had eight

or nine of their best players participate in that Olympic tournament they would have been the same team in June. No way.

So perhaps it's no coincidence that Carolina and Edmonton, which also had just three Olympians, wound up as Stanley Cup finalists, while teams such as Ottawa and Philadelphia, each loaded with Olympians, bowed out early.

In effect, Gary Bettman's great experiment is screwing with the competitive integrity of the NHL product.

Which is why I say let's end this marriage now and stop pretending it's a great step forward for hockey. I don't blame Bettman for trying, but enough is enough.

32. Commissioner Gary Bettman insists the National Hockey League lockout was about ensuring competitive balance for all 30 teams. Bob wonders what league Gary was watching.

IN JUNE OF 2004, the Stanley Cup final featured the Tampa Bay Lightning and the Calgary Flames in a thrilling seven-game series that saw the Cup go to Florida for the very first time.

Three months later, Gary Bettman and the National Hockey League owners shut down the game—in large part, they claimed, because the league's competitive balance was out of whack.

Right.

You can debate whether or not you want parity in the league. I've already said you'd better be careful what you wish for when you start dreaming about parity. But this inane argument that small-market teams can't have a legitimate chance to win the Cup without economic parity is ridiculous.

In making the assertion that the league needed to level the economic playing field in the interests of competitive balance, Bettman had to ignore a flood of evidence at his feet that would have suggested otherwise. Not the least of which was the fact that the Flames and Lightning ranked 16th and 17th in league payrolls during the 2003–04 season. Or that, of the final four teams that season, only the Philadelphia Flyers ranked among the upper half in spending.

But the NHL, Bettman insisted, was going to hell because the big teams were winning everything.

Of course they weren't. In 2002–03, the final four playoff teams featured three in the lower half of league payroll when Ottawa, Anaheim and Minnesota all reached the conference finals. And though big spenders Colorado, Detroit and Toronto were all there in 2001–02, most would agree the Leafs are hardly a threat to the competitive balance of the NHL.

If spending money was a guarantee of a Cup in the old NHL, then someone should have told the New York Rangers. The Rangers, despite spending more money than anyone in hockey most seasons, somehow managed to miss the playoffs seven years in a row heading into the lockout. Over those same seven seasons, the Ottawa Senators, in one of the league's smallest markets, surviving a puny Canadian dollar and a bankruptcy, somehow managed to make the postseason every year.

The Rangers, oddly enough, didn't get back into the playoffs until after the lockout, when they no longer held an economic advantage over the rest of the league's teams.

Truthfully, 2005 was an illogical time for the league to get on a soapbox over competitive balance. After decades of dynasties, the NHL had witnessed just one repeat winner (Detroit 1997 and 1998) in 12 seasons.

Not only was the NHL's competitive balance problem a myth, but hockey actually had *more* competitive balance than any of the major professional team sports.

In the final five seasons heading into the lockout, exactly half of the NHL's 30 teams reached the championship semifinal. That's higher over the same period than Major League Baseball, where 13 of 30 did so; the National Basketball Association, where 13 of 30 did so; or the NFL, where 13 of 32 made it that far.

In fact, the National Football League, that beacon of fairness held up by hockey people on countless occasions as the model for parity because of its salary cap, had far more of a competitive-balance problem than the NHL.

Think about it. One NFC team, the Philadelphia Eagles, went to four conference championship games in a row. An AFC team, the New England Patriots, won three Super Bowls in four years. So of eight possible appearances in the conference finals from 2002 to 2005, the Eagles and Patriots made it seven times.

Nothing in hockey could compare to that.

What most people fail to recognize is that while much was amiss about the old NHL collective bargaining agreement, including an economic advantage for some teams, that advantage didn't guarantee success on the ice.

By limiting unrestricted free agency to players 31 years of age and older, the NHL ensured that big-spending teams would have free access to players only once they were past their prime years. So while the Rangers and other teams were certainly able to buy up some of the biggest names, they weren't necessarily getting the best players. And those players past age 31 were often on the downside of their careers, meaning teams got stuck with long-term contracts for players with diminishing skills and overinflated price tags.

Smaller-market teams weren't always able to retain their stars up until age 31. But by striking the right deal on the trade market, they could often find fair value in return through younger, cheaper talent that made them as—or more—competitive than they'd been previously.

Of course, not everyone bought into this logic. Especially in a place like Edmonton, where fans accepted wholeheartedly the notion that all the Oilers' shortcomings could be blamed on the evils of NHL economics. Fix the system, they argued, and we'll be right back on top. And sure enough, in 2006, under the new economic model, the Oilers were right there, one game away from their first Stanley Cup in 16 years.

That all sounds wonderful, until you recall that during the regular season the Oilers finished eighth in the Western Conference, which is about where they used to finish under the old economic system. Without points from shootouts, which didn't exist until the 2005–06 season, the Oilers wouldn't have made the playoffs at all. And by the next season they missed the playoffs and finished with one of the poorer records in the NHL.

I'm not saying that teams with bigger budgets didn't have an advantage if they did most things right. But that's different than having a competitive-balance problem in the NHL.

During the spring of 2006, when Gary Bettman was a guest on my *Prime Time Sports* radio show, he had the nerve to remark how thankful he was that the lockout had restored competitive balance to the NHL.

My co-host that day, Stephen Brunt, had the best retort for the commissioner.

"Congratulations, Gary," Stephen said, "for finally finding an economic system that allows the New York Rangers to make the playoffs."

33. There has been nothing but euphoria since the National Hockey League introduced the shootout. But Bob says there's a much better way to rid hockey of tie games.

THERE'S NOTHING MORE exciting in hockey than overtime.

Whether it's the second round of the Stanley Cup play-offs or a good overtime battle in November, there's a different kind of energy about playing hockey past the scheduled three periods.

Overtime is better in hockey than in basketball or baseball because those sports don't have the sudden-death element. And while the National Football League's overtime is cut-throat, it's also patently unfair because a team can lose without ever getting the ball.

But in hockey, overtime works. Which makes me wonder why in the world the National Hockey League thinks that anything more than five minutes of overtime is too much? Here you have a winner-take-all battle, a contest in which one mistake or one great play can end the game. And then, five minutes into it, with the adrenaline soaring, you shut it down and resort to a skills competition.

If hockey is bent on getting rid of ties, then would someone please explain to me why teams can't play more than five minutes of overtime? With the four-on-four format, it's not as if teams don't have enough fresh bodies to play longer. As we've seen during the playoffs, teams are perfectly capable of occasionally playing one, two or even three periods of overtime and then bouncing back the next night. But the fact is that, playing four-on-four overtime, teams would almost never be required to play more than one extra 20-minute period. Especially since, with one point in the standings guaranteed, teams tend to go more for the win and worry less about allowing a goal.

Consider that during the 2005–06 regular season, there were 281 games that went past regulation time. Of those, 136 ended within five minutes of four-on-four overtime. So if 48.4 percent of four-on-four overtime games end within five minutes, how many are going to go a full period? How about approximately none? A second period of four-on-four overtime would be as rare as a 20-innning baseball game.

The only potential problem would be the need to flood the ice just in case overtime went the full 20 minutes. Well, from the start of a flood until the puck drops is about 14 minutes. With most games now ending in under two and a half hours, do you really think anyone is going to go home or stop watching on television because they have to wait 14 minutes?

The NHL doesn't need the shootout. It doesn't need to decide its game with a gimmick, a skills competition that bears no resemblance to the game of hockey whatsoever.

I was interested in the shootout the first few times I saw it. But by about the third one I was completely bored. And now we've got guys trying goofy moves, backing into the crease in mid-flight, carrying the puck like a lacrosse ball, flipping the puck from between their feet. It's ridiculous. Not because I don't like neat tricks, but because a hockey game should be decided by guys playing hockey, not guys impersonating Siegfried and Roy.

I mean, was there anything worse than watching the Toronto Maple Leafs' playoff hopes vanish in a shootout between New Jersey and the New York Islanders on the final day of the 2006–07 season? It takes a lot for me to feel any sympathy for the Leafs. But is that any way for a team to watch its season be decided?

The shootout has also had the unintended effect of taking the excitement out of penalty shots. It used to be that penalty shots were like kick-return touchdowns in football. You might go half a season without seeing one. And then you might see two in a week. Either way, it was special. Now a penalty shot feels just like another shot in a shootout.

Look, four-on-four hockey is the most entertaining form of the game there is. Everyone pretty much agrees on that. So why not give the fans more of it? Instead, you've now got people talking about using the shootout to decide playoff games partly—you guessed it—to please American television.

Presumably, this would happen only after a period or two of scoreless overtime. But just the same, you're messing with the most dynamic element of the Stanley Cup playoffs.

Playoff shootouts would eliminate the uncertainty that binds us to great playoff hockey games. It's that notion of never knowing when a game will end, as we watch the clock creep past midnight. Playoff shootouts would erase such moments as Pat LaFontaine's goal against Washington in the fourth overtime of a seventh game in 1987, or Brett Hull's famous "no goal" in triple overtime of Game 6 that won the 1999 Stanley Cup for Dallas.

It's not like there's a ridiculous number of playoff games that go past two periods of overtime. In fact, over the past two playoff years there has been exactly one. So what exactly is the problem we're trying to correct?

You probably heard the outcry for a playoff shootout after Vancouver and Dallas took four periods of overtime to decide their first-round opener in 2007. But games like that are part of what define the Stanley Cup playoffs and make them unique.

Anyone who has ever sat in an NHL rink during overtime knows there are only two sounds that interrupt the flow of play when an overtime goal is scored. It's either jubilation or the thump of chair seats flipping up by the thousands as people rise towards the exits.

And those are the only ways a playoff hockey game should end.

34. **There's no more critical decision for a National Hockey League team than making the first-overall selection in the entry draft. For some teams, it's the beginning of a beautiful relationship. For others, it's the moment they look back on and wonder what might've been. Bob looks at teams that would love a mulligan.**

EVERY TEAM THAT picks first overall would love to be in the same position as the Pittsburgh Penguins of 1984. The whole world knew they would select Mario Lemieux. And what do you know? Lemieux turned out to be not just the greatest player in the history of that franchise, but among the greatest ever to play the game.

Unfortunately, it's rarely that easy. In many instances, teams end up looking back at what they could've and should've had. And what might have been, had they chosen someone else.

In grading the first picks overall, it's not just important to consider what that player turned out to be. You also need to keep in mind the players the GM and scouts passed over.

So here are the five top instances where a mulligan off the tee would have changed the course of hockey history.

5. Brian Lawton, F, Minnesota North Stars, 1983. Lawton became the first American player to go first overall when Minnesota selected him out of high school and then ushered him into the National Hockey League that fall. He played 58 games in his rookie year, scoring 10 goals and adding 21 assists. Injuries plagued Lawton throughout his career, part of why he never scored more than 21 goals in a season and failed to crack the 50-point barrier even once. At the start of his sixth season, he failed to make the North Stars out of training camp and then rejected the club's attempt to demote him to the minors. His career ended before he was 30, unlike that of the player Minnesota could have taken with the top pick: Steve Yzerman, who went fourth overall.

4. Alexander Daigle, F, Ottawa Senators, 1993. The Senators, despite having no money, were in such a rush to sign this guy that they blew the league's rookie salary structure along the way, inking him to a five-year, $12.5 million contract. Daigle never fit the franchise player part, and was apparently interested in few things about hockey besides the paycheque. He broke the 25-goal plateau just once, and registered

50 points just twice. Had Ottawa picked Chris Pronger, Paul Kariya or Scott Niedermayer, who went second, third and fourth in 1993, the Senators' early history would have been much different.

3. Greg Joly, D, Washington Capitals, 1974. The first player drafted in Washington Capitals history, Joly failed to develop into the kind of franchise building block the Caps were hoping for. Injuries played a part in his shortcomings, as he rarely played a full season. Traded to Detroit after two seasons with the Caps, Joly finished his career with more games logged in the American Hockey League than the NHL. There is no shortage of players the Capitals could have taken in '74, including Clark Gillies, Pierre Larouche, Mario Tremblay and Bryan Trottier.

2. Gord Kluzak, D, Boston Bruins, 1982. The Bruins actually received two players (Brad Palmer and Dave Donnelly) from Minnesota just for selecting Kluzak first overall, since the North Stars wanted Brian Bellows with the second pick. It turns out Belllows was the better choice, playing in nearly four times as many National Hockey League games as Kluzak and narrowly missing the 500-goal club. Kluzak, meanwhile, resembled Bobby Orr on the Bruins' blue line only by virtue of his chronic knee injuries, which limited him to 299 career games. Donnelly and Palmer, meanwhile, had no impact in Boston. The Bruins could have done even better than Bellows had they taken either of the two defencemen who went fourth and fifth that year: Scott Stevens and Phil Housley.

1. Doug Wickenheiser, F, Montreal Canadiens, 1980. Wickenheiser scored 89 goals and 170 points during his final year of junior hockey but never found that scoring touch in the pros. He scored 25 goals as a member of the 1982–83 Canadiens, and 23 two years later with St. Louis, a season that was interrupted by a freak off-ice knee injury. Wickenheiser's career went downhill from there, and he ended up with just 111 National Hockey League goals. Denis Savard, who finished with 473 career goals, went third that year. Fourth and sixth, respectively, were Larry Murphy and Paul Coffey, a pair of defencemen who combined for 683 goals between them.

35. Eric Lindros received so much attention during his teen years, he seemed destined for the Hall of Fame before he played a single NHL game. So was it all hype? Bob says history won't be kind to Lindros, but for a while he was as good as they said he'd be.

GIVEN HIS DIMINISHED status in today's hockey world, it's easy to forget the anticipation that preceded Eric Lindros's arrival in the National Hockey League.

There was, of course, the refusal to play in Quebec, the year of sitting out and, finally, the trade that sent him to Philadelphia.

But all that aside, this was a player who many believed would eclipse Wayne Gretzky as hockey's greatest scorer. As a member of the Oshawa Generals, he sold out junior hockey arenas across Ontario because fans wanted a glimpse of this once-in-a-lifetime combination of size, strength and skill.

At age 18, Lindros was added to Team Canada's roster for the 1991 Canada Cup, bumping established veterans like Steve Yzerman a full year before he played his first NHL game.

Now that Eric Lindros is merely a shell of the player he once was, it's fair to ask the question: Was he oversold? Did he in any way live up to the hype? And, if it hadn't been for the eight concussions, would we be talking about one of the all-time greats?

I think it's fair to divide Eric Lindros's career into two halves: before and after the Scott Stevens hit during the 2000 playoffs, which forced him to miss the entire 2000–01 season. Though his first recorded concussion occurred more than a year before Stevens hit him in Game 7 of the Eastern Conference finals, it was that moment that marked the beginning of the sharp decline of Lindros's career.

His teammates watching from the bench thought it might have marked more than that.

"I believe I said I just watched that kid's career end," teammate Keith Primeau told the Philadelphia *Daily News*, years later. "I really believed that I had watched Lindros play his last game."

It turned out to be just Lindros's last game as a Flyer. But he was never the same player from that point forward.

Up until the Stevens hit, Lindros had scored 290 goals in 486 regular-season games through his first eight seasons, a pace of .60 goals per game.

By comparison, Wayne Gretzky scored 524 goals in 632 regular-season games during his first eight seasons, for an average of .83 goals per game.

While that may seem like a wide margin, you have to consider the decrease in overall NHL goal scoring that coincided with Lindros's arrival. During Gretzky's first eight seasons, the average NHL game had 7.67 goals scored. During Lindros's first eight seasons, however, that number had dipped to just 5.98, a decrease of 22 percent. Take 22 percent off of Gretzky's total and you get .647 goals per game, a rate much closer to Lindros's.

And when you consider that Gretzky played on the highest-scoring teams of all time during his Edmonton years, it's fair to say that he and Lindros were, at the very least, comparable goal scorers during their first eight seasons.

Gretzky is, of course, the NHL's all-time goal-scoring leader with 894, so it may be unfair to use him as the only basis for comparison. Well, here's how Lindros stacks up against the NHL's top 10 goal scorers of all time in terms of goals per game during their first eight seasons. These figures are adjusted to reflect the differences in NHL goal scoring during Lindros's first eight seasons and those of the other players. (For example, Gordie Howe's average has been increased to reflect the fact that goals were harder to come by during his first eight seasons. Conversely, Mark Messier's rate has been lowered to reflect that scoring was more plentiful during his first eight seasons than in Lindros's.)

PLAYER	GOALS/GAME
Brett Hull	.648
Wayne Gretzky	.647
Mario Lemieux	.638
Eric Lindros	.60
Phil Esposito	.584
Luc Robitaille	.512
Marcel Dionne	.477
Gordie Howe	.463
Mike Gartner	.405
Steve Yzerman	.404
Mark Messier	.362

When you look at numbers like those, you can certainly conclude that Eric Lindros hasn't received his due.

Or you could say that his greatest weakness—perhaps his *only* weakness—has been longevity. In his prime, he played a young man's style of game; he was a virtual bull in a china shop who wasn't afraid to go anywhere on the ice. Which is part of what made his scoring pace during those first eight seasons unsustainable. But it was fun to watch.

Eric Lindros won't end up in the Hockey Hall of Fame. His numbers don't warrant it and he hasn't done much in his career to generate much goodwill with the voters.

But he still deserves to be mentioned right alongside the all-time greats. And in terms of what the public was sold when he was still a teenager, he came pretty much just as advertised.

36. For most of its existence, the National Hockey League has been all about dynasties. But Bob says forget those great teams from the 1940s, '50s and '60s. The only dynasties worth measuring are those that came later.

IT IS VERY LIKELY that we've seen the last of the National Hockey League's dynasties. Under a system that includes a salary cap and broader free agency, great teams are likely to be taken apart and sold at a yard sale when the players' salary demands can no longer be accommodated and free agency beckons. Powerhouse teams will fade from memory quickly.

Which perhaps makes the matter of the NHL's single greatest dynasty all the more significant.

You could certainly argue that the distinction of greatest dynasty should go to the Detroit Red Wings of the early 1950s, which boasted Gordie Howe, Sid Abel and Ted Lindsay, among others, on the roster. And of course there's the dynasty in Montreal that followed with Rocket Richard, Jean Beliveau,

Doug Harvey and many others who wound up in the Hockey Hall of Fame.

But as great as those teams might have been, you can't compare their road to the Stanley Cup with the grind that teams endure today, with its four rounds of seven-game series and transcontinental travel.

Beating out just five other teams and having to endure only two playoff series to hoist the Cup just doesn't cut it. So I'm limiting my candidates for greatest dynasty to those that came after the league expanded to 12 teams in 1967–68.

Which leaves us with three dynasties to consider for greatest ever:

Montreal Canadiens, four consecutive Cups from 1976 to 1979. The first thing that jumps out at you about the Montreal Canadiens of the 1970s is the consistency they maintained over their four Stanley Cup years. Montreal never won fewer than 50 regular-season games, at a time when only three other teams—the Islanders, the Flyers and the Bruins—reached that plateau even once. And in one of those years, 1976–77, the Habs were an astounding 60–8–12, which is an unparalleled mark in the modern NHL. The Canadiens also won two other Stanley Cups leading up to their string, in 1970–71 and '72–73, which has to count for something. And while any dynasty is sure to be stacked with great players, Montreal's Guy Lafleur has the distinction of being the best pure scorer of the pre-Gretzky era. And the defencemen on that team—led by Larry Robinson, Serge Savard and Guy Lapointe—comprised one of the greatest units ever.

New York Islanders, four consecutive Cups from 1980 to 1983. Unlike the Canadiens, the Islanders weren't completely dominant during the regular season, winning 50 games just once during their Stanley Cup years. In 1982–83, they finished tied for seventh overall, but wound up winning the Cup in a four-game sweep of the final. Which is part of why the Islanders stand out as perhaps the greatest playoff team of all time. From the spring of 1980 until they lost to Edmonton in the 1984 finals, the Islanders won 19 consecutive playoff series. And not once during that span did they play a best-of-seven series that went the full distance. No team has ever seemed as mentally tough when it mattered most; this was a group of players emboldened by the sense that they could not lose once spring rolled around.

Edmonton Oilers, five Stanley Cups in seven seasons from 1983–84 to 1989–90. The Oilers had the greatest offensive player of all time in the prime years of his career, which says a lot in itself. But the fact that they never won more than two Stanley Cups in a row is a bit of a knock. The Oilers played in a 21-team NHL in which 16 teams made the playoffs, meaning they were able to wrap up a playoff spot months before the end of the regular season—and, presumably, rest up for the postseason. That's not their fault, but it made for some very cushy matchups in the early playoff rounds for Edmonton, such as the 31–38–11 Winnipeg Jets of 1983–84.

The verdict: There's not much to choose between these teams. But I'm going with the Canadiens. And here's why: during their four Cup-winning years, the Canadiens averaged 125.75 points during an 80-game regular season, compared to 103.75 for the Islanders and 104.6 for the Oilers. Montreal never missed a beat for four complete seasons. And that kind of consistency, when you're winning four Cups in a row, is beyond remarkable. It's the greatest team feat in the history of the sport. And one unlikely to ever be surpassed.

37. Goaltenders get more than their share of the credit and the spotlight when their teams win.

Bob tells you which ones deserve to be named as the greatest of all time.

A LOT OF IMPORTANT ingredients, beyond the mere skill of stopping the puck, go into a being great goaltender. First of all, the guy's got to be mentally tough, not just in a way that allows him to handle criticism, but in a manner that allows him to intimidate the other team.

The greatest goaltenders have an edge, because shooters are intimidated by their mere presence. These goalies can get inside the heads of opposing players and make them believe they'll only score if they take the perfect shot.

The best goalies also embolden their teams to be a little more aggressive, to cheat just a little bit if need be on the offensive end, because players know the guy between the pipes can bail them out.

But more than anything, great goalies are guys who win. There's no virtue in a goaltender who plays consistently all year long but surrenders the softies that break the spirit of a team when it matters most.

With those qualities in mind, here's my list of the greatest goaltenders of all time.

5. Georges Vezina. I'll be honest. I never saw him play and I don't know a heck of a lot about him beyond the fact he recorded the NHL's first shutout in 1917–18. But anybody who gets the award for top goaltender named after him deserves to make my list.

4. Terry Sawchuk. Sawchuk makes my list just for what he accomplished during the first five years of his career with Detroit: a Calder Trophy, three Stanley Cups and two Vezinas. Injuries hampered him throughout his career, but he retired as hockey's all-time leader in goaltender victories, while his 103 career shutouts remains untouched.

3. Martin Brodeur. He gets knocked for playing during

a low-scoring era on a team where defence is the major pre-occupation. But consistency defines Brodeur; the first post-lockout season was the only year of his career in which his goals-against average (2.57) exceeded 2.50. He's won three Cups, an Olympic gold medal and a World Cup title. He's played a tonne of hockey—2006–07 was the 10th season in 11 that he's played at least 70 regular-season games. And, with 92 shutouts at age 35 at the end of that campaign, he was also within striking distance of Terry Sawchuk's all-time career mark of 103.

2. Jacques Plante. Plante was the all-time innovator in goal, the first to come out of his crease to play the puck and the first to regularly wear a mask (evidently, he was the smartest of his era as well). All of that, however, makes it easy to forget the standards for success he set with five consecutive Stanley Cup championships and five consecutive Vezina Trophies. The Cup thing is less of a deal to me than the Vezinas. There were only six teams back then, but being the best goaltender in the world meant the same thing then as it does now. His 1962 Hart Trophy win wasn't repeated by a goaltender for 35 years. And we'll never see another goaltender lead the league in goals-against average eight different times in his career.

1. Patrick Roy. By any standard, Roy is the greatest National Hockey League goaltender of all time. He played in and won more NHL games than any goaltender in history and did it over a 20-year career. His three goals-against average titles were spread out over 14 years. And he stayed at the top of his game right through his career, playing at least 61 games in each of his last seven seasons. The biggest thing about Roy was that he was a winner who made everyone around him feel like one, too. He may not have been the greatest team guy in the world, but that wasn't his role. By his presence, he challenged teammates to be as confident as he was, and that made them better. Not only did Roy win two Stanley Cups in

Montreal and two in Colorado, but his teams missed the play-offs just once, during the lockout-shortened season of 1994–95. And his Stanley Cup final performances were stellar—he allowed an average of fewer than two goals a game over 21 contests. Here's the other thing I love about Roy, and it has nothing do to with his goaltending: when he was done playing, he went back and coached junior hockey! Guys of his status usually act like they're ready to step behind the bench without any sort of learning curve at all (a certain Number 99 comes to mind), and yet there's the supposedly arrogant Roy, back in Quebec, riding the buses with a bunch of teenagers.

What? No Hasek??? That's right, Dominik Hasek doesn't make this list. Look, the guy *could* be great, but he has been a headache everywhere he's played. One of the ingredients of a great goaltender is dependability, and Hasek was anything but. He pulled the chute at various times in Buffalo, Detroit and Ottawa, leaving his teammates guessing each time what was or wasn't really wrong with him. And despite all the accolades, he won just one Stanley Cup, and that was with a Detroit team that was probably good enough to win one without him in 2002. The Wings had won two before he got there, and no one is suggesting Chris Osgood or Mike Vernon should go into the Hall of Fame.

What about Glenn Hall? His streak of 502 consecutive games is impressive, but for part of his career teams didn't even dress backup goaltenders.

Grant Fuhr? I know he played in a high-scoring era, but any goaltender with a save percentage consistently below .900 and who allowed an average of almost four goals per game some years can't make my list. Fuhr had a great record because the Oilers were a scoring machine. But they *had* to be, just to make up for the deficiences of their goaltender. His short-lived post-hockey career in golf was more impressive than his exploits with the Oilers.

38.

European hockey players have become so common that no one even remarks when one wins an NHL award or is selected first in the entry draft. Bob tells you which are the greatest of all time.

NOTHING HAS DONE more in the past three decades to change hockey—and the level at which it's played—than the influx of European talent. In fact, Canadians owe Europeans a debt of gratitude. Because it was their dominance in the skill areas that forced Canadians to rethink the way they were learning and playing the game. Europe has yet to produce a Bobby Orr, a Wayne Gretzky or a Gordie Howe. But it's only a matter of time. So until that player arrives, here's my list of the greatest European players ever to suit up in the NHL.

5. Jari Kurri. Kurri probably doesn't get his due because many view him as a byproduct of Wayne Gretzky. In fact, he actually scored one more goal the year after Gretzky left for Los Angeles than he did during Gretzky's last season in Edmonton. It's tempting to rank countryman Teemu Selanne ahead of him. But that would require that we ignore Kurri's contribution to five Stanley Cups with the Oilers. He ranks 18th all-time in points as of the end of the 2006–07 season, and 17th in goals.

4. Borje Salming. The first Swede inducted into the Hockey Hall of Fame, Salming was everything the Toronto Maple Leafs were not. He was gutsy, durable and one of the most skilled two-way defencemen ever to play. And the sacrifices he made with his body to prevent goals left no doubt about his toughness.

3. Jaromir Jagr. The only reason Jagr ranks this low is that there are still too many nights when he seems not to care. If he were motivated each and every night he'd probably be number one on my list. Still, how do you argue with a guy who was a hit the moment he broke into the NHL as a teenager, has won five NHL scoring titles (including four in a row beginning in 1997–98) and helped lead his country to an Olympic gold medal? During the 2006–07 season, he became the all-time leader in goals and points by a European at just 35 years of age.

2. Peter Stastny. Stastny was 24 years old when he joined the Quebec Nordiques in the fall of 1980 and took almost no time to adjust to the NHL. Unlike a lot of Europeans, he claimed to like the smaller North American ice surface because he could get to the net faster. Stastny, like Gretzky, was a great scorer but a better passer. I give him credit for turning the Nordiques from a basket case into a good hockey club and, along with brothers Anton and Marian, earning his success at a time when many people still doubted Europeans could excel in the NHL. Stastny was just the second NHL player ever to record 1,000 points in a decade. If the guy who did it first hadn't grabbed so much attention, Stastny wouldn't be overlooked so often.

1. Nicklas Lidstrom. The thing I love about Lidstrom is that he's become a superstar in the NHL by playing defence in a manner that is true to the European game. He doesn't deliver thundering body checks, and his physical presence doesn't strike fear into anybody. But he can skate, handle the puck, shoot and create turnovers like no other defenceman in hockey. He is the first and only European to win the Norris Trophy, capturing it five times in six seasons after being a three-time runner-up. He's won three Stanley Cups, an Olympic gold medal and was the first European ever to win the Conn Smythe Trophy as playoff MVP. He's been the rock of the great Red Wing teams of the past decade, rarely out of the lineup due to injury and consistently leading Detroit in ice time. Which is why he was the logical choice to replace Steve Yzerman as captain at the start of the 2006–07 season, and why he gets my vote as best European ever.

39.

Fans these days think most professional athletes are selfish jerks who are out of touch with reality. Except for hockey players. People say they're different. Bob says they're right.

HOCKEY PLAYERS DO a lot nasty things to one another on the ice. They hook and they spear one another, and occasionally they'll break off a nasty slash when they think an official isn't looking. And when their tempers flare, the things they scream at one another would make cowboys blush. Sometimes they even take their gloves off and fight.

And yet, off the ice they've managed to be portrayed as decent guys, as somehow different from the ego-driven jerks in baseball, the NBA and NFL who couldn't care less about the fans.

Not only are most hockey players more than willing to go into their communities and engage with fans, they even treat the media with respect. Ask anyone who has covered the four major team sports in North America and they'll tell you the same thing: when it comes to dealing with athletes who treat you fairly, who will give you the time of day and who regard the fans in a sincere way, no one comes close to hockey players.

Funny that, when baseball, football and basketball players disgrace themselves, it's almost always away from the field of play. Conversely, hockey players mostly get in serious trouble only during games. But away from the ice, you rarely hear a complaint about them.

So how come hockey players don't become the same spoiled brats other athletes do?

Well, for one, professional hockey gets its culture from Canada. And while NHL players now come from around the world, the coaches, the management and the culture of professional hockey is still Canadian. And in Canada, there really isn't a celebrity culture. I mean, besides some hockey players and a few musicians or politicians, who really qualifies as a Canadian celebrity? And even celebrities in Canada, such as they are, don't get the same privileges that come with being famous in the United States.

And hockey players in Canada, as popular as they are, aren't really fawned over by anybody but hockey fans. Stop for a second and try to name the number of hockey players during the last 25 years whose celebrity status has transcended the sport into the larger culture. Wayne Gretzky, sure. Maybe Mario Lemieux, Guy Lafleur or Patrick Roy at the height of their runs. But who else beyond Sidney Crosby?

They're not like Magic Johnson or Michael Jordan or Pete Rose or Barry Bonds or Joe Namath, people you could put on the cover of any magazine in America and they'd be instantly recognizable to anybody—within *or* beyond the culture of sports.

Hockey players are really only celebrities to people who follow the game religiously—which, in Canada, is a lot of people. But in the United States this group represents a very slim percentage of the population.

Which is another part of why hockey players stay so humble. Hockey players are constantly reminded of where they rank in the United States, the country that crowns celebrities. I mean, it's hard to get your ego out of whack when you can go about your business in most any of the 24 NHL cities in the U.S. without anyone recognizing you.

Even the athletes who play in the fishbowls of Canadian cities are reminded each time they cross the 49th parallel of just how insignificant they are in the North American professional sports landscape.

It's a very big deal to be on *Hockey Night in Canada*. But when that plane touches down in Raleigh, Anaheim or Miami, no one really cares who they are. Hockey players are very big fish in a very small pond. And most of them know what a small pond it is.

NFL, NBA and major league baseball teams try to shelter their players from publicity, but NHL clubs in the U.S. troll for it. And so the players understand, either subtly or not so subtly, that it's the fans who buy the tickets and keep the cash flowing.

There's also something about the way hockey players are developed that keeps their egos in check.

Canadian kids get all kinds of special attention for playing hockey. But when your road to the pros involves riding a bus for four years and living in places such as Brandon, Moose Jaw, Sault Ste. Marie or Val d'Or, it's a bit humbling. I'm not saying these players are hard done by. But when you compare that experience to what athletes in college football or basketball experience—from the crowds to the television to the boosters wanting to do them favours—it's completely different.

In the United States, a teenage star in baseball, basketball or football will have thousands of fans turning out to watch him play high school games, with college recruiters reminding him how great he is. And once in college, star athletes in the big three sports tend to live a pretty unreal existence. In fact, in football and basketball in particular, the celebrity status bestowed upon some college athletes is bigger than that awarded to many professionals.

If you're a Heisman Trophy candidate or a player leading his team to the Final Four in college basketball, everyone in America knows your name. So is it any wonder that, by the time a player reaches the pros, he's already convinced himself he's the greatest thing since sliced bread?

Hockey players at U.S. colleges, meanwhile, are way, way down on the list of importance. Quick, hockey fans, name the last three winners of the Hobey Baker Award.

I think it's the same for Europeans. Hockey may be a big sport in Sweden or Finland or the Czech Republic. But on that continent the biggest game is still soccer, so hockey players are second-class athletes in Europe.

Lastly, I think there's something in the nature of hockey that keeps players on an even keel. Look, basketball and baseball have always been "me" sports. In basketball, one player can have such an influence over his team's performance that he can get away with being a jerk. And in baseball, it's always been about the individual and his stats. You can be a great baseball player and a horrible teammate, and teams will still want you. And in football, while it's a great team sport, most of the attention goes to the quarterback, running backs and receivers. Which is probably why those guys always seem to be the biggest crybabies.

But in hockey, where all 18 skaters are on the ice every night, where the culture of the team reigns supreme, there's no room for "me" players.

I'm not saying there aren't jerks or selfish players in hockey. Because there are. But overall, if you had to spend a month with a group of professional athletes, you'd want them to be hockey players.

40. It seems the National Hockey League just can't make everyone happy with the way it arranges its regular-season schedule. But if the goal is to create and strengthen rivalries, then Bob says the focus should be on the playoffs more than the regular season.

THE NATIONAL HOCKEY LEAGUE is correct when it maintains that rivalries are the engines that drive interest in hockey.

Which is why, coming out of the lockout, the league was so keen to adopt a schedule in which teams face each of their division rivals eight times during an 82-game regular season.

The only problem is that rivalries aren't created during the regular season. They're born in the playoffs. So I don't care how many times the Atlanta Thrashers play the Washington Capitals during the regular season; teams with no geographic or historical link are never going to build a rivalry unless they play at playoff time. Which, under the NHL's current playoff format, could be next year. Or it could be 30 years from now.

You need only look at the NHL today to understand how rivalries work. The Toronto Maple Leafs and Montreal Canadiens have a strong historic connection. But Toronto's true rival of late has been Ottawa, because the Leafs and Senators faced each other four times in five years during the playoffs. Meanwhile, even though Ottawa and Montreal are just two hours apart, there's relatively little buzz when the Canadiens and Senators face each other during the regular season because they've never met in the playoffs.

In Dallas, they can't find Edmonton on a map. Yet fans there know who the Oilers are, thanks to meeting five times in five years in the playoffs from 1997 to 2001.

The problem with the NHL's current playoff format is that teams rarely face each other two or three years in a row at playoff time. And until that changes, I don't care if you face the teams in your division 20 times during the regular season, you're never going to get a good rivalry going.

Which is why if I ran the NHL, I'd put a little bit more balance into the schedule and take some out of the playoff format.

Here's what I mean.

Playing each team in your division eight times during the regular season is a fine thing when you've already got a rivalry going. So no one is complaining about Calgary facing Edmonton that number of times. But a schedule weighted this way gives a distinct advantage during the regular season to good teams that play in lousy divisions.

So, the first thing I'd do is go back to a balanced schedule within each conference, where each team faces every one of their conference rivals four times a season. That would take up 56 games of the schedule. To fill out the other 26 games of the regular season, teams would play home-and-home with 13 of the 15 teams in the other conference.

This would address most of the grumbling about there not being enough balance in the schedule, about teams playing the same opponents too often, and about the league's best players—Sidney Crosby and Alexander Ovechkin, for example—rarely travelling to the other side of the continent.

As for playoff seeding, I'd scrap the league's current three-division format in favour of two divisions in each conference, one with seven teams and one with eight.

Then, I'd go back to the way the NHL structured its play-offs during the 1980s, when four teams from each division reached the playoffs and teams had to play their way out of their divisions to reach the Stanley Cup semifinals.

You only need to look at what happened the last time the NHL used a division-based playoff format, from 1981–82 to 1992–93, to see what would happen. During the first few years of this format, the Montreal Canadiens and Quebec Nordiques met four times in six years, the Edmonton Oilers and Calgary Flames met four times in seven years, the Philadelphia Flyers and New York Rangers, five times in six years. Now *that's* how you build a rivalry, and it's what the NHL needs today.

Going back to a division-based format almost guarantees that the best teams in each division will clash at playoff time, and it increases the likelihood of teams meeting on several occasions over a short time span. The playoffs are what stick in the memories of players, fans and coaches. It's simply a different kind of hockey, one that produces a different kind of emotional response between two teams.

And after they meet a few times in the playoffs, it might even get someone fired up about Atlanta playing Washington in the regular season.

41.

They were two of the most vicious on-ice incidents in hockey history: Marty McSorley's stick to the head of Donald Brashear and Todd Bertuzzi's attack on Steve Moore. There was no shortage of people rushing to insist the incidents had nothing to do with fighting in the game. Bob says they couldn't be more wrong.

VANCOUVER'S DONALD BRASHEAR was not engaged in a fight when Marty McSorley of the Los Angeles Kings hit him over the head with a stick by during a game in February of 2000. Nor was Colorado's Steve Moore exchanging blows with Vancouver's Todd Bertuzzi when Burtuzzi nearly killed him during the latter stages of a contest in March of 2004.

Yet it seems that every time these two incidents are discussed, someone feels obliged to remind us that neither one had anything to do with fighting. What a load of bull. Both of these incidents, like almost every similar incident in the history of the game, are directly attributable to the culture of fighting in hockey—a culture that allows payback and instigation, both of which are central to most of hockey's worst on-ice events.

There are all kinds of examples of this. But the McSorley–Brashear and Bertuzzi–Moore incidents best illustrate my point.

McSorley and Brashear were two tough guys who'd fought on multiple occasions, and had in fact already fought twice in the game that ended for Brashear when his helmetless head bounced off the ice.

McSorley has insisted time and again that he was not try-ing to injure Brashear with a stick to the head. What he wanted to do, he said, was start another fight with Brashear.

"I had never intended to hurt him," McSorley said. "I wanted to whack him hard enough to make him mad enough to turn and fight me, as I'd done hundreds of times in the past."

Whatever your thoughts are on the merits of fighting, or even of hitting guys in the head hard enough to make them want to fight you, the fact is that without fighting in the game, there would have been no two-round build-up to the event, and no need for McSorley to provoke Brashear into a third fight.

In fact, all it would have taken to prevent the McSorley–Brashear incident is a rule stating that players who fight are tossed from the game. If the NHL had that rule, the same one that exists in virtually every other professional sport, the league would have avoided one of its more unflattering moments of all time.

The same is true of the Bertuzzi–Moore incident. It's often suggested that fighting in hockey is harmless because it usually involves two tough guys squaring off with no one get-ting hurt.

But the Bertuzzi–Moore incident was different. Three weeks earlier, Moore had laid a legal hit on Vancouver captain Markus Naslund—though the Canucks deemed it a dirty hit. Hence, according to hockey's code, he had to pay for what he'd done. When the two teams met on March 9, Moore, who had not a single NHL fight on his resume, was confronted by Vancouver's Matt Cooke early in the game. He accepted the challenge and held his own.

Since Moore seemed not to have suffered enough, Bertuzzi felt it necessary for Moore to pay again. I think we can assume that Bertuzzi wasn't trying to end Steve Moore's career when he skated up behind him in the third period of an 8–2 hockey game. What seems more logical is that he was looking to do exactly the same thing McSorley had been hoping to do four years earlier with Brashear: he wanted to start a fight.

It's even been suggested by some that Moore is partly to blame for what occurred because he didn't answer the call, didn't turn around and fight when the bigger man grabbed his sweater from behind. After all, they say, what did he expect?

How much more obvious can it be that this incident grew out of the code and the culture of fighting in hockey?

Just ask McSorley, who provided this poignant insight into the Bertuzzi–Moore incident just days after it occurred.

"I'm 100 percent sure Todd had zero intention of doing what has actually happened," McSorley explained. "He wanted to fight the guy, have him turn and face him so he could beat him up like every other hockey fight."

Okay, so let me get this straight. Neither incident had anything to do with fighting, although both guys were apparently in the process of starting fights when these incidents occurred.

Trying to separate the McSorley–Brashear and Bertuzzi–Moore incidents from the issue of fighting is a cop-out by those who don't want to admit that the culture of fighting produces serious and ugly incidents. Anyone who doesn't see that is an idiot.

And then there's that laugher about fighting in hockey never leading to serious injuries. The fact is that it does. It's just that the combatants aren't always standing face-to-face when those injuries occur.

42. Coaching in the National Hockey League has always been a what-have-you-done-for-me-lately kind of business. Bob says that's going to get worse—not better—as the league moves forward.

BY MID-DECEMBER of the 2006–07 National Hockey League season, four head coaches had already been fired.

Get used to it, folks.

Coaching in the NHL may have been a tough business in the old league, but it's about to get much, much worse.

Here's why:

Back in the NHL's former economic order, teams had different expectations of success. In the big markets, they always expected to win, no matter what. In the smaller cities, it was mostly about being competitive from year to year and hoping for an occasional run at the Cup.

But now, with every team competing on a theoretically equal playing field, everyone thinks their team should be a Stanley Cup contender all the time.

In big markets, the economic advantage under the old system taught fans and owners to anticipate and demand success. But while the economic advantage no longer exists, the high expectations remain. Detroit and Dallas and Philadelphia no longer hold the hammer to go out and buy whomever they want to plug a hole in their lineup, but fans and owners in those cities still expect their teams to be dominant. Which is why Ken Hitchcock barely survived the drop of the puck to start the 2006–07 season when his Flyers looked dreadful. And why, when fans in playoff-spoiled St. Louis wouldn't come to games later that season, Mike Kitchen took the fall.

Things have changed in the smaller markets as well, where expectations of success used to be more modest. Fans and owners in those markets understood that economics put their teams at a disadvantage and that rebuilding was not an overnight process. Which is why teams like the Edmonton Oilers were praised each and every year they either scraped into the playoffs or missed them by only a whisker.

But that's all changed. Small-market teams no longer have excuses. When the Columbus Blue Jackets can't compete with the Dallas Stars, Gerrard Gallant is looking for work and Ken Hitchcock is hired to replace him.

What's also becoming clear in today's NHL is that some teams are able to go from losers to winners from one year to the next. Coaches who took over losing teams used to get three or four seasons to turn things around. But with more liberal free agency and a salary cap, the window can be much, much narrower for some teams. Every time a team such as Pittsburgh or Atlanta turns things around in one year, other owners in the league wonder why *their* teams can't do it. I don't think we'll ever see coaches granted the kind of leeway they once enjoyed to rebuild a team slowly through the draft. Now they're on the clock from day one.

The other factor putting the squeeze on coaches is the pressure general managers operate under these days. Under the old order, general managers had to oversee the draft, make a trade or two and handle a few roster changes each off-season. You didn't see teams bidding adieu to seven or eight players each off-season and then adding seven or eight new ones. There weren't as many trades forced purely by economics.

In short, general managers today have to be much more hands-on and have far more decisions to make from one season to the next. So when, at the end of all their work, a team stinks, what are they going to do? Well, they've got to blame somebody. And that leaves just one option: axe the coach.

The Chicago Blackhawks reworked their roster before the 2006–07 season. So, when the team went into the dumper, what did general manager Dale Tallon do? He fired head coach Trent Yawney, even though Chicago's team had been decimated by injuries through the early part of the season.

It's doesn't help coaches one bit that barely half the teams in the NHL make the playoffs these days. Fifteen years ago, owners could be patient and allow teams to work through difficulties during the regular season because the schedule really didn't matter that much. Every team, except the very worst, would have a chance to redeem itself in the playoffs.

But that's no longer the case. Managers are just now beginning to understand that being a good team doesn't guarantee a playoff berth anymore. That for the first time in hockey history, every game really does count. And that winning in the regular season means more than ever.

Of course, not even making the playoffs is any guarantee that a coach's job is safe. I mean, just look at what New Jersey general manager Lou Lamoriello did to Claude Julien with three games remaining in the 2006–07 season. Julien had his team in first place in the Atlantic Division with a 47–24–8 mark, yet Lamoriello fired him and stepped behind the bench himself to finish the season. Lamoriello may be unique, but is there a better example of the sense of power and entitlement that general manager's operate with these days.

Even early in a season, there aren't many ways in today's game for teams to shake things up beyond firing a coach. There are lots of early-season trade rumours, but precious few early-season trades. The salary cap won't allow them. Dumping players outright costs teams money against the salary cap. But there's no cap on coaches. Which makes them that much more disposable than ever.

43. Remember the days when Canadian hockey players could dismiss Americans? It wasn't so long ago. But no more. Bob says cracking the top five among U.S. hockey players is no easy chore.

LOOK DOWN THE roster of virtually any National Hockey League team these days and you're bound to find two or three players born south of the 49th parallel. They're no longer novelty acts, as we saw when 10 Americans were drafted in the first round in 2007. And as Canada found out during the final of the 1996 World Cup, their best can play hockey as well as or better than ours can.

Yet owing to hockey's waning popularity in the United States, the best American hockey players are far more recognizable in Canada these days than they are at home. In fact, I'm guessing that outside of a few cities, most are unrecognizable to the average sports fan in the U.S. Yet if Chris Chelios or Brian Leetch walked into a shopping mall in Winnipeg, there'd be a mob scene.

Well, if Americans won't give them their due, I will. Here are my all-time greatest U.S.–born NHL players.

5. Mike Modano. It's hard not to like a guy who's been a number one centre his entire career, a consistent point producer, a two-way player and a Stanley Cup champion. He also became the all-time leading goal scorer among Americans during the 2006–07 season. About all there is to knock about Modano is that, while he's always been a great player, he's never been a superstar, nor carried home any of the league's annual awards. He had 50 goals and 93 points in 1993–94, but he's never hit 40 goals in any other season, and the 93 points was a career best, despite playing on a consistent winner.

4. Joe Mullen. He was better than a point-per-game player during his career, scoring 1,063 in 1,062 regular-season games, including 502 goals. His 51 goals and 110 points with Calgary in 1988–89 set the stage for his 16 goals and 24 points in 21 playoff games that spring, as the Flames claimed their first Stanley Cup. He added two more Cups with Pittsburgh, evolving his game to combine with Ron Francis and give the Penguins a pair of outstanding two-way players behind the firepower of Mario Lemieux, Kevin Stevens and Jaromir Jagr.

3. Brian Leetch. Certainly the best Texas-born hockey player ever, Leetch was a key to the Rangers' 1994 Stanley Cup win, becoming the first and only American to win the Conn Smythe Trophy as playoff MVP. He had greatness, becoming just the fifth defenceman to record a 100-point season, and longevity, cracking the career 1,000-point barrier during his final season of 2005–06 with Boston. Like Mark Messier, Leetch missed the playoffs during the latter stages of his career, including six straight years from 1998 to 2003. But no one seems to hold that against Messier, so I won't let it tarnish Leetch's reputation either.

2. Chris Chelios. Hard to believe it was way back in June of 1990 that Montreal decided it had to send a draft pick with Chelios to Chicago in exchange for Denis Savard. Four years later Savard had retired, but Chelios has taken the Gordie Howe career path. The guy has essentially had three NHL careers: one with Montreal, another with Chicago, and he's well into one in Detroit, where he won his second Stanley Cup in 2002. Most impressive is how he's adapted his game to remain productive at an age when most players have retired. What else could you say about a guy who won his third Norris at age 34, was a first-team all-star at age 40 and captained his country's Olympic team at age 44?

1. Pat LaFontaine. LaFontaine's NHL career was the opposite to that of Chelios: short and sweet. While his career numbers don't shine, he was the most talented American player ever before concussions ended his career at age 33 in 1998. It's tantalizing to ponder what LaFontaine could've been had he been able to stay healthy. In the seven seasons in which he dressed for at least 74 games, he averaged 45 goals. And that doesn't count the year he scored 46 in just 57 games with Buffalo in 1991–92. Not the greatest career by an American, but the greatest American player ever.

What about in net?

Frank Brimsek, a two-time Vezina winner from Minnesota who retired in 1950, is considered by some to be the best. But in the modern era there are really just two choices: Tom Barrasso and Mike Richter, both of whom played on Stanley Cup winners. I'm taking Barrasso. He broke into the NHL during a high-scoring era, winning the Vezina and Calder trophies while posting five shutouts and a 2.66 GAA as a 20-year-old rookie with Buffalo in 1984–85. His two Stanley Cup wins with Pittsburgh in 1991 and 1992 came at a time before teams compulsively played with a defence-first mentality. Mario Lemieux and Jaromir Jagr got all the headlines for those teams, but they all knew Barrasso was the unheralded hero. Had Barrasso not battled injuries and had a strained relationship with the media, his legend would loom much larger. I like Richter, but he played in and won fewer games than Barrasso and had just one Stanley Cup win, compared to Barrasso's two.

44. Hockey is a game that requires quick thinking and a sharp mental edge at all times. When players or coaches let their minds slip, it can be ugly. Bob gives you his favourite playoff brain cramps.

THEY SAY EVERYTHING gets magnified at playoff time. I couldn't agree more. Score a highlight-reel goal during the 38th game of the regular season and it'll be forgotten by next week. Do it in the seventh game of a playoff series and it'll be one for the ages.

Same thing with bonehead plays. Score into your own net in mid-January, and the clip will be good for a few jokes. Do it in the playoffs and your grandchildren will be asking you about it.

Here are my favourite playoff moments that some would like to forget.

5. Alex Kovalev, Montreal vs. Boston, Game 4, Eastern Conference quarterfinal, 2003. This one makes the list purely for how bizarre it was. The Canadiens and Bruins were tied 3–3 in double overtime, with the Bruins leading the series two games to one.

Midway through the second overtime period, Boston's Travis Green slashed Kovalev on the wrist as he skated by. Kovalev, in obvious pain, simply stopped playing, as if the whistle had blown. Of course, this being overtime in the old NHL, there was no call. Kovalev, however, acted like a nine-year-old, bending over at the waist and gliding straight into teammate Sheldon Souray, knocking him off the puck near the Montreal blue line. Souray could only watch in stunned disbelief as Boston's Glen Murray picked up the idle puck, raced in on goal and scored a breakaway winner. The gaffe could have cost the Canadiens the series. But the Russian forward got a reprieve when Montreal rallied with three consecutive wins to capture the series in seven games.

4. Don Cherry, Boston vs. Montreal, Game 7, Stanley Cup semifinals, 1979. The Bruins still haven't lived this one down. Boston was less than three minutes away from snapping a 14-game losing streak in Montreal and ending the Canadiens' string of three consecutive Stanley Cups. But with 2:34 to play, the Bruins took a penalty for too many men on the ice. That opened the door for Guy Lafleur's game-tying power-play goal and the eventual winner by Yvon Lambert in overtime. Instead of being dethroned, the Canadiens went on to win their 22nd Stanley Cup. Who was behind the Bruins' bench? None other than Don Cherry. This infamous gaffe is relived every Saturday night during *Hockey Night in Canada*'s first intermission when Cherry is shown responding to the jeering crowd as part of the intro to "Coach's Corner." Cherry was subsequently fired, thus ending his five-year tenure with Boston.

3. Marty McSorley, Los Angeles vs. Montreal, Game 2, Stanley Cup final, 1993. With 1:45 to play and the Canadiens on the verge of falling behind 2–0 in the series, Montreal coach Jacques Demers requested a measurement of the stick of Los Angeles enforcer Marty McSorley. McSorley's stick was ruled illegal and Eric Desjardins scored to tie the game 2–2 with 73 seconds to play. Desjardins's third of the game, in overtime, marked the first hat trick by a defenceman in Stanley Cup final history and tied the series at 1–1. This one was a killer because Los Angeles lost the next three games as Montreal captured its 24th Stanley Cup. McSorley was having a great postseason, but how he thought he was going to help his team with that stick is a mystery.

2. Patrick Roy, Colorado vs. Detroit, Game 6, Western Conference final, 2002. Up 3–2 in the series against Detroit, Patrick Roy's cockiness got the best of him with 39 seconds to play in the first period of a scoreless sixth game at home. After making a strong save off a wrist shot by Steve Yzerman, Roy lifted his glove into the air, showboating like the Statue of Liberty, in mocking triumph.

One little problem. The puck wasn't actually in Roy's well-displayed glove. It was lying on the ice, where it was easy pickings for Brendan Shanahan to poke it home for what turned out to be the game-winning goal. One bad goal seemed to turn the series. Colorado never scored again as the Red Wings went on to capture Game 7 in a 7–0 blowout en route to their third Cup in six years.

1. Steve Smith, Edmonton vs. Calgary, Game 7, Smythe Division final, 1986. It's hard to beat this one, given the teams involved, the rivalry and the interruption of a dynasty. The Edmonton Oilers and Calgary Flames were tied 2–2 early in the third period of the seventh game, when rookie defenceman Steve Smith took the puck behind his own net from goaltender Grant Fuhr. Instead of playing it safe, Smith tried a diagonal breakout pass that hit Fuhr's left leg and the puck bounced into the net. There were still 15 minutes to play, but the Flames managed to hold on, advancing to win their first Stanley Cup against Montreal. There's no telling whether Edmonton would have won the Cup that spring if it hadn't been for Smith's screw-up. But considering that the Oilers won the next two, you have to think it may have cost the Oilers a chance for five in a row.

Honourable mention: To Ottawa's Chris Phillips who followed in Smith's skates 21 years later by bouncing a puck in off Senators goalie Ray Emery from behind the net in what turned out to be the deciding game of the Stanley Cup final in Anaheim. The Senators were headed for a loss in game 5 anyway, but Phillips' screw-up was a backbreaker. "Now I know how Steve Smith felt," said Phillips afterward, who was just eight years old when Smith made his gaffe with the Oilers.

45. **There are lots of great things that go on around a National Hockey League game—and a few that can get under your skin. Here are some things Bob could live without.**

1. Players refusing to emerge for the announcement of the three stars at the end of a game. There was a time when the three stars of a hockey game meant something. People would remain in their seats or stand in the aisles, waiting to see which three players would be honoured. Nowadays, no one cares. The selections are never the subject of debate after a game. They have no relevance to anything. Not even to the players, many of whom can't be bothered to come out for a three-second skate at the end of a game— especially the visting players after a loss. We could solve this by getting rid of the three stars altogether, since neither the fans nor players seem to care. Because the only thing more ridiculous than introducing the three stars after a game is doing so without them there.

2. NHL attendance figures. Why doesn't the NHL just do us all a favour and refuse to announce attendance figures for teams that play to half-empty houses? That would be preferable to what it does now, which is to allow its teams to pick whatever figure they want, even when it bears no resemblance whatsoever to the size of the crowd. I mean, you see games on television all the time where the building is empty. But in the papers the next day, the attendance is reported as something like 15,000. I guess we now know what happened to the propaganda ministers from the old Soviet Union—they're in charge of announcing the NHL's attendance figures. During Super Bowl week in Miami in 2007, a reporter went to a Florida Panthers game against Washington and counted the fans. The figure he came up with: 5,500. The figure the Panthers announced: 11,300. It's insulting to our intelligence. Look, if the NHL can't give us the real numbers then it shouldn't give us any at all.

3. Ridiculous homer choices for the three stars. I wish I could count the number of times I've seen a game where the home team wins 2–1 and is badly outplayed, but somehow the three stars all come from the same team. It's ridiculous. In close games, there shouldn't be three stars from one team and none from another. And when a home team is outplayed definitively, it shouldn't have two of the three stars. Yet it happens all the time. Don't even get me started on home team goaltenders being named game stars for mediocre performances. (Did I mention we should just rid of the three-star selections altogether?)

4. Goal judges. Can someone please explain to me why the National Hockey League still has goal judges? It's quaint and all. But no one pays them any attention—not even the referees. I've seen games where the red light goes on and no one even reacts to it. Not the fans, not the players, not the announcers—nobody. So how about showing the goal judges the door and selling that seat to someone else for $300?

5. The Gear Daddies' song "I Want to Drive the Zamboni." Please, someone, write another song about a Zamboni. This tune was sort of cute when it first surfaced a few years back. But now you can't go to a hockey game anywhere without hearing it. Enough.

6. Teams refusing to disclose the nature of minor injuries at any point in a season. I understand why teams like to keep injuries secret at playoff time. Players often play through pain at that time of year and they don't want opponents knowing where they might be a little or a lot sore. But now a groin pull in October is referred to as a "lower body injury." It's ridiculous. If only people bet on hockey. Then National Hockey League would have to do something about this insanity to protect the interests of the betting public.

46. **Remember the days when teenage hockey players lived for the thrill of playing the game? The days before 15- and 16-year-old kids needed agents and demanded trades, forgetting about the good of the team? Bob says thank heaven those days are gone.**

LET'S UNDERSTAND ONE thing right away: junior hockey is a business. A *big* business in which everyone gets a piece of the action, from the coaches to the owners to the sponsors to the arena landlords. Everyone, that is, except the players, who get about $50 a week from a multimillion-dollar industry.

In essence, they are powerless entities in a sport that revolves around them but offers them no say in the manner in which they're used.

So I welcome the idea that players, some of whom are not old enough to drive, have agents. After all, someone needs to advise them and look after their interests. Agents are nothing more than advocates, people whose job it is to guide a player's career. And no one needs someone like that more than young hockey players. Because you know teams and coaches, whose business comes down to winning games, can't be counted on for that.

The culture of hockey is all about putting the team before the individual. Which is fine when you're being paid hundreds of thousands or millions of dollars. And it's fine when you're a kid and it's all about fun, or you're in your thirties and you're playing for beer after work. But junior hockey is all about getting as much attention for yourself as possible so you can become a pro. So if you were a player and your coach stuck you on the fourth line in perpetuity, what would you do? Take one for the team, or call your agent and demand a trade?

If I'm a player in junior hockey, I want to be in the absolute best situation to make it to the next level. And if I'm not in that position, then I want out.

Yet it seems every time there's a story about a junior hockey player demanding to be traded, commentators in the media and fans go on about the gall of teenage hockey players who've lost touch with team values. They scream about how players in the good old days played for the love of the sport and how today's kids have forgotten all that.

What a bunch of hooey.

Junior hockey players are the least powerful athletes on earth. Unlike college athletes, they don't choose their teams. Their teams choose them in a draft that has never been collectively bargained. They are often billeted far from home. Their coaches hold their futures in their hands. They have no power at all, save for one thing: they can refuse to play. And if we deny them that one and only right, then it's called slavery.

So when a player sees his chances to move to the next level going down the tubes because his team is a basket case or the coach has him in the doghouse, he ought to want out. If he doesn't, he's crazy, because all that team loyalty stuff is going to earn him nothing at the end of four years.

Jason Spezza's experience with the Mississauga Ice Dogs in 2000–01 is a perfect example of a player who needed to have a me-first attitude in order to protect his career. Spezza played the entire 1999–2000 season on a Mississauga team that won just nine games all year. So when it became clear the Ice Dogs were no better the next season (they ended up winning all of three games in 2000–01), Spezza had had enough. He packed up his gear and went home, called his agent and demanded a trade to send him somewhere he could better display his skills.

Lots of people said he was spoiled. They said Jason Spezza should get out on the ice and put the team on his back.

Not on your life. Jason Spezza needed out of Mississauga to protect all that he'd worked for and his future. There's no reason he should have had to suffer just because Don Cherry's team in Mississauga was an absolute mess.

Nor should any other player who feels he's not in the best situation for career advancement.

It may be a game, but no one has more at stake in junior hockey than the players. Which is why they shouldn't be shy about looking after their own interests first.

47. Home-ice advantage in a playoff series means playing the first two games at home. But is that really an advantage, or would teams do better if they could open on the road? Bob has the answer.

IT'S THE OPENING NIGHT of a playoff series and all the pressure is on the home team.

And it's not always good pressure. It's often pressure of the we-better-win-or-we're-in-trouble kind.

Which is why some National Hockey League coaches and executives have argued they'd rather their teams open up on the road, away from the pressure, than have to do so at home.

Which makes sense when you think about it. Nearly everything seems to play to the psychological advantage of the visiting team.

If the home team doesn't win the first game, then the pressure really looms large in Game 2 because no team can like its chances heading out on the road down 0–2 in a series.

Meanwhile, dropping the first game on the road is no big deal for the visiting team. A win in Game 2 still sends a team home for Games 3 and 4 with a home-ice advantage over the rest of the series. Even when a visiting team loses both road games to open a series, it doesn't seem like the end of the world. After all, the anguish of a pair of losses is easily absorbed by the prospect of "going back to our barn, where we own 'em."

Sounds right, except for one thing. There's absolutely nothing to back up any of that philosophy when you look at what's occurred over the past 10 seasons of Stanley Cup playoffs.

Over that span, there have been 48 times when a team has gone down 0–2 on the road to open a series. According to some thinking, those teams shouldn't be in such dire straits. After all, they're headed home. The only problem is that teams going home 0–2 have won just two of those 48 series. In other words, coming home is little consolation. When a team goes down 0–2 on the road, the team in the lead almost always wins the series.

Strangely, teams actually have a much, much better chance of coming back from 0–2 in a series when they lose the first two games on home ice. Over the past 10 seasons, there have been 14 instances in which a team has dropped the first two games of a series on home ice. Yet in six of those, the team having to go out on the road down 0–2 for Games 3 and 4 has come back to win the series.

Does that make any sense? No, it doesn't. Except for the fact that teams that go down 0–2 at home are always the higher playoff seeds and therefore presumably better teams. Conversely, teams that go down 0–2 on the road are always the lower playoff seeds and presumably weaker teams. Still, that hardly explains the remarkable statistical disparity between a team's chances when dropping the first two games at home, compared to the first two on the road.

It's clear that starting a series on home ice is not a disadvantage at all. In fact, it's a huge advantage, even when things start off badly during the first two games of a series. So teams that dismiss it might want to be careful what they wish for.

48.

Much was made of the changes to NHL hockey after the lockout. But Bob says you ain't seen nothing yet. Here's what the NHL game will look like in the 2016–17 season.

WHEN PLAY RESUMED following the National Hockey League lockout, fans and commentators couldn't stop marvelling about the product that was unveiled.

The game had flow and it had speed. Players with skill were allowed to use it. And while a new crop of stars was emerging, others who'd excelled in the old NHL were now on the way out.

Gone were players such as Peter Worrell, the six-foot-seven enforcer once considered a valuable commodity in the NHL despite the fact he could barely skate and had hands with which he could barely handle the puck. Meanwhile, players such as Buffalo's Daniel Briere, who was a decent centre in the old NHL, suddenly became a star.

But I believe the full evolution of the new NHL is a long way from being complete. In fact, it will probably take a decade before we see the full impact of the changes to the game that began with in the 2005–06 season. That's how long it's going to take to weed out the old-style players and old-style thinkers, until everyone accepts and understands the way the game is going and how to take advantage of it. Not just in the NHL, but all the way down the development chain to the grass roots.

People forget that the habits of hockey players, things like clutching and grabbing, are formed at a young age. And since junior hockey develops players for the pros, and minor hockey develops players for the juniors, there is a direct correlation between how the pro game is played and what is being practised at the grass roots.

At the start of the 2006–07 season, Hockey Canada began instituting the same changes to minor hockey that took the NHL by storm one year earlier. And guess what? Minor hockey went through the very same adjustment phase the pro game did. Lots of penalties, parents screaming at referees, and players struggling to understand what they can or can't do.

It has been a bit disruptive. But the end result will be a redefinition of what the ideal hockey prospect looks like.

There are all kinds of kids—usually undersized—who for years have been walking away from hockey at age 12 or 13 because they see the writing on the wall. They know they're not big enough or strong enough to be taken seriously as prospects. And so they figure, why bother?

But that will no longer the be the case with the game now opened up, with the NHL now more interested in skill than grit.

The 2006 draft represented the first time NHL teams were selecting players with the knowledge of how the new rules would affect the game. The players they were drafting, however, had still come through a development system based on the old ideas of how hockey should be played.

Now, however, you've got players who are eight, nine and ten years old being developed in a system that mirrors the new style of NHL game. It's going to be about another decade before those players are eligible for the NHL draft. And I'm guessing that by the time they are, their skill sets will be very much in tune with the way the game is being played at the professional level.

You can see that in junior hockey already, because junior teams are compensated financially based on the number of their players who are drafted by NHL teams. If they don't adjust and produce players to fit the NHL game immediately, scouts will turn their attention more to Europe or the U.S. college ranks. And that would cost junior teams money.

Speed is the most common element between the first two Stanley Cup champions of the post-lockout era, Carolina and Anaheim. And since champions in professional sports tend to spawn imitators, a few more speed-oriented Cup winners should weed out the last of the dinosaurs and put an even larger premium on players with speed and skill.

In 10 years, there will be no lumbering defencemen taken high in the draft—only those who can skate, shift gears and move the puck with lightning speed. Forwards will be noted mostly for their wheels and their hands.

There will be few or no goons, because teams simply won't be able to afford to dress players who can't compete in all areas of the ice. There will be fewer penalties called as the NHL fills its ranks with those who've grown up with the new rules and officials who know how to call them properly. And where once players relied on clutching or grabbing to play defence, blocking shots will become second nature for every NHL player.

Yes, it's going to be a very different and much better game a decade or so from now. All we need to do is wait for it.

49. Hockey players have been able to escape the law, even when committing dangerously and intentionally violent acts on the ice. Bob says it's time the law put hockey's worst offenders in something more restrictive than the penalty box.

THE NATIONAL HOCKEY LEAGUE has always insisted it is fully capable of policing itself and exacting its own form of discipline on those who perpetrate acts of violence on the ice.

And in the vast majority of cases, where the incidents are minor and the repercussions not so severe, that is true.

Yet despite some serious efforts by the NHL and other hockey leagues in the past 25 years to eliminate gratuitous violence from their game, we still are plagued by incidents that make us cringe. Incidents that go far beyond what anyone expects to see at a sporting event. Attacks that put the well-being, if not the lives, of some players in danger.

Maybe it's time the NHL and other leagues changed their tunes and encouraged law enforcement to take a role in handing out discipline. I'm not suggesting that police get involved in anything that takes place in the normal course of a hockey game. But for those rare few incidents, the kind that happen every few years, the ones that clearly go beyond the reasonable expectation of what should occur in the sport, there needs to be a higher authority.

If acts of outright violence in hockey resulted in players doing time—as in jail time—instead of serving suspensions at their mansions, it would accomplish overnight what hockey has been trying to get rid of for the better part of a quarter century.

Sounds like a radical step, but I believe there are people in the game who'd love to see it. Including some players, such as Vancouver's Mattias Ohlund, who watched teammate Donald Brashear being whacked over the head by Marty McSorley in 2000 and reacted this way: "That guy should be treated the same as if he tried to kill a guy on the street, because that's what he could have done had his stick hit [Brashear] across the neck."

(Of course, Ohlund—or any other Canuck—made no such comment when Todd Bertuzzi assaulted Steve Moore.)

The problem is that the law has been hesitant to get involved with cases of sports violence. And where it has stepped in, the results have been almost meaningless.

McSorley was charged with assault with a weapon and found guilty by a jury. But his sentence of 18 months' probation was hardly the kind of message that struck fear into players.

Similarly, Todd Bertuzzi was charged with assault causing bodily harm for his attack on Steve Moore in 2004. After a plea bargain, Bertuzzi was given a conditional discharge and one year's probation.

And when Dino Ciccarelli hit Toronto's Luke Richardson in the head during a game back in 1988, he spent a few hours in jail and paid a $1,000 fine.

"It is time now that a message go out from the courts that violence in a hockey game or in any other circumstances is not acceptable in our society," said Judge Sidney Harris in the Ciccarelli case. That was two decades ago.

Look, hockey players on the ice are entitled to the same societal protections that you and I enjoy when we're walking down a sidewalk. They do not consent to assault when they strap on the pads each night.

Which, by the way, was the argument used by McSorley's lawyer, Bill Smart, who stated that NHL players give "explicit consent" to the risk of on-ice contact.

Really? Cite the evidence, Mr. Smart. Where does it state in their contracts that they consent to being cold-cocked from behind?

The sport of hockey has inherent risks, just like boxing, baseball or football does. Getting hit in the head with a punch in boxing is part of the risk that every athlete accepts in that sport. In baseball, getting beaned with a pitch is part of the risk, even though that's not the object of the sport. And in football, a player who gets laid out, even with a cheap shot, understands that in a game that fast, involving players with such immense strength, there are going to be times when not every hit is clean.

But to suggest that there's any relationship between a marginally dirty hit and other, more blatant acts of violence is ridiculous.

Take the Ontario Hockey League case involving Plymouth's Jesse Boulerice and Guelph's Andrew Long from a playoff game in 1998. During that game, Boulerice delivered a deliberate slash across Long's face that sent him to the ice and into convulsions. Long suffered a broken nose, a broken nasal cavity, a cut requiring 20 stitches between the tip of his nose and his upper lip, a concussion accompanied by seizures, plus a blood spot on his brain.

In short, it was the kind of slash that could have killed Long.

Yet when Boulerice was charged with assault to do great bodily harm less than murder, his lawyer, James Howarth, replied this way: "If what Jesse Boulerice did was criminal, then thousands of 'hockey crimes' are committed on a daily basis. Every penalty for slashing, high-sticking or cross-checking must, of necessity, be considered to be at least a felonious assault."

Well, excuse me, Mr. Howarth, but I disagree. To suggest that all slashes are the same is like saying someone who pushes to get onto a crowded subway should be treated the same way as a person who shoves someone down a flight of stairs.

What Jesse Boulerice did to Andrew Long was nothing like an ordinary slash. It was an act of violence intended to injure. There is no way that Andrew Long or any other hockey player consented to being deliberately slashed in the face.

And it's time all hockey leagues faced up to this fact.

Instead of resisting the input of law enforcement, hockey should work with the legal system to define which sorts of incidents should fall under its jurisdiction. If leagues were so willing, I think the law would be more apt to step in. And you'd have an effective deterrent in place that would allow leagues to wash their hands of the ugliest on-ice incidents. Boulerice initially faced a penalty of up to 10 years in prison and a $5,000 fine, but he was able to plea-bargain his way down to a reduced charge of aggravated assault and he served only three months' probation. If he'd got something more than a slap on the wrist, other players might have learned a different lesson.

When someone deliberately swings a stick and hits an opposing player in the head, as the Islanders' Chris Simon did to New York Ranger Ryan Hollweg in March of 2007, that's not a hockey matter. And when a player skates up behind another and sucker punches him, breaking his jaw in the process, that's not a hockey matter.

Those types of incidents should be treated exactly the same way as they would if they occurred between two players who met in the parking lot after a game. Why, because they happened to be standing on the ice wearing skates, should it be any different?

It's a game. We all acknowledge that. But when it stops being a game and becomes a crime, hockey needs to acknowledge that the penalties should be different.

50.

So, your kid wants to be a pro hockey player. And at age 16 he can't decide between waiting for a U.S. college scholarship and playing for a major junior team. Bob weighs in on which development system is best for whom.

WHEN IT COMES TO which hockey development system is best for a young player who wants to reach the National Hockey League, one thing should be understood: if a kid has extraordinary talent, if he's a hard worker and he's got his head on straight, the scouts are going to find him no matter which way he goes.

Junior hockey people love to slag the U.S. college system by suggesting it doesn't prepare players for the pros. And the colleges really pour on the scare tactics when they recruit, portraying the three Canadian major junior leagues as hockey sweatshops.

But whether it's Dany Heatley and Paul Kariya, who both went the U.S. college route, or Vincent Lecavalier and Rick Nash, who played Canadian junior, both roads will get the best players to the top of the mountain.

Here's my advice if you and your 16-year-old ever face the fork in the road, having to choose between major junior hockey or waiting for a scholarship in the National Collegiate Athletic Association.

For a kid with otherworldly talent, I don't think there's much doubt about the best way to go. If a kid is capable of playing with the best teenagers in the world by the time he's 16, then that's what he should do. In major junior hockey he gets some of the best coaching there is, plays 70 games a year and learns a style of game that's akin to what is being played in the NHL.

The problem with young phenoms wanting to wait for U.S. college hockey is that they've got to bide their time for two years playing Provincial Junior A or Junior B against lesser competition while they finish high school. That's fine for a lot of kids. But it would have been silly for Sidney Crosby to play two seasons of Junior A hockey when he was capable of dominating major junior by the time he was 16.

On the other hand, for those kids who aren't going to be sure-shot pro prospects—which, by the way, is the vast, vast majority of players—it's best to go to college.

There are a couple of things to bear in mind. First of all, major junior hockey is a business built on a foundation that puts hockey first. That means kids are going to be on the ice whether they're trying in the classroom or not. So if you've got a kid who's smart but lacks discipline, then leaving home to play junior hockey at age 16 isn't necessarily the best option. Lots of junior teams talk about their players being encouraged to take school seriously. But I've yet to see a team that has pulled a player off the ice for scholastic reasons. If a kid doesn't want to study, no one is going to bench him until he gets his grades in order. It just doesn't work that way. And until it does, the education part of the junior hockey experience remains at the player's whim.

The major junior leagues have gone to great lengths to shed the image of teams being full of high school dropouts who've risked everything to make it in hockey. They now provide academic support for players who want it during the season. And there are varying degrees of scholarship money put aside for players to be used for post-secondary education after their junior careers are over.

The problem is that the best education packages, the ones that pay the full shot for college or university, are reserved for the top prospects—who are the least likely to need them because they're the guys who usually turn pro. If you're a low draft pick, the kind of player unlikely to eventually be drafted by an NHL team, your education package is likely to pick up only a portion of the costs of going to school after junior hockey, which leaves some players footing a bill.

And those education packages vanish if a player signs a contract with an American Hockey League or National Hockey League team. Players can sign in one of the lower minor leagues—such as the Central Hockey League, the East Coast Hockey League or the United Hockey League—without blowing their scholarships. But they've got just 18 months to give up the minor pro life and go back to school, or *their* funds are cut off as well.

If you're 21 years old, playing minor-league hockey and living the life—eating, drinking and living for free, making a few bucks and possibly making the acquaintance of young women—it may not be easy to give it all up and walk on back to school. But if you don't, you wake up one day at age 30 with nothing more than a high school diploma and a minor-league hockey resume.

If a player goes the college route and the NHL doesn't call, he can go to one of those minor leagues with degree in hand. That way he lives the dream—so to speak—without being out on a limb when it all ends at age 28 or 30.

Which is why, unless my kid was the second coming of Gretzky, Lemieux or Crosby by age 16, he'd be going the college route. Period.

51. **There was a time when hockey's regular season was nearly meaningless. But with only 16 of 30 teams reaching the playoffs, even great teams can no longer afford to mail it in over 82 games. Still, Bob says the regular season is rarely the place to judge which team will win the Stanley Cup.**

DURING THE 1995–96 SEASON, the Detroit Red Wings finished the regular season with 131 points and a record of 62 wins, 13 losses and 7 ties. They then survived two tough playoff rounds before being eliminated by the Colorado Avalanche in the Western Conference final.

The next season, Detroit finished with 37 fewer points during the regular season, including 24 fewer wins, and won the Stanley Cup.

Which raises the question of how much performance during the regular season actually matters towards what happens in the playoffs? As it turns out, very little.

Coaches and players talk nicely about the Presidents' Trophy, the award for best overall regular-season record. And they'll wax pragmatic about the need to peak at the end of the season. But they'll also tell you that the playoffs are an entirely different setting, where all that has occurred previously is meaningless.

The last statement is the most true, since there is no consistent correlation between performance in the regular season and performance in the playoffs. Sometimes the best team from the regular season wins the Cup and sometimes it doesn't. Sometimes teams that go all out to get every point they can during the regular season run out of gas in the postseason. And sometimes they just keep on rolling.

The table on page 151 shows what's happened at playoff time over the past 16 seasons to the team with the best overall record during the regular season.

Four teams have won both the Presidents' Trophy and the Stanley Cup. But in six instances, the team that won the Presidents' Trophy didn't get past the second round of the playoffs. And overall, only five times, or less than a third of the time, did the team finishing first overall even reach the Stanley Cup final. Similarly, the table on page 152 shows where the past 16 Stanley Cup champions finished overall during the regular season.

YEAR	TEAM	POSITION
2007	Buffalo	lost, third round to Ottawa
2006	Detroit	lost, first round to Edmonton
2004	Detroit	lost, second round to Calgary
2003	Ottawa	lost, third round to New Jersey
2002	Detroit	won Stanley Cup
2001	Colorado	won Stanley Cup
2000	St. Louis	lost, first round to San Jose
1999	Dallas	won Stanley Cup
1998	Dallas	lost, third round to Detroit
1997	Colorado	lost, third round to Detroit
1996	Detroit	lost, third round to Colorado
1995	Detroit	lost, Stanley Cup final to New Jersey
1994	New York Rangers	won Stanley Cup
1993	Pittsburgh	lost, second round to New York Islanders
1992	New York Rangers	lost, second round to Pittsburgh
1991	Chicago	lost, first round to Minnesota

YEAR	TEAM	POSITION
2007	Anaheim	fourth
2006	Carolina	fifth
2004	Tampa Bay	second
2003	New Jersey	fourth
2002	Detroit	first
2001	Colorado	first
2000	New Jersey	fourth
1999	Dallas	first
1998	Detroit	third
1997	Detroit	fifth
1996	Colorado	second
1995	New Jersey	tied for ninth
1994	New York Rangers	first
1993	Montreal	seventh
1992	Pittsburgh	sixth
1991	Pittsburgh	seventh

While finishing first doesn't necessarily correlate with winning the Stanley Cup, similarly, very few Cup winners of late have come from near the bottom of the playoff pool. (In the lockout-shortened 1995 season, New Jersey did it after finishing ninth.) Twelve of the past 16 Cup winners have finished with a top-five record during the regular season, including the last 10 in a row. That's a reflection of both talent and the importance of having home-ice advantage through most of the playoffs. But I would also suggest it means that teams that have to fight like crazy just to get into the postseason pay a price during the play-offs. It sounds nice to say you want to be playing meaningful hockey during the final few weeks of the season, but it's better to be coasting at least a bit and resting up for the games that matter.

Which is perhaps why eventual Stanley Cup winners rarely have overly-impressive records during the final 10 or 20 games of the regular season. Logic might suggest that the best teams want to be shooting the lights out during the March and April games. But rarely is that the case. In fact, most Cup winners have had very mediocre records during the span when one might expect they should be peaking.

The table on page 154 shows how the past 16 Stanley Cup winners fared down the stretch. Not exactly scintillating, are they? Only the 2000 New Jersey Devils and 1994 New York Rangers were overly dominant during the final 10 games of the regular season. Detroit in 2002 was simply awful, winning just one of its final 10 games before going on to capture the Stanley Cup.

Back up as far as the final 20 games of the regular season, and only the 2000 Devils blew the field away. So, while most eventual Cup winners are generally playing well during the final 10 or 20 games, lots of them are hovering around .500 and almost none of them are tearing it up in a way that suggests they can't be stopped in the playoffs.

Keep all this in mind when, at the end of the next hockey season, the clichés come out about the importance of finishing first overall and the need to peak at the right time of year. Remember, most Stanley Cup winners really can just flick the switch when the playoff lights shine.

	RECORD IN FINAL 10	RECORD IN FINAL 20
2007 Anaheim	5-5-0	13-7-0
2006 Carolina	5-5-0	9-11-0
2004 Tampa Bay	5-5-0	13-6-1
2003 New Jersey	5-1-4	8-7-5
2001 Colorado	6-3-1	13-7-0
2000 New Jersey	8-2-0	17-2-1
1999 Dallas	6-4-0	11-7-2
1998 Detroit	6-4-0	10-8-2
1997 Detroit	4-3-3	7-7-6
1996 Colorado	6-4-0	12-8-0
1995 New Jersey	5-4-1	11-6-3
1994 New York Rangers	8-1-1	12-6-2
1993 Montreal	4-6-0	9-11-0
1992 Pittsburgh	6-3-1	12-7-1
1991 Pittsburgh	5-3-2	10-9-1

* records include wins and losses in overtime and shootouts

52.

The 2006–07 season fuelled debate on the kinds of hits to the head that often leave players concussed and unconsious. Bob says most of the debate around this issue misses the mark.

THERE'S NOTHING MORE chilling than watching a player being struck in the head by a body check and knocked out cold.

Everyone loves a big open-ice hit in a game. But no one enjoys what sometimes follows it.

The opening 25 games of the 2006–07 National Hockey League season included four incidents in which players had to be carried off the ice following blows to the head. Montreal's Aaron Downey, Carolina's Trevor Letkowski, Detroit's Jason Williams and his teammate Johan Franzen all had one thing in common when they were concussed.

Not one of them was carrying the puck.

Which is why, if you want to solve the NHL's concussion crisis, if you want to make the game safer for players without detracting from it, there's an easy way to do it. The NHL simply needs to do stop allowing players who've passed or shot the puck to be targets.

In football they call it roughing the passer. In hockey it's called finishing the check, which has always seemed to me like a euphemism for interference with a player who no longer has the puck. The purpose of a body check should be to separate the puck carrier from the puck.

Yet most concussions are sustained when a player passes the puck up ice, then gets set to join the rush up ice and all of a sudden—*boom!*—he's clobbered by a check he didn't know was coming, often delivered to the head by a shoulder.

And yet the debate around hits to the head usually still involves someone saying something like, "If these guys can't keep their heads up while they're skating with the puck, then they deserve to get drilled."

And I agree. But it is rare indeed to see a player being concussed while he's carrying the puck. The overwhelming majority of these guys have been skating without it.

It's ridiculous that hockey now enforces rules to protect every player on the ice without the puck except the most vulnerable guy on the ice, the player who's just made a pass or taken a shot.

Allowing this to happen rewards players who are too slow to get to an opposing player while he still has the puck. They get there late and are rewarded with a free shot.

So let's offer a challenge to players: If you want to deliver the bone-crushing hit, you must do so to a player who is carrying the puck. To run a player after he's gotten rid of the puck is easy and, frankly, bordering on cowardly.

When Vancouver's Willie Mitchell delivered a late hit on Franzen, it marked one of the few times interference was called on such a play. It usually takes something as blatant as the hit New Jersey's Cam Janssen threw at Toronto's Tomas Kaberle in March of 2007. Most times these kinds of hits go unpenalized altogether.

But as none other than Detroit defenceman Chris Chelios suggests, suspensions for those types of hits should be the norm, not the exception.

"Anytime a guy passes the puck and starts watching the play and you want to run and hit him, you can do it," Chris Chelios told the *Detroit Free Press* after the incident involving Franzen. "If it's only going to be two minutes—I mean, look at the seriousness of the injury it can cause. There was intent there. The defenseman knows it was late. You can do that every game if you want to."

The NHL's decision at the end of the 2006–07 season to allow referees to assess a major penalty and game misconduct when an injury results from an act of interference is but one small step in the right direction. It also needs to redefine interference.

Remember the famous Scott Stevens hit on Paul Kariya in Game 6 of the 2003 Stanley Cup finals that laid out the then Anaheim forward? The NHL reviewed the hit and determined it was legal. And I'm sure, by their definition, it was.

Hockey needs to take a page from football's book. When a quarterback releases a pass, the attacking defensive player is allowed to make contact as long as he attempts to let up. In hockey, the defensive player shouldn't be allowed to lower his shoulder into a guy's jaw to "finish" the hit once the puck is gone.

Look, I don't want to see hitting taken out of hockey. But it's got to be purposeful hitting and it's got to be fair. And I can't see how removing the blindside hit on unsuspecting players who are skating without the puck diminishes the game one bit.

53. Everyone remembers watching Raymond Bourque raise the Stanley Cup above his head in triumph with Colorado in 2001. But what about those players whose great careers were never capped by such a moment? Bob looks at the best players who never got to lift Lord Stanley's mug.

WINNING THE STANLEY CUP, especially in a 30-team league, comes down in large part to luck. There are players who win it their first year in the league and others who go for years without a sniff. Then there are those for whom disappointments are never avenged and who retire with outstanding careers, but no lap around the ice with Lord Stanley's mug.

It's unfair that so often, the way players are remembered comes down to a series or two played in the spring. Unfortunately, players who never got to enjoy those moments are far easier to dismiss or forget, especially when it comes time for induction into the Hockey Hall of Fame.

Lots of fantastic players have never had the pleasure of lifting the Cup in a moment of glory. Here's my top five of those who had great careers but rarely, if ever, had even a sniff of the Stanley Cup.

5. Darryl Sittler. It's almost redundant to say a player who spent most of his career with the Toronto Maple Leafs never got close to the Stanley Cup. Most who've worn the blue and white didn't deserve anything better. But Darryl Sittler did. Sittler played 11-plus seasons in Toronto, three in Philadelphia and one in Detroit before retiring at the end of the 1984–85 season. Despite his prowess as a Maple Leaf, Sittler's teams reached the third round of the playoffs just once: in 1978, under Roger Neilson. When he finally escaped Toronto and the wrath of owner Harold Ballard, Sittler was part of four consecutive first-round exits with the Flyers and Red Wings as his career wound down. The Leafs had three promising playoff runs during Sittler's prime, from 1976 to 1978. And that's when we got a glimpse of what kind of playoff performer he could have been with a better team, watching Sittler rack up 44 points in 32 games during those years.

4. Gilbert Perreault. Perreault spent his entire 17-year career in Buffalo with a Sabres team that was usually competitive but never great. The Sabres reached the Stanley Cup final just once with Perreault, losing to Philadelphia in six games in the spring of 1975. Beyond that, Buffalo reached the third round only once, losing to the first Cup-winning New York Islander team in 1980. Perreault scored 33 playoff goals and added 70 assists in 90 games, which is certainly respectable. During the two deepest playoff runs with the Sabres he had 36 points in 31 games.

3. Dino Ciccarelli. The empty spot on his finger where a Stanley Cup ring should be is probably the reason he's not in the Hockey Hall of Fame, despite scoring 608 goals in his career. Ciccarelli might have won a couple of Cups early in his younger days had his Minnesota North Stars not run smack into a pair of dynasties. In his rookie campaign, the North Stars reached the Stanley Cup final only to lose to the New York Islanders in five games in 1981. They reached the conference final three years later but were snuffed out by the first Cup run of the Edmonton Oilers. His closest call came more than a decade later with Detroit, when he was part of the Red Wings' loss in the Stanley Cup final to New Jersey in 1995 and to Colorado a year later in the Western Conference final. The Wings won the Cup the next two seasons, but by then Ciccarelli had departed for Tampa and Florida, where he finished his career by missing the playoffs in three straight seasons. Ciccarelli doesn't wear much blame for failing to win the Cup. He scored 14 goals in 19 playoff games as a rookie when the North Stars went to the final, then had 15 goals in 33 games during his two deepest runs with Detroit.

2. Marcel Dionne. When you think of Dionne, the word "superstar" comes to mind immediately. But there are no classic playoff moments to crystallize his image among the all-time greats. Dionne missed the playoffs all four years he played in Detroit before his move to Los Angeles, and with the Kings, he never got past the second round in 11 seasons. His final three seasons in New York were marked by the Rangers missing the playoffs once and being eliminated in the first round twice. Dionne has to share some of the blame in Los Angeles, where he scored just one playoff goal in 12 playoff games from 1978 to 1981. His career ended with just 21 playoff goals in 49 games to go with the 731 goals he scored during 1,348 regular-season games.

1. Phil Housley. You've got to feel bad for Phil Housley, who, like Dionne, had a fantastic career but spent the spring of most seasons watching the playoffs. He didn't just fail to win the Stanley Cup—most years, he didn't get anywhere near it. With Buffalo, Winnipeg, St. Louis and Calgary, Housley got past the first round of the playoffs just once in 13 years, and that was in his rookie year with the Sabres. Housley finally made a run to the Stanley Cup final with Washington in 1998, when the Caps were swept in four games by Detroit. With Calgary, Housley missed the playoffs three times and then twice more with Chicago. In a 21-year career, he got past the first round of the playoffs twice. That's hard to fathom from a defenceman—and sometimes centre—who played nearly 1,500 NHL games, scoring 338 goals and 894 assists.

54. Canada is easily the greatest hockey nation on earth. We win more championships and produce more players, coaches and executives than any country in the world. But Bob says there's no excuse for it not being that way.

THERE IS JUST ONE nation on earth that directs most of its best athletes towards ice and pucks.

Canada. That's it. Only here is the game most prominent in the minds of kids, parents and sports fans. Only here are the very best and brightest of our athletic stock encouraged to become hockey players above and beyond all other sports.

And only here does the training and development in the sport dwarf that available for any other athletic endeavour.

Which is why if Canada wasn't the greatest hockey nation on Earth, it would be a pretty sad comment on us as a sporting nation.

Because when it comes to devoting resources and talent towards hockey, only the United States is comparable to Canada. In that country, we know that most of the best athletes are driven to sports such as basketball, football and baseball. And in a whole lot of the U.S., hardly anyone plays the game. So, while hockey may be played in the United States in numbers comparable to those in Canada, only here are we guaranteed of attracting most of the very best athletes from coast to coast.

And while I don't want to diminish the fact that we are dominant in most things hockey-related, you can't ignore the fact that hockey has by far the shallowest talent pool of any major team sport in the world.

In fact, it's actually shocking to consider just how few hockey players there are outside of North America.

A 2004–05 survey by the International Ice Hockey Federation reported that Canada had 543,390 registered hockey players, followed by the United States (435,737), the Czech Republic (83,589), Russia (77,202), Sweden (67,747), Finland (62,886) and Germany (30,344).

So, with more than half a million players playing the game and the best coaching in the world, I would certainly hope we end up on top more often than not.

And that's before you consider the huge disparity in available hockey facilities between Canada and everywhere else in the world.

Consider that for a population of roughly 33 million people, Canada has 3,000 indoor rinks and another 11,100 outdoor rinks. That's one rink for every 2,357 Canadians. It's an astounding ratio when you think of it. In fact, we have a lot more rinks per person than we do hospitals.

Second on that list would be the United States with its 2,400 rinks, 2,000 of which are located indoors. On a per-capita basis, you're talking about one rink for every 123,000 Americans.

The rest of the world doesn't even come close. According to the IIHF, Sweden has 445, Finland has 253, Russia has 145, the Czech Republic has 143 and Slovakia comes in at 51— about as many rinks as Toronto.

Sweden, with the third most hockey rinks on Earth, has one rink for every 20,225 of its citizens. In Russia, our supposed rival, it's one rink for every 986,000 people.

I won't dare to suggest that Canada isn't the greatest hockey nation on Earth. But when you handicap that debate against the actual numbers of players and facilities in each country, you could make a pretty good argument that, pound for pound, Slovakia deserves the title.

Here's a country of 5.5 million, with just 9,402 hockey players and 51 rinks according to the IIHF survey. Yet it produced 22 players who began the 2005–06 season on NHL teams—among them such stars as Marian Hossa, Marian Gaborik, Zdeno Chara, Miroslav Satan, Pavol Demitra and Andrej Meszaros. Hossa and Chara alone are among the very best scorers and defencemen, respectively, in the world.

The start of that same season featured 371 Canadians in the NHL, making up 52.3 percent of the player pool. Which is great. But remember, it is far easier for someone to reach the NHL than it is to make it in any other major professional team sport.

Consider that there are about 1.5 million hockey players in the world, with roughly a third in Canada, another third in the United States and another third in the rest of the world combined. That's minuscule compared to the millions participating in baseball, basketball, rugby, cricket and soccer—and even football—around the world.

That's right: there are roughly three times as many football players in the United States as there are hockey players in the world. So even a sport that is limited to basically two countries has a deeper talent pool than hockey does.

And in a sport like soccer, which has 250 million participants worldwide, the World Cup champion really can claim to be world champion, since the whole world plays the game in some form or other.

Here's another point worth making carefully: I think

we've arrived at a time when it is fair to suggest that any sport that does not involve the significant participation of athletes of African descent has a weaker talent pool than those that do.

In baseball, we now acknowledge that the game was weaker before integration. Imagine football, basketball, boxing, track and field and other sports without black athletes in the competition. It's not the same thing, is it?

Since hockey is the one global team sport that remains nearly 100 percent white at the elite levels, I think it's fair to suggest its talent pool is lacking something compared to those of other sports.

And that doesn't seem about to change anytime soon. The nations that produce elite hockey players have remained remarkably consistent over the past 25 years, with no sense that the membership will expand beyond the core that competes every four year at the Olympics.

So, take a bow, Canada. You deserve it as the undisputed greatest hockey nation on Earth. Every now and then, however, it's worth recognizing how heavily the playing field is tilted in our favour.

55. **Remember the days when people debated whether two referees made for a better National Hockey League game? Well, Bob says there's no debate anymore. Unless you want to go back the old NHL.**

PEOPLE WHO DID not grow up with hockey often had the same reaction the first time they watched one referee trying to officiate a game.

"How in the world can one guy keep track of everything that's happening on the ice?" they'd ask.

As we now know, they didn't. I mean, in football you've got officials all over the field. In baseball, every base has its own umpire. And basketball requires three guys to officiate a court that is just 94 feet long and 50 feet wide.

Yet in hockey, which is much faster and is played on a far bigger surface, it was determined that while two people were needed to watch for offside calls, it took just one to call all the potential infractions on the ice, those around the puck and away from it. Does that sound right?

You have to think that one of the reasons the National Hockey League resisted efforts to enforce its rulebook for so many years was that it couldn't. With just one referee, there was simply no way to enforce a crackdown on all the stuff that goes on during a game.

I mean, really, how do you call hooking and interference behind the play if you're the only guy out there and your job is to follow the puck?

When the NHL went to the two-referee system back in 1998–99, it was essentially confirming what all of those neo-phyte hockey fans saw when they watched the game. You can't officiate this game with one person.

So let's agree that the league's successful post-lockout crackdown on obstruction and interference would never have been possible with one referee. Not a chance.

First of all, one referee wouldn't be able to see all the things that must be kept in mind the way the game is being called right now. Under the two-referee system, officials take positions that allow them the very best sightlines from which to view the game. These sightlines weren't as critical under the way the game used to be officiated, but they are today.

Second, going back to one referee in today's NHL would mean an explosion in the amount of diving. Hockey fans are already up in arms about the degree to which players are willing to fake or exaggerate a fall to the ice to draw a penalty.

Well, with just one referee out there trying to call every infraction, there'd be more diving going on than at the Summer Olympics, as players took advantage of the officials' lack of positioning.

Then there's the physical factor. With no red line for offside purposes, play moves through the neutral zone far faster in today's game than it used to. And without obstruction to slow attacking players as they cross through the zone, it would be nearly impossible for one referee to keep up with the flow of the game. And keeping up with the play is more important than ever, because referees must now be able to spot more than just egregious fouls.

Thirty-year-old officials would have to be fitness superstars in order to keep up with today's NHL as lone referees. Meanwhile, referees past their mid-forties would be forced into retirement—they wouldn't be able to skate fast enough to keep up with the play. Since teams are always complaining about the number of inexperienced referees in the game, why would anyone want to see the good ones pushed out of their jobs earlier than they have to be?

There's also a critical support factor when you have two referees out on the ice together. When there's one guy working alone, it's only natural that when fans, players and coaches are working him over for an entire game, telling him he's missed calls and blown others, a little self-doubt can surface. The pressure to bend or soften up, the way NHL officials routinely used to do as a game moved along, is much easier to withstand when there's another guy out there with you, reinforcing what you're doing and trying to uphold the same standard from his end of things.

So forget this debate, because there's no going back. Two referees is the only way to go. And frankly, it's something that should have happened a long, long time ago.

56.
Everyone loves to bet on sports—except hockey fans, it seems. Bob explains why the fastest game on ice doesn't attract much action in the betting world.

TRY THIS EXPERIMENT the next time you're with friends taking in a hockey game on television: hands up, everyone who bets on the National Hockey League.

Chances are no one does. Which should be surprising, since fans of nearly every other sport love to lay a little action to boost their interest.

And some sports, such as the National Football League, are positively driven by the passion to gamble that is shared by football fans. Betting on a Super Bowl, for instance, is so widespread that half of everybody watching on television has some sort of wager on the game. And while basketball and baseball are distant behind the NFL in terms of betting, there's still a significant amount of gambling on those sports every day.

But betting on hockey—whether here in Canada or in the United States—is almost nonexistent.

I think a big part of it is cultural. I would suggest that if you surveyed 10,000 hard-core hockey fans in the United States (assuming you could find them), you'd find a much higher percentage of them betting on games than you would with 10,000 hard-core fans in Canada. That's because in the United States, wagering on a particular sport is part and parcel of loving that sport.

In Canada, it's not that way. In fact, you're almost a traitor if you wager on a game that involves your team instead of just cheering out of loyalty. I'm always amazed by the purity of devotion Canadians show their favourite teams, especially if those teams happen to be the Maple Leafs or Canadiens. So loyal are they, it seems, that fans are hesitant to lay a bet on a game for fear of spoiling the experience.

Now they may play Pro-Line for a few bucks here and there. Or they may be in a hockey pool of some kind. But serious wagering on hockey is pretty rare among fans in Canada.

In the United States, the gambling culture among fans is far more widespread. But most hockey fans south of the border tend to be the same people who watch other sports as well. And so, when given a choice between betting on hockey, football, basketball or baseball, they'll almost never choose hockey. One reason is that they generally know less about hockey than those other sports. And secondly, they won't bet hockey because its odds are by far the worst on any board.

Here's what I mean.

Under normal circumstances, with what is known as a 10-cent line, a gambler has to bet $110 on a team to win $100. In other words, the bookmaker who collects one bet on the Maple Leafs and another on the Canadiens would take in $220 in total. He would then pay out $210 to the winner, leaving himself a profit of $10. That's also known as the "juice" or "vigorish," which in the case of a 10-cent line is about 4.5 percent.

When betting with a 10-cent line, a gambler has to win 52.4 percent of his bets to break even. That doesn't sound like a lot, but it's actually difficult to achieve.

In hockey, however, the bookmakers almost always post 20-cent, 30-cent or even 40-cent lines. With a 20-cent line, you've got to bet $120 to make $100. Which means the negative expectation is double what it is with a 10-cent line. It's 9 percent, which is very, very tough to beat. In fact, in order to beat a 20-cent line you'd need to win almost 55 percent of the time. And with a 30-cent line, that rate grows to almost 57 percent. Anything higher than that and you're talking about lottery-type odds of taking home any money.

Which is why no intelligent bettor would touch hockey. It's just there for suckers, like the fan from Toronto who stumbles off a vacation charter to Las Vegas and bets on the Leafs without knowing the difference between a 10-cent line and a 40-cent line.

Betting lines on hockey are a service for tourists on which the casinos make a bit of money. But there's no real market for hockey betting, which is why the casinos aren't interested in doing the work necessary to produce a 10-cent line. If there were more demand, you'd get competition and a better line for bettors. But there's not. In fact, you can assume that a marquee NFL game on a Sunday attracts more money from bettors than does an entire season of hockey.

The casinos are only interested in using hockey to lure in blind bettors. Which is exactly what they get every time someone places a puck wager.

Now, if I were the National Hockey League, I'd be lobbying the casinos to make hockey wagering more competitive with other sports. I'd beg for a 10-cent line, because the promotion of gambling would be a positive for hockey, as is anything that fuels interest in the sport.

What you have right now is a culture in Canada that loves hockey but doesn't embrace wagering on it. And a culture in the U.S. that loves gaming but not hockey. So until the pure economics of betting hockey improve, and that doesn't seem likely anytime soon, hockey betting will continue to be a magnet for suckers.

57. ■ **The biggest hockey story of all time has yet to occur. But when it does, it will be bigger than "Gretzky traded to Los Angeles" or "Leafs finally win Cup." Bob explains.**

THE BIGGEST HOCKEY story ever might break tomorrow. Or next week, next year, 20 years from now or beyond.

But it will happen, and perhaps sooner rather than later.

And when it does, you will see the media from all over this country mobilize like never before on a sports story. It will be as much a news story as a sports story and it will fuel debate and criticism within and beyond hockey like nothing before.

I am talking about the day a player dies as the result of injuries sustained in a hockey fight.

It's something that's rarely discussed, but something many people in the game quietly fear. For in today's game, with the size of the men who bare-knuckle fight for a good part of their paycheques, it's hardly a stretch to assume someone is going to suffer a catastrophic injury.

Many of the men who throw punches for a living these days are giants, far bigger than the hockey pugilists of a generation ago. Players such as Ottawa's Brian McGrattan, at 6-foot-4 and 220 pounds, Pittsburgh's Georges Laraque at 6-foot-3 and 240 pounds or Buffalo's Andrew Peters at 6-foot-4 and 240 pounds can pack far more powerful punches than those who preceded them. You just can't allow men of that size to battle one another and not expect serious injuries to occur.

I mean, when a guy like Minnesota's Derek Boogard, at 6-foot-7 and 254 pounds, crushes Todd Fedoruk's face as he did in October of 2006, are we really surprised that Fedoruk needs facial reconstruction afterward? And just how thin is the line between needing facial reconstruction from a fight and getting brain damage? That's certainly what a lot of people were wondering after watching Fedoruk get his face pummelled again, five months later, this time by New York's Colton Orr.

Just how close do we have to get to seeing a guy get his face taken apart before people say enough? I applaud the NHL's vice-president of hockey operations, Colin Campbell, for coming out after the second Fedoruk incident in March of 2007 and suggesting it was time to ask whether fighting still had a place in hockey. But you didn't hear a chorus of support for that position from within the sport, did you? And in a moment of unsurprisingly horrible judgment, Commissioner Gary Bettman came forward a few days later to reassure everyone that the NHL will always have fights.

It will be up to Bettman, or whomever is leading the NHL the day a player is killed by the bare fists of another, to answer the questions that will be asked over and over again: Why did so few see this coming? Why was this risk allowed to be run?

Don't think it can happen? Sorry, but to suggest that something will not occur in the future just because it has not in the past is a sign of stupidity in itself.

Back in March of 2002, a 13-year-old girl named Brittanie Cecil was attending a Columbus Blue Jackets game—something millions of fans have done for decades. But Cecil turned out to be the unluckiest hockey fan ever when a puck came flying out of the rink and struck her in the left temple. She walked out of the arena but died two days later from injuries sustained from the puck.

The reaction was predictable. Why had a risk so obvious been ignored by the NHL? Why had the sport knowingly subjected its fans to such risks? And why didn't it do something before someone was killed? By the start of the next season, every NHL building had netting at both ends of the ice to protect fans from pucks coming their way at high speeds.

There had been lots of *injuries* sustained as a result of pucks flying out of NHL rinks, just as there have been lots of injuries in hockey fights.

In fact, in recent years Nick Kypreos, Jeff Beukeboom, Ryan Flinn and Steve Moore have all suffered injuries that could have had tragic consequences from punches thrown on the ice. In three of those cases careers were ended, which is certainly bad enough.

When a death does occur as a result of a hockey fight, the debate will be loud and long, because the issues that surround fighting have plagued the game since its earliest days. And should it happen in a junior hockey game—where, remarkably, players as young as 16 years of age fight each other with bare fists before paying crowds—the condemnation will be that much more severe.

And when the smoke clears, there will be no debate about fighting in hockey. The arguments about enforcers as protectors and safety valves and other such garbage will be moot. The abolitionists, long marginalized in the sport, will get their way, and they'll wish they'd been wrong about a tragedy occuring.

58. The National Hockey League game is vastly improved since before the lockout, without a doubt. It's faster, more skilful and more exciting. But Bob says there's one simple change that would make it so much better.

I FIND IT REMARKABLE how many people recoil at the notion that the National Hockey League should increase the size of its nets.

It's as if someone were trying to mess with a sacred measurement. You'd almost think that "four feet by six feet" was found scribbled on an ancient glacier by some hockey god 100 million years ago.

Which just goes to show you how hidebound the NHL is to tradition and how closed-minded hockey fans can be. Remember, this is a league where it took years to remove the red line for offsides. And since that has occurred, not one negative thing has resulted from that change. Imagine.

Increasing the size of the nets would have the same effect.

Not only would it improve the game, but it would solve the biggest problem there is with post-lockout hockey, which is the disproportionate number of goals scored on power plays.

The NHL managed to achieve its goal of increased scoring after the lockout, going from 5.14 goals per game in 2003–04 to 6.17 in 2005–06. The problem is, most of the scoring increase has taken place with the man advantage. And that is largely because the new officiating standards have produced more power plays.

When teams were playing five-on-five, scoring went up just .13 goals per game in 2005–06, which proves that the new NHL game depends far more on special-teams performance than ever before. It also raises the question of what might happen in five years, when players have fully adjusted to the new rules and the number of power plays presumably drops towards previous levels.

Will we not then see a corresponding drop in goal scoring? Sure we will, unless there's a significant increase in five-on-five scoring.

The NHL may have cleaned up all the interference in the game, given it more flow and put more of an emphasis on skill, but what's that really worth if it doesn't result in more goals when teams are playing at even strength?

The simplest and least disruptive solution to all of this is to make the nets bigger. Though traditionalists would scream, a bigger net would do more to restore the game to its roots than anything. Because it's not the size of the net that matters, but the area of the net that's visible to shooters. And as long as the target at the other end of the ice—the visible part of the net—is still far, far smaller than it was even 20 years ago, the game can never be what it once was.

The NHL has done its work by reducing the size of goal-tending pads by 11 percent. But the players who occupy the nets these days, just like players at every position, are a lot bigger than they were even a generation ago. The only way to fix this is with bigger nets. Even a couple of inches of both height and width would be enough.

With bigger nets, coaches will be far more likely to breed offence into the game because they'll believe they have a good chance of scoring. There was lots of evidence that, by the second year of post-lockout hockey, many teams were already starting to revert to more defensive styles of play. Which is part of why scoring was down roughly a quarter of a goal per game from 2005–06 to 2006–07.

Growing the nets wouldn't require a different type of player, a different skill set or even a different style of goaltender. It would simply give shooters back some of the advantage they once had. And, combined with the crackdown on interference, I believe that would produce the best game we've seen in at least a generation. Let's get back to the days when a shooter could beat a goalie with a clean, hard shot instead of relying on there being a crowd in front of the net before the puck is put on goal.

I'm sure goalies wouldn't welcome the change, and lord knows they would lobby to fight it. But they should be flattered. It's like when baseball lowered the mound for pitchers in the late 1960s or the National Football League decided that teams should kick off from their 30-yard line instead of the 35. Those sports simply recognized that one set of skills in the sport had advanced beyond others, so the game had to adjust.

Goaltenders are so much bigger and better than they were a generation ago. Let's make them protect a larger target.

59. ■ They are the "coulda, shoulda" teams of the National Hockey League. Teams that had great chances to lift Lord Stanley's mug but instead let an opportunity pass. Here are the teams Bob says should have won it all.

THE DIFFERENCE BETWEEN a team winning or not winning a Stanley Cup is simple. Teams that win it are immortalized in at least some small way. Whether it's that moment when players raise the Cup above their heads, the victory parade or the Cup-clinching goal, it becomes part of Stanley Cup lore. Yet the teams that don't win it, great as they may be, tend to fade from our memories very quickly.

Hockey fans can easily recite all kinds of details about the dynasties of the Montreal Canadiens, New York Islanders and Edmonton Oilers. But ask them to recall whom those teams beat during their Stanley Cup runs and it gets much tougher.

So here are my rankings of the best teams that could easily have won a Cup or two over a period of years but did not.

8. St. Louis Blues, 1967–68 to 1969–70. These Blues weren't exactly a powerhouse during their initial three seasons. But the National Hockey League's decision to group all six expansion franchises into one division guaranteed that one of them would reach the Stanley Cup final each year. The result was that St. Louis got a golden opportunity three years in a row. Scotty Bowman became the first coach to figure out that talent-poor teams could improve their chances by focusing on defence. Goaltender Glenn Hall was fantastic during the '68 playoffs before the Blues bowed out in four games to Montreal in the Stanley Cup final. The next season, St. Louis added Jacques Plante, who promptly won the Vezina Trophy as the Blues allowed by far the fewest goals in the NHL, going to the final and losing again to Montreal in a sweep. Bobby

Orr finished them off in next year's final with the famous goal that ended with him soaring through the air. St. Louis lost that one in four games as well, and has never been to the Cup final since.

7. Boston Bruins, 1989–90 to 1991–92. These Bruins got to the Stanley Cup final once and played in two other semifinals, losing all three times to offensive juggernauts. First it was the 1990 Edmonton Oilers, who did the damage in a 4–1 series victory in the Stanley Cup final. The Oilers then passed the torch, not to the Bruins but to the Pittsburgh Penguins, who defeated Boston in back-to-back semifinals en route to Cup wins in '91 and '92. Losing to three consecutive Cup winners was little consolation for a quality Bruin team that included few stars beyond Ray Bourque and Cam Neely (who played just nine games in '91–92) and had former Oiler Andy Moog in goal. The Bruins managed to dump Montreal in three consecutive playoff years, which in itself should have been cause for celebration. But their new nemesis, Pittsburgh, went 8–2 against them over two series meetings.

6. Ottawa Senators, 2000–01 to 2006–07. If the NHL used a college-football style of voting over this span to determine its champion, Ottawa would have won at least three Stanley Cups. The Senators were consistent pre-season favourites and would look the part throughout each regular season. Then the magic would disappear at playoff time. They didn't always get the necessary clutch goaltending, but a far bigger ill was their inability to score goals in the postseason. Ottawa was favoured in all three of their playoff matchups with Toronto during this time but somehow lost them all, including two in Game 7. Game 7 also wasn't kind to Ottawa in the conference final. The Senators had the lead on home ice against New Jersey in 2003, but let a chance to compete for the Cup slip through their fingers when the Devils went ahead late in the third period. The Sens were better in

2006–07 but still not good enough, losing to Anaheim in five games in the final.

5. St. Louis Blues, 1999–2000 to 2002–03. Over four seasons these Blues finished with no fewer than 98 points but got to just one conference final series, losing to eventual champion Colorado in 2001. In '99–00 they became one of the few teams to win the Presidents' Trophy for best overall record and then bow out in the first round of the playoffs. Pavol Demitra and Pierre Turgeon were the offensive stars for a team anchored by Al MacInnis and Chris Pronger on defence. Goaltending, however, was a significant issue. Neither Roman Turek nor Brent Johnson, who followed him, could put St. Louis on a par with the league's elite playoff teams.

4. Philadelphia Flyers, 1984–85 to 1986–87. This is the case of a team that ran smack into a dynasty. The Flyers eclipsed the 100-point mark three times from '84–85 to '86–87 and reached the Stanley Cup final twice. Unfortunately, their opponents in both final series were the Oilers, who featured the game's greatest player and one of the best supporting casts of all time. Philly had Tim Kerr, Brian Propp, Mark Howe and youngsters Rick Tocchet and Scott Mellanby. Though the Flyers won just three fewer regular-season games than Edmonton over that three-year span, they were no match at playoff time, losing in five games in 1985 and seven in 1987.

3. Chicago Blackhawks, 1970–71 to 1972–73. The Blackhawks benefited greatly from divisional realignment in 1971, which grouped them with six expansion teams (plus a seventh, Atlanta, in '72). Backed by the goaltending of Tony Esposito, Chicago reached the Stanley Cup final twice in three years, the first in '71 with Bobby Hull and the second, in '73, without him. But while Hull was the headliner in Chicago, he was hardly the only star. Brother Dennis Hull, Pat Stapleton, Bill White, Stan Mikita, Pit Martin and Keith Magnuson were all stars in their own right. The Hawks had a 2–0 lead on home ice halfway through Game 7 against the Habs in '71, but Montreal tied the game after two periods and won it 3–2 with an early third-period goal. Two years later the Habs took them again in a six-game final, after which the Blackhawks entered a period of decline.

2. Boston Bruins, 1975–76 to 1978–79. Oh, what the Bruins of the late 1970s would have accomplished were it not for the Montreal Canadiens. Boston reached either the Stanley Cup semifinals or final in four consecutive years from '76 to '79, with three of those losses, including the two defeats in the Stanley Cup final, coming at the hands of the dynastic Montreal Canadiens. The post Esposito–Orr Bruins had lots of blue-collar style to them, what with the likes of Gregg Sheppard, Stan Jonathan and Terry O'Reilly. But with Gerry Cheevers in goal, Brad Park on defence and Jean Ratelle playing with the ageless Johnny Bucyk (who retired after the '77–78 season), the Bruins also had talent, finishing with 100 points for five consecutive years. History would have been different if the Bruins could have won a game or two on the road against Montreal. Instead, they lost all nine playoff games at the Montreal Forum from '76 to '79. The '79 semifinal loss was the most painful, as the Bruins blew a third-period lead in Game 7 after being penalized for having too many men on the ice.

1. Philadelphia Flyers, 1994–95 to 2005–06. Where to begin listing the great players who wore a Philadelphia uniform over a period during which the Flyers were one of the most consistent teams in hockey? How about Eric Lindros, John LeClair, Mark Recchi, Eric Desjardins, Rod Brind'Amour, Paul Coffey, Mikael Renberg, Simon Gagne, Keith Primeau, Chris Therien, Jeremy Roenick, Kim Johnsson, Tony Amonte and Peter Forsberg? The Flyers never dipped below 93 points in the standings and were regularly over 100. But they reached just one final series and three conference finals, losing their best chance for a Stanley Cup in 1997 in a four-game sweep against Detroit. The one constant? Despite playing with one of the biggest payrolls in hockey, the Flyers never went to the bank for a marquee goaltender. With Patrick Roy, they'd have won at least three Cups over this span.

60. They say you can't fix a team overnight. Well, you can if you hit the jackpot in a single draft year. But how many NHL teams do that? Bob looks at the greatest single drafts.

THE NATIONAL HOCKEY LEAGUE has changed a lot over the past 40 years. So have the methods by which general managers build their teams. In the days before free agency, before multi-million-dollar contracts, it was a different kind of puzzle to solve. And now, in the salary cap world, it's all changed again.

Yet for all the changes in hockey and the business of the sport, one constant has remained true: teams that draft well will be rewarded handsomely for their efforts. And conversely, teams that draft poorly have almost no chance of success, even if they happen to have unlimited budgets.

Most years, success means getting one quality NHL player out of a draft. If you happen to get two or three, especially in today's 30-team league, that's remarkable. And of course, everyone is ecstatic when they're able to pull a star from one of the later rounds once the obvious prospects have been picked over.

Here are the teams that had the best results ever from any single year of looking into their crystal balls and predicting the future.

5. Calgary, 1984: Gary Roberts (12th), Paul Ranheim (38th), Brett Hull (117th), Jiri Hrdina (159th), Gary Suter (180th). Pulling five decent NHL players out of one draft is amazing. When four of them wind up playing more than 1,000 games, it's incredible. Jiri Hrdina is the only name on this list that doesn't jump out at fans, but he did score 22 goals for the Flames in '88–89 and, after moving on to Pittsburgh, retired with three Stanley Cup rings in five years. The other four combined for over 3,300 points in their careers, with Roberts and Suter instrumental in the Flames' only Cup win in '89. Just imagine how this draft would be recalled in Calgary if the Flames hadn't traded Hull.

4. Montreal, 1971: Guy Lafleur (1st), Chuck Arnason (7th), Murray Wilson (11th), Larry Robinson (20th). The Canadiens kept up their flow of great players by snagging two of the all-time best on draft day in 1971. Beyond the Habs of the Original Six era, Guy Lafleur remains the greatest player to wear a Canadiens uniform and was the top offensive player in the game before Wayne Gretzky arrived. Robinson, meanwhile, was the best player on one of the greatest defensive units ever to play together, as the Habs won four consecutive Cups in the late 1970s. Murray Wilson played on three of those teams. Only Chuck Arnason, who spent just a year in Montreal before bouncing around the NHL, was a disappointment.

3. Edmonton, 1980: Paul Coffey (6th), Jari Kurri (69th), Walt Poddubny (90th), Andy Moog (132). In one swoop the Oilers found Wayne Gretzky's future right winger and the defenceman who would be his playmaking partner on the highest-scoring teams of all time. They weren't just great players; Coffey and Kurri both brought unique skills to the game, enjoying long and distinguished careers. Along with being part of all five Oiler Stanley Cups, Kurri and Coffey combined for 40 seasons, 16 Stanley Cup final appearances and 12 championship rings. Moog, not to be completely overshadowed, won three Cups with the Oilers, mainly as a backup, in a 16-year career. Poddubny, meanwhile, left Edmonton early and was not terribly missed.

2. Edmonton, 1979: Kevin Lowe (21st), Mark Messier (48th), Glenn Anderson (69th). Between the drafts of 1979 and '80, the Oilers selected five skaters who played on all five of their Stanley Cup-winning teams. That kind of draft success is simply unparalleled in back-to-back years. Coincidentally, all three of their 1979 draft picks were also part of the New York Ranger championship in 1994, giving the trio a combined 18 Stanley Cup rings. In addition, Messier ranks second all-time in NHL points scored, Anderson cracked the elite 1,000-point club and Lowe was a seven-time all-star who became the team's captain and general manager. Not a bad day's haul.

1. Detroit, 1989: Mike Sillinger (11th), Bob Boughner (32nd), Nicklas Lidstrom (53rd), Sergei Fedorov (74th), Dallas Drake (116th), Vladimir Konstantinov (221st). The most remarkable thing about the six NHL players the Red Wings managed to find in the 1989 draft is that the best ones came late. In Lidstrom, Fedorov and Konstantinov, the Red Wings found three franchise players who helped lay the foundation for the dominant team of the later 20th and early 21st centuries. Any team would be thrilled to get a defenceman like Lidstrom, a five-time Norris Trophy winner, or Konstantinov, a Norris Trophy finalist before the accident that put him in a wheelchair in 1997, in any round. And the same could be said of Fedorov, who, like Lidstrom, is destined for the Hockey Hall of Fame. Getting all three after every team in the NHL had passed on them at least twice (in Konstantinov's case, 10 times) will likely never happen again. Finding Sillinger, Boughner and Drake in one draft would be a fine year for any team. In this case they turned out to be the supporting cast in the greatest single draft by any team in history.

61. You can't get through a week without hearing someone complain about diving in the National Hockey League. Bob says that before you can get rid of it, you have to understand it.

WHEN YOU TALK about diving, there is one incident in recent National Hockey League history that stands out above all others.

During Game 3 of the opening round of the 2003–04 playoffs, Montreal was clinging to a one-goal lead over Boston with less than a minute to play and Bruin goaltender Andrew Raycroft on the bench. Suddenly, Montreal centre Mike Ribeiro was lying on the ice as if he'd just been stabbed, the apparent result of a collision at centre ice with Boston's Mike Knuble. The skinny forward flailed like a fish that had just been hauled ashore, clutching his throat and kicking his legs as if struggling for air.

Understandably, play was halted.

The Bell Centre crowd fell to a hush as players on both teams looked on with grave concern, the thrilling finish to a close game all but forgotten. That is, until Ribeiro jumped up and skated towards his team's bench, laughing and taunting the Bruins as he left the ice.

To just about anyone who saw it, either live or on highlight reels, it was despicable. You can bet that even some of the Canadiens privately shared the thoughts of Boston defenceman Nick Boynton, who didn't hesitate to express his opinion.

"You can only cry wolf so many times, and he'll get his," Boynton said. "Whether it's in this series or sometime else. People have to play exhibition games. That's what those are for. If I were him or his teammates, I'd be embarrassed. It's not hockey. I thought he'd swallowed his tongue and then he got up and taunted the bench."

Ribeiro, however, managed to stop play, giving his team a rest at a critical juncture of the hockey game, and helped them emerge with a win in what eventually became a seven-game series victory for Montreal.

I'd like to point out here that Mike Ribeiro, while born and raised in Montreal, is the son of a former Portuguese professional soccer player. Why is that relevant? Because what Ribeiro did in that game was stolen right from the soccer pitch, a point that was made by Don Cherry later that week.

And while his tactic may have been unique in the NHL, it's the kind of thing you're likely to see at least once, if not two or three times, when watching an elite soccer match.

The difference is that it is obviously tolerated to a much greater degree in soccer. I mean, this is a sport that has accepted forever and ever that players will periodically go down as if they've been shot from behind the grassy knoll. You saw it all the time in the 2006 World Cup.

Now, I won't suggest that diving didn't exist in the NHL before the influx of European players, because guys like Bill Barber and Steve Shutt were certainly known to embellish in order to get a call. But I don't think it's a coincidence that nowadays, with roughly 30 percent of the NHL made up of players from overseas, it's become one of the hot-button issues in the game.

I understand that the gut reaction of North American sports fan is to suggest that the European tolerance of diving is gutless and shameful. And, at first glance, I tend to agree.

But you've got to remember that diving in hockey is, in some ways, no different than fighting, excessive stickwork or trying to intimidate your opponent physically. It all falls under the umbrella of trying to get away with something that you believe gives your team an advantage.

Viewed through a North American lens, we would never cast aspersions on a player who gets caught hooking behind the play. And God knows some of the dirtiest hockey players ever—Tie Domi comes to mind—have been wildly popular in the cities where they've played. We simply accept or applaud certain things that players do beyond the rules to gain an edge for their team. And others, such as diving, we do not.

In North America, the macho culture hasn't allowed players to be bred as divers. We come from a culture where playing hurt is a virtue. Where tolerating pain is heroic. And, therefore, to go down in a heap in the middle of play is considered weakness.

We learn that bad things will follow if you pretend you are hurt.

Think for a second of the career of Sidney Crosby thus far. He's lived up to everyone's expectations as the NHL's next superstar. What's the only knock on him? He's a diver, some say, as though that's a serious flaw in a guy who's lighting up the league and fighting off checks to score every goal he gets.

But in soccer it would certainly appear that no one is terribly afraid of being called a diver.

And the influence of soccer runs throughout European sport, something that's difficult for those of us raised in North America to appreciate. Just as Canadians tend to play other sports the way they play hockey (ask the South African rugby team at the 1995 World Cup, who started to run up the score against the overmatched Canadians, with predictable results), Europeans play hockey the way they play soccer. While young Canadian athletes are being taught that you need to be tough to succeed, a lot of Europeans are learning it's smart to dive.

Not surprisingly, some North American players have adopted the practice as well. And they've done so, no doubt, with the same rationale as if they were trying to send a message by hitting a guy after the whistle. It's all in the name of giving your team an edge.

What's the solution? I think it's the same as with any other problem in the game of hockey: you've got to breed it out of the sport.

Players will dive until they learn it won't give them an edge. It's really no different than trying to breed out the instincts to clutch, grab and hook that have infected the game for years.

Just as with those other infractions, the league has to be vigilant, proving to players that they're far more likely to be penalized for a dive than to gain an edge. Only then will we see it disappear from hockey. Already we've seen the NHL more willing to penalize divers for embellishing on plays where a hook or a slash in already being called, sending both the slasher and the diver to the box at the same time. At first, that seems absurd. But by using diving penalties to negate a man advantage a team would have received without such a show, the league is sending the right message.

Because you're just never going to shame diving out of the hockey as long as it works.

62. You hear all the time that today's hockey players don't have the respect for one another that they did in the good old days. But Bob says people forget how nasty the good old days could be.

EVERY TIME THERE'S a dirty hit in a National Hockey League game, we inevitably hear the "R" word.

Respect. As in, "Players don't respect each other in today's NHL like they used to back in the 1950s, '60s and '70s." We are supposed to believe that players in those days played the game with a concern for their opponents that no longer exists. That back then, players viewed opponents as fellow hockey players first and rivals second.

Which is a bunch of bull.

First of all, this argument is rooted in a cultural myth that suggests that every generation is less respectful than the ones that have come before. Think of any field of endeavour and I will guarantee you people will say there was more respect 30 years ago. Politics? Music? The National Basketball Association? The business world?

I mean, when is the last time you heard anyone suggest that people are more respectful today than they were a generation ago? You didn't hear that in the 1970s, '80s or '90s, and you sure don't hear it today.

So I'm not surprised to hear people say respect has gone out of hockey even though, as you can see at a glance, there has never been more respect among hockey players than there is in today's NHL.

Here's why: these days, players see themselves as businessmen. They understand their market value and the notion that everyone is playing for money and not just loyalty to the sweater. They are union brothers before they are Leafs or Flames or Oilers. And they get chummy with one another through players' association business, off-season events or the modern churn of player movement in the league.

Which is a huge difference from the days when hockey players saw themselves as soldiers fighting for the crest on their sweater. Back then, respect was reserved for teammates, fans and the owners who paid them—not for players on the opposing team. And those sorts of feelings were easy to maintain when players often spent their entire careers with the same team. They didn't want to fraternize with opponents. And, in fact, many of them refused to.

It's simply not like that today, an age where players share agents, vacations and an understanding that they're all in this together. If you've ever stood between two NHL dressing rooms after a game, you'll notice the numbers of opposing players who seek each other out for a handshake and a conversation. It's like old home week.

You think that happened in the days of the Original Six rivalries? Was Detroit's Ted Lindsay going down the Maple Leafs dressing room to shake hands with George Armstrong and find out how the wife and kids were doing? Not on your life.

And if you want to talk about a lack of respect in the game, Ted Lindsay is a good place to start. Here's a guy whom his coach, Jack Adams, once described as a player who would be "a great guy to throw into a game where there were no rules."

One time, during a fight with Boston's Bill Ezinicki, Lindsay knocked his opponent out cold. When teammate Gordie Howe alerted Lindsay to this fact, he apparently fired back, "I don't give a damn, I'm going to kill him," before being hauled off and taken away.

Does that sound like respect to you?

Of course, that incident, and the others like it, weren't picked up by 24-hour sports channels and repeated over and over and over again.

Back in the 1960s and '70s, if you butt-ended someone with your stick behind the goal, you'd be surprised if the primitive TV coverage of the day picked it up. And that's if the game was even being broadcast.

But today, with every game on television and cameras all over the ice, every cheap shot is a highlight, complete with reaction the following day from around the league and the pundits in television studios.

And so, when retired players are asked to comment on a well-publicized cheap shot and whether today's players have as much respect for one another as they used to, what do you think they're going to say? It's ludicrous.

You hear all the time that the number of injuries caused by high sticks in the game today is all about a lack of respect.

I would suggest it's far more about a generation of players that has grown up with full facial protection playing in a league that allows players to remove it when they become professionals.

When Marian Hossa allowed his stick to come up high and straight into the eye of Bryan Berard in a game between Ottawa and Toronto in 2000, was that because he didn't have enough respect for his opponent? Of course it wasn't. In fact, Hossa had so much respect for Berard that he visited him in the hospital after the incident and was so shaken by what happened that his game went into the crapper for several weeks afterward.

There are times I think people have wiped their minds clean of the stuff hockey players used to do to each other 30, 40 and 50 years ago.

So let me take a moment to refresh some memories.

Where, exactly, was the respect when Philadelphia's Broad Street Bullies of the 1970s used to terrorize opponents by pounding them into submission? Was respect what Dave "The Hammer" Schultz was displaying when he pounded New York's Dale Rolfe with a dozen unanswered punches to the face during a game in 1974? I'm sure Rolfe felt respected as he fell gasping to the ice, blood streaming down his face.

As Brian McFarlane wrote when he described the incident in his Original Six series, "The Flyers stood around, not smirking, perhaps, but confident that their teammate's rampage, his furious attack, would enhance their chances for victory."

That does sound like respect, doesn't it?

When Rocket Richard punched a linesman and delivered a pair of retaliatory slashes at Boston's Hal Laycoe in 1955, was that respect?

Or was it respect when when Wayne Maki and Ted Green swung sticks at each other in a 1969 pre-season incident that nearly killed Green?

Or how about the time in 1978 when Colorado's Wilf Paiement broke the nose of Detroit's Dennis Polonich by swinging his stick at his face? Detroit general manager Ted Lindsay testified that Paiement hit Polonich like a baseball player swinging a bat. Nothing, I would suggest, says respect quite like a baseball swing to the face.

The respect was so long-lasting in this incident that Polonich told McFarlane years later that "Paiement never showed any remorse for clubbing me." This despite the fact that Polonich's career went on a downhill spiral after the incident.

Or was Winnipeg's Jimmy Mann showing respect when he jumped over the boards to sucker punch Pittsburgh's Paul Gardner in 1982, breaking his jaw in two places?

Look, I could go on and on about the way hockey used to be played, about the viciousness of what occurred on the ice and the complete and utter lack of respect many players had for anything but winning games.

The issue in this debate isn't a lack of respect in the modern NHL game. It's the lack of respect being shown for just how nasty hockey used to be.

63. They are perhaps the two most thrilling stories in the history of hockey: Canada's 1972 triumph over Russia and the United States' Miracle on Ice at the 1980 Olympics. So it's time for the ultimate fantasy showdown. One game only. Team Canada '72 faces off against the 1980 U.S. Olympic team. Bob tells you how it all shakes out.

IT OFTEN SEEMS that Canadians can't get enough of reliving the 1972 Summit Series. In fact, I'm sure that 200 years from now, Foster Hewitt's famous call of Paul Henderson's winning goal will still be a cultural signature in this country.

America's "Miracle on Ice" hasn't quite become part of the national fabric in the United States. But any team that can get American popular culture fired up about hockey gets my respect.

They were two teams that seized the moment with dramatic wins. One did after starting out as an overwhelming favourite, the other as a team that beat seemingly insurmountable odds. Both teams wore national pride on their sleeves and believed they were serving a cause beyond hockey by sending a message to the evil empire that was the Soviet Union.

So there you have the backdrop to the ultimate hockey fantasy matchup. One game, winner takes all.

On paper, it's no contest. Canada wins.

Yet we need to remember that the Soviet team the Americans beat was considered far greater than the one the Canadians narrowly edged.

In fact, in 2002, the International Ice Hockey Federation ranked the top 10 Russian hockey players of all time. Of those players, only four—Vladislav Tretiak, Boris Mikhailov, Valery Kharlamov and Alexander Maltsev—played for the Russians in 1972.

Comparatively, there were eight players from the IIHF alltime list on the 1980 Olympic squad (Tretiak, Slava Fetisov, Mikhailov, Kharlamov, Sergei Makarov, Vladimir Krutov, Alexei Kasatonov and Maltsev).

Leading up to that 1980 tournament, the Russians were as dominant as at any point in their hockey history. They'd crushed the NHL all-stars 6–0 in the deciding game of the Challenge Cup in 1979. In the 1978 and '79 World Hockey Championships, the Russians had gone 17–1, outscoring opponents 122–40. And after the Olympic loss to Team USA at Lake Placid, the Russians didn't lose a game at the World Championships until 1985—a five-year winning streak. Never mind the 1981 Canada Cup final in which the Russians destroyed Team Canada by an 8–1 score.

So, the Americans would have had to get up pretty early in the morning to beat these guys.

All that being said, I don't think there's much doubt that in a seven-game series the Canadians from '72 would win. Canada would have more size, skill, experience and talent. They'd be better with the puck, better without it, better in goal and better on the attack.

But a one-game event is a different matter altogether.

Let's assume for moment that the '72 Summit Series and 1980 Winter Olympic hockey tournament never occurred. And as a result, none of the lessons that either team might have learned through those experiences exist, either.

The Canadian team, even without Bobby Hull and Bobby Orr in the lineup, was a juggernaut. In players such as Phil Esposito, Gilbert Perreault, Bobby Clarke and Ron Ellis, we're talking about a team full of all-stars and future Hockey Hall of Famers. If you include head coach Harry Sinden, 13 members of Team Canada went on to be inducted into the Hockey Hall of Fame.

But having that much talent on a hockey team for the first time ever had a downside for Canada as well. The Canadians believed they could not be beaten. They had that Canadian sense of hockey superiority and they assumed that facing the Russians would be a cakewalk.

Moments after the puck dropped during that first game at the Montreal Forum, it appeared it would be just that. Instead, Canada's early 2–0 lead only set the table for the Russians to stage their comeback in what was considered a shocking 7–3 win for the visitors.

The Canadians were out of shape, and their mental focus was nowhere near what it should have been. In short, they didn't afford their opponents the respect they deserved.

It was arrogance that nearly undid Canada's efforts in 1972. And eight years later it was arrogance that cost the Russians against the Americans at the Lake Placid Olympics.

Team Canada thought that all it really needed to know about the Russians was that guys like with names like Yakushev, Petrov, Mikhailov and Kharlamov couldn't possibly be a threat.

So if the Canadians were willing to dismiss a team representing a country that had won nine of the past 10 World Hockey Championship titles, just how might they regard a bunch of American college kids? Would the greatest collection of hockey players ever put together be likely to spend a moment considering how to shut down Neal Broten, Dave Christian or Mark Johnson, or how to beat Jim Craig? Not a chance.

I mean, these were kids. The oldest player for the Americans was Buzz Schneider, and he was 25. The Canadians would have dismissed the Americans from the outset. They would have considered them merely play toys—boys taking on men.

Compare that to the attitude American head coach Herb Brooks would have drilled into his charges for a game with Team Canada. Brooks was a fanatic when it came to preparation. He understood in 1980 that his team's slim chance relied on preparedness, conditioning and discipline. He studied the Russians, knew their strengths—and their few weaknesses—intimately. His players respected their opponents but never feared them. And Brooks used psychology to make them believe the unthinkable could occur.

It would have been much easier for Brooks and his staff to scout the likes of Henderson, Esposito, Cournoyer and Savard than the mysterious Soviets. Brooks would have understood where the Canadians might be vulnerable and that, with speed and unrelenting checking throughout a game, the Americans had a shot.

Brooks would spend every minute during training camp designing tactics to counter Canada's superior skill while reinforcing to his players the opportunity for a knockout.

Juxtapose the Canadian sense of invulnerability against the preparedness of the Americans and you have the first necessary ingredient for an upset.

I imagine that, like in that first game against the Russians in '72, Team Canada would pull out in front of the Americans quickly. And from there, that sense of self-assuredness would kick in fully. Which would certainly be dangerous, because if there's one thing the Americans proved in Lake Placid it's that they wouldn't just go away.

Of course, the U.S. would need outstanding goaltending to stay close against Canada. And while Jim Craig may have been an NHL bust, he proved he could stand up to the world's best over a short period of time. When it was all on the line in 1980, Craig held one of the most potent Soviet attacks ever assembled to three goals, shutting the door to hold a one-goal lead throughout most of the third period.

Yes, the Americans would need some luck. But it's not hard to imagine them getting to the late stages of the second period trailing 2–1 or 3–2, as was the score at that point of their victory over Russia. And so, if they were close to Canada at that stage, when stamina becomes more of a factor, there's no doubt they'd be able to capitalize on any letdown in the Canadian game brought on by a lack of conditioning.

What's often forgotten about Team USA is the degree of talent on its roster. History has painted these guys as a bunch of overachievers who had no business even being in the tournament. But that's simply not true.

They *were* young and inexperienced. But when you look over the roster and consider that Ken Morrow went from Lake Placid to Long Island and won four straight Stanley Cups with the New York Islanders; that Mike Ramsey went on to a 17-

year career, spent mostly as a stalwart of the Buffalo Sabres' blue line; that Neal Broten also played 17 seasons in the NHL, including a 105-point season with the Minnesota North Stars in 1985–86; that Dave Christian had four seasons with at least 70 points in his 14-year NHL career; or that there were at least a half dozen others who had very decent NHL careers, it's clear this was not a team of nobodies.

Team USA was in fact 4–0–1 heading into the medal round at the Olympics in 1980. And after defeating the Russians, they went on and won the gold against the Finns.

Would it be improbable that they'd knock off the vaunted Team Canada '72 squad? Perhaps. But in our hypothetical world I'd be laying my money on the U.S.A.

Team Canada underestimated its foe in 1972 at its peril and was fortunate to have seven games to recover from its hubris. But in a one-game showdown with the Miracle on Ice crew, they'd be hard pressed to avoid an upset until it was too late.

Ken Dryden famously suggested after the Summit Series that Team Canada had dodged a bullet. If this one game could take place, he would have to concede that the Canadians had taken one.

64. **Wayne Gretzky and Bobby Orr both left us in awe at how they could dominate a game. But Bob says not even the Great One was as great as Number Four.**

NOTHING DEFINES TRUE greatness like an athlete who comes along and does things that have never been done before.

Which is why, despite their differences, Bobby Orr and Wayne Gretzky have far more in common than most people might think. Orr and Gretzky weren't just great players at their respective positions. They challenged us to rethink what was possible in ways we never imagined.

With Orr it was that ability to control the offensive flow of a hockey game from the back end. In Gretzky's case, it was his innate ability to anticipate what was going on around him at all times, making the puck come to him almost magically. No one had ever seen a defenceman rush the puck the way Orr did, or witnessed a player with Gretzky's instincts for where to be on the ice at any given moment. They were each one of a kind when they arrived on the scene, and still are today.

Both players were prodigies in their early teens. They performed under the glare of a tremendous spotlight from the start of their careers. And though neither was a dominating physical specimen, each brought to the table things that can't be measured. And each was a gamebreaker pretty much from the moment he hit the ice in the NHL.

Gretzky versus Orr divides hockey fans like no other debate. Consider what happened when *The Hockey News* assembled its panel to judge the 100 greatest players of all time. With 50 voters casting opinions, Gretzky placed first with 2,726 voting points. Orr was second with 2,713. That's a difference of 0.48 percent among people who've spent their lives around the game and had ample chance to study both players.

So, no one said this would be easy.

THE CASE FOR ORR

Bobby Orr burst onto the scene in 1966–67 as an 18-year-old and won the Calder Trophy. Harry Howell of the New York Rangers won the Norris that season, and bid the trophy a fond goodbye. "I'm glad I won it now," he said, "because it's going to belong to that Orr from now on."

Howell was right. The next season, Orr began a run of eight consecutive Norris Trophies, as the Bruins went from perennial losers to Stanley Cup winners in 1970 and 1972. He scored 100 points in six consecutive years, and his 46 goals in '74–75 was the best ever by a defenceman until Paul Coffey scored 48 with Gretzky's Oilers in 1986.

By that time, when Gretzky was in his prime, there were roughly 1.5 more goals scored per game than in the early 1970s. In other words, Orr's goals were harder to come by than Gretzky's or Coffey's.

The only qualifier to any of Orr's accomplishments is that they coincided with the NHL's expansion from six to 12 teams, a degree of growth unparalleled in professional sports at a time when there was no new influx of player talent. The result was that the 100-point barrier, previously unbroken, was shattered repeatedly by several players immediately after expansion.

That, however, doesn't take away from Orr winning two scoring titles as a defenceman, something no one could have imagined before he arrived.

Which brings us to the most remarkable thing about Orr. He simply did things that no one had ever seen a defenceman do. And the fact that he was able to accomplish his amazing scoring totals without being considered a defensive liability defies explanation.

Orr changed hockey by giving defencemen a much greater offensive role in the game, beyond simply chipping in on the power play. From the moment Orr changed the game, defencemen have been measured not just by how they prevent goals but also by how they help create them by joining or leading the rush up ice. In Orr's case, he often *was* the rush, starting with the puck deep in his own end and gaining a head of steam while opposing players watched helplessly.

And yet, because Orr was a defenceman, he had to play a more physical game than Gretzky, who always got more than his share of protection from both officials and teammates. And Orr, when he had to be, was tough.

It's that versatility that sets Orr apart from other players. On any given night, he could be the top shooter, skater, checker or passer on the ice. For one player to be so remarkable at so many different aspects of the game, at both ends of the ice, is the genius of Bobby Orr.

Orr was also a standout playoff performer, tallying 92 points in 74 games, including 44 points in 29 playoff games during Boston's Cup-winning years of 1970 and '72. He scored both Stanley Cup–winning goals and captured two Conn Smythe Trophies as well.

THE CASE FOR GRETZKY

Gretzky didn't so much change hockey as he perfected it. His skill set seemed so innate, so instinctual, that it's hard to imagine anyone coming along and seeing the game better than he did.

Gretzky, like Orr, entered the NHL during a period of expansion, when four World Hockey Association teams were added to the league before the European wave was in full force. It's fair to suggest, however, that going from 17 teams to 21 wasn't nearly as dramatic for the NHL as going from six to 12 had been when Orr came along.

Gretzky, like Orr, played at a time that coincided with an increase in NHL scoring. But while Orr's era featured several players who broke through new statistical barriers, Gretzky alone pushed his totals to unprecedented heights. Marcel Dionne won the scoring title during Gretzky's rookie year of 1979–80 with 137 points, a figure consistent with the highest individual tallies from the second year of expansion (1968–69) until that time. From there, Gretzky won seven consecutive scoring titles, eclipsing the 200-point total four times. The top individual point totals among other NHL players during that span, however, remained consistent with those of previous years. In fact, not a single player cracked the 150-point barrier during those years. In other words, Gretzky was moving the bar at a time when it remained in place for every other player.

Fans see hockey mostly as a game about creating goals, and nobody was better at that than Gretzky. He could put the puck in the net, and he was a wizard of the assist. Anyone would be an offensive threat on a line with Gretzky.

And Gretzky was judged to be the greatest player in the game for a much longer span of his career than Orr was. Gretzky won the Hart Trophy nine times and was without peer until Mario Lemieux rose to prominence. Orr, conversely, was judged to be the game's most valuable player just three times.

Like Orr, Gretzky was as good in the playoffs as he was during the regular season. He twice won the Conn Smythe Trophy and set numerous records while leading the Oilers to four Cups.

And for a guy who didn't look all that durable, Gretzky played an enormous amount of hockey during his career when you factor in playoffs and international commitments. Yet he never seemed fatigued, and his game never dropped off for any length of time. He was at least a point-per-game player throughout his career except for his last season, 1998–99.

THE VERDICT

I have a hard time not wondering what Orr might have been had knee injuries not hampered him throughout his career, eventually forcing him to retire at age 30. During much of his career he was forced to gauge what his knee could withstand, which limited his ability to play to his full potential every night. Maybe that's why there were nights, when the Bruins were winning handily, that you didn't notice Bobby Orr so much. It was almost as if during those games, when things were going Boston's way, he would save himself for when he was needed.

Because, so often, when the Bruins were behind, when they needed a critical goal to tie a game or pull ahead, Orr would make that happen. I've got to assume we'd have seen more of that on a consistent basis had he played on two good knees throughout his career.

The deciding factor is going to be subjective, and it's going to go down to a razor's edge: comparing Gretzky to what Orr would or should have been. Here's why I have to pick Orr: at his best, no one was better or more fun to watch than Bobby Orr. Not even Gretzky.

65.

During the 1990s, no story got more attention in Canada than the possibility that every one of its National Hockey League teams—save Toronto—might eventually move south. Bob tells you what happened to Canada's NHL crisis.

IT'S EASY TO FORGET how recently Canada was gripped by fear that its National Hockey League franchises would, one by one, relocate to the United States.

Conventional wisdom around the turn of the millennium suggested that the Ottawa Senators, Edmonton Oilers, Calgary Flames and maybe even Vancouver Canucks would all one day move south. There were even those who wondered aloud whether the Montreal Canadiens would survive in the long term in the city where they are a cultural institution.

It was considered a national crisis, one that involved discussion at the highest levels of government in this country. And so, when George Gillett Jr. became the first American owner of the Canadiens in 2001, he could feel the anxiety in Montreal on the cold January day when he was introduced.

"These are the Montreal Canadiens," said the Colorado businessman, "not the Oklahoma City Canadiens."

Just a few short years later, the idea of the Montreal Canadiens heading to Oklahoma City or anywhere else in the

U.S. seems preposterous. As does the thought that any of Canada's five other NHL teams might be enticed to move south.

So what happened? Where did all those stories about teams preparing to call in the moving vans go? What happened to the national crisis? Why do Canada's NHL teams now seem as secure as they've ever been?

Leading into the lockout, NHL commissioner Gary Bettman went out of his way to frame the league's fight with its players' union as a battle for the small-market teams, particularly those in Canada.

He got a standing ovation for delivering that message in Edmonton, where the Oilers had said in the years preceding the lockout that they were simply holding on for dear life until a salary cap could be secured. And if there was no cap? Well, Oilers chairman Cal Nichols said, the team would study its options, which included suspending operations or moving.

So, as we all know, the NHL shut itself down and got its cap. And sure enough, by the start of the second post-lockout season, things seemed mighty rosy in Canada.

Talk about Canada's teams being in dire straits was gone. The dominant sports story in Canada for about a decade had simply vanished. Just as Gary Bettman had promised, the lockout had solved everything in the home of hockey.

But had it really?

The truth is that the lockout and the salary cap have had almost nothing to do with the solid footing on which Canada's NHL teams find themselves these days. In fact, you can tie the stability, or in Toronto's case the immense profitability, of Canada's NHL teams almost entirely to the value of the Canadian dollar, which has soared over the past five years.

Consider that on January 21, 2002, the Canadian dollar hit an all-time low of 61.79 cents U.S. At the time, the Calgary Flames' payroll was about $26.9 million (U.S.) for the 2001–02 season. Yet to pay that amount with 62-cent dollars, the Flames had to spend $43.39 million in Canadian funds.

Fast forward to the post-lockout world of 2005–06, by which time the Flames' payroll had soared to $36.59 million U.S., which appears to be a 36 percent increase from four years earlier. However, when you consider that the Canadian dollar was trading at close to 90 cents U.S. in 2005–06, the Flames' payroll in Canadian dollars was $40.65 million. That actually represents a decrease of $2.74 million from four years earlier. If Calgary had had to meet that $36.59 million payroll in 2005–06 with the 62-cent dollars of 2001, the Flames would be spending just over $59 million in Canadian funds.

By the 2006–07 season, the payrolls of all six Canadian teams were around the $40 million (U.S.) mark. A 62-cent dollar would run that tab up to $64.5 million Canadian. There'd be no trouble swallowing that in Toronto. But everywhere else in Canada, teams would be in crisis, even with the limited amount of revenue sharing they might be entitled to.

The truth is that in U.S. dollars, five of the six Canadian teams are actually spending more on salaries in the post-lockout world than they were before there was a salary cap. Ottawa, Calgary and Edmonton—supposedly the three most vulnerable teams prior to the lockout—have boosted their payrolls by more than 50 percent. Only the favourable exchange rate has made any of this possible. Without that development, Canada's teams would be in jeopardy—with or without a cap.

At the 2007 Stanley Cup final in Anaheim, Bettman had the audacity to say the improved plight of Canada's teams was due to the salary cap and revenue sharing. Yet salaries have gone up in Canada under the cap system and not a dime of the league's shared revenue has flowed north of the border. The salary cap has done nothing for the economic viability of Canada's teams. That still lies in the hands of international bankers.

66. No debate rages in minor hockey quite as fiercely as the one about when kids should begin bodychecking. Bob says the answer is simple. For most kids, the answer is never.

FOR ALMOST AS LONG as kids have been playing hockey, people have been debating whether or not they should be allowed to bodycheck. But to me it all comes down to how you think of minor hockey.

If you think of 10- or 11-year-olds as being part of a professional development stream, then of course they should hit. Why wait to introduce them to what they'll need to know one day to earn a living in the NHL? Let them knock each other's brains around, just like their heroes on television.

Of course, if we want to get realistic about what minor hockey really is, especially at the house-league level, there's no argument for bodychecking at all. And yet Hockey Canada allows kids to bodycheck at the age of 11, and in some parts of the country it's still endorsed at age nine.

I'm sure there are people who sit back and wonder what damage 11-year-old kids can do by running into one another. Well, the evidence suggests it's significant. In 2006, the *Canadian Medical Association Journal* published a study that suggested that the number of injuries, including severe ones like concussions and fractures, more than doubled among 11-year-olds after bodychecking was introduced. At 11 years of age, most kids are still working on their skating and learning how to do different things with the puck. The last thing they need is to worry about some kid—usually a bigger kid—running them over.

Bodychecking in minor hockey tends to be a really great experience for two or three kids on every team, and a terrible one for all the rest. And those kids who enjoy it are the bigger kids, the ones whose growth spurts have come early. They're often the same ones who might enjoy pushing someone around a schoolyard. But for the majority of kids, it's something they want no part of.

So the only reason to force it on them is to prepare them for a future that probably doesn't exist.

What proponents of bodychecking fail to recognize is that 99.9 percent of kids who play the game are simply there for recreation. It's not about making the NHL. I mean, they can dream—but so what? Most kids who play hockey do so into their early teens, step away from the game for a few years and then maybe they go back to it later in life as adults.

By allowing bodychecking, you are catering to the notion that minor hockey players are all someday going to be pros and therefore must be trained in the pro version of the game from the first moment they step on the ice.

There's no need for kids to play an adult version of the game. And the irony is that most adult beer-league hockey doesn't allow bodychecking. And why is that? Because people get hurt when there's hitting and no one wants to take that risk when they're 30 years old. Yet we're willing to subject our kids to what we as adults refuse to endure?

The only kids who need to learn to bodycheck are the ones who graduate from minor hockey into the competitive streams, which includes everything from the lower levels of Junior C and D hockey right up to the major junior system that feeds the NHL.

Those kids should be learning to bodycheck by age 14. At the triple-A level, for the elite kids who look like they've got a realistic chance of having some kind of future in the sport through their teens, I can see allowing it at 13. But that's it. Which is basically what they do in Quebec right now, and somehow that province manages to produce NHL players. Some of them even become stars.

By waiting to introduce bodychecking until age 14, you'll drive fewer players away from the sport at a young age when all they want is fun. And you're still giving the competitive kids plenty of time to learn the physical game that they'll need to master as they climb up the development ladder.

All of this flies in the face of that absurd argument from some parents and coaches, the one about kids being done a disservice if they aren't taught to hit—or absorb hits—at a very young age. That somehow we're endangering our children down the line because we haven't schooled them early enough in the arts of giving and taking hits.

What a bunch of garbage. It's the nonsensical, dinosauric crap that hockey people come up with all the time to justify their own beliefs.

There's no sport where contact is as important as football, yet lots of professional players don't begin playing tackle football until they're 14 years old. Do football players need to be hitting each other at nine and 10 years old in order to develop into professionals some day? Of course not.

And in hockey that's even more true, because the most important skills kids need to develop have nothing to do with hitting. They are, in this order: skating, skating and more skating. Followed by puck handling and, lastly, checking. If some kids never learn to bodycheck, so what? Most will never need it.

Let's let kids play the game. Let them enjoy themselves. Let them score goals and make rushes with the puck. Bodychecking can wait. And for most, it can wait forever.

67. ■ **Each year, before the entry draft, speculation mounts about whether we are about to witness a deep or shallow draft. But that determination isn't made the day of the selections. Bob looks back and rates the deepest drafts in NHL history.**

I'M ALWAYS AMUSED when I hear hockey people suggest that the top 10 picks of a particular draft are far more valuable than the remaining players because there's supposedly a sharp drop-off in talent beyond that point. Or other years it's supposed to be good to have a mid-round pick because, after all, this is a deep draft.

We all know that once you get past the top five or six picks, the entry draft is nearly impossible to predict. Some teams do it better than others, but to suggest how strong a draft is once you get past the first dozen players or so is a mug's game at best.

That's because some of the very best talent in many drafts comes long after the first few names are called. The only way we can evaluate drafts is with a rear-view mirror.

Then there's the debate about criteria for what makes a great draft.

Mine is to look first at the number of all-time great players who come from a particular year. Are there guys who left their mark on the game and are in, or almost sure to be in, the Hockey Hall of Fame? Every draft is about possibilities and whether a once-in-a-generation type of player might be somewhere among those fresh faces.

After that, drafts should be evaluated based on the number of front-line NHL players that come from a particular year. These are guys who aren't going to be remembered 50 years from now but were great players in their day, racking up decent numbers and helping their teams significantly, even if they never quite achieved true greatness.

With that in mind, here are my picks for the best draft years in NHL history.

5. The "Stanley Cup Draft," 1983. An amazing number of prominent players taken in this draft not only had great careers but also wound up hoisting the Stanley Cup.

Steve Yzerman and John MacLean were taken with the second and sixth picks overall, eventually helping lead Detroit and New Jersey, respectively, to hockey's top prize.

Tom Barrasso, who won a pair of Cups with Pittsburgh, was the first goaltender taken when he went fifth. The best one, however, went 194 choices later when Chicago took Dominik Hasek in one of the all-time steals in NHL history.

Esa Tikkanen won Cups with both Edmonton and the New York Rangers, while Claude Lemieux won championships in Montreal, New Jersey and Dallas. Kevin Stevens and Rick Tocchet were teammates with Pittsburgh when the Penguins won the 1992 Stanley Cup—Stevens finishing his career with 329 goals, while Tocchet had 440.

Among non–Cup winners, 1983 included a pair of players whose careers were shortened by injuries in Pat LaFontaine and Cam Neely, both of whom were taken within the top 10.

While this draft isn't as star-studded as some, it produced a strong supporting cast that includes Sylvain Turgeon, Russ Courtnall, Dave Gagner, Dan Quinn, Peter Zezel, Bob Probert, Gary Galley and Uwe Krupp.

4. The "European Draft," 1990. With Petr Nedved and Jaromir Jagr taken among the first five, this draft also included Slava Kozlov, Peter Bondra, Alexei Zhamnov and Sergei Zubov. Only 1989 (Mats Sundin, Bobby Holik, Robert Reichel, Sergei Fedorov, Nicklas Lidstrom and Pavel Bure) is comparable to that group in terms of import talent. Otherwise, 1990 saw seven of the first eight picks turn into to front-line NHLers, which is a dynamite batting average. A group that includes Owen Nolan, Keith Primeau, Mike Ricci, Darryl

Sydor and Derian Hatcher sounds like the lineup at any all-star game from about the early 1990s onward. Further down, Keith Tkachuk and Martin Brodeur were also first-rounders in a class that included Doug Weight and Geoff Sanderson later on. The only knock on this draft is that Jagr and Brodeur are the only two all-time greats.

3. The "Defenceman Draft," 1979. Nine defencemen were taken with the 21 picks of the first round, and six of them went on to play at least 1,000 NHL games—Rob Ramage, Ray Bourque, Mike Ramsey, Brad McCrimmon, Jay Wells and Kevin Lowe—which is why this draft stands alone in terms of rearguards. The other three taken early—Craig Hartsburg, Keith Brown and Paul Reinhart (who also played some forward)—were no softies, either. Beyond the defencemen, forwards Brian Propp, Michel Goulet, Dale Hunter and Dave Christian were all taken in the first or second rounds. But the stunning thing about the 1979 draft was the quality of players available later on. Neal Broten, Mark Messier and Guy Carbonneau were all third-rounders, while 400-goal scorers Glenn Anderson and John Ogrodnick went in the fourth.

2. The "Goal Scorer's Draft," 1988. How's this for firepower: five of the top 10 players taken scored at least 350 goals in their careers, and six got at least 250. Mike Modano and Trevor Linden went first and second overall, combining for over 2,000 points in their careers. Four more forwards who went in the top 10—Martin Gelinas, Jeremy Roenick, Rod Brind'Amour and Teemu Selanne—have enjoyed long and distinguished careers. The scoring prowess yielded in this draft extends further, to Mark Recchi, Tony Amonte and Alexander Mogilny. Overall, this draft included nine players who scored at least 33 goals in a season and five who hit 50. Nor was it all about forwards that year: Rob Blake was a bit of an afterthought when taken with pick number 70.

1. The Best Draft in History, 1984. With Mario Lemieux as the headliner, the '84 draft was unlike any before or since. The early part of the first round was light on true superstar-quality players, with Kirk Muller, Ed Olczyk, Al Iafrate and Shayne Corson among the names that followed Lemieux. There was still much to come, however. Patrick Roy's name didn't grab much attention when he was taken with the 51st pick, but his place in the game's history is right up there with Lemieux's. On defence, Kevin Hatcher and Gary Suter were stars in the NHL and with Team USA in international play. A remarkable collection of forwards includes—besides Lemieux—Gary Roberts, Scott Mellanby, Stephane Richer, Ray Sheppard, Brett Hull and Luc Robitaille. Lemieux (1st), Hull (117th) and Robitaille (171st) went a long time between hearing their names called at the 1984 draft. They're much closer in the NHL record book, where they rank ninth, third, and tenth, respectively, in all-time goal scoring.

Now, just for fun, let's apply the same criteria to see which year produced the weakest crop of players. There are lots of candidates—1976, 1985, 1992, 1996—but the winner is 1975. After Mel Bridgman went first overall, the rest of the top 10 went like this: Barry Dean, Ralph Klassen, Bryan Maxwell, Rick Lapointe, Don Ashby, Greg Vaydik, Richard Mulhern, Robin Sadler and Rick Blight. Of that group, only Bridgman and Lapointe got to 500 NHL games in their careers. Of the 217 players taken that year, exactly four managed at least 200 career NHL goals. The best player taken in 1975? No question about it: Dave Taylor, taken in the 15th round with the 210th pick, scored 431 goals and was the only player drafted in 1975 to play 1,000 games in the NHL.

68.

Major junior hockey gets great exposure, huge crowds and is touted as the breeding ground for the next generation of National Hockey League stars. Just don't tell anybody it's not the best amateur hockey in the land.

HERE'S SOMETHING YOU will never see in this day and age: a top major junior hockey team accepting a challenge from a decent Canadian university squad.

Why? Because the junior team would lose. And in doing so, it would shatter the myth that junior hockey is a higher grade of the sport than that played by Canada's mostly ignored university players.

The superiority of university hockey comes as a shock to a lot of hockey fans who've been brainwashed into thinking that most of the players in major junior hockey are serious NHL prospects. After all, junior hockey is where you go to see the next generation of NHL stars, right?

University hockey players in Canada, conversely, couldn't be more anonymous, playing in what is perceived as a dumping ground for those who couldn't become pros, which is why almost no one goes to see them.

In fact, the perceptions of both brands of hockey are completely wrong.

Junior hockey teams are not full of future NHL stars. Many teams have no future NHL players on their rosters at all, while the best teams are lucky to have two or three players capable of reaching either the American Hockey League or possibly the NHL. At best, a handful from each team are good enough to join one of the low minor pro leagues that dot the southern half of the United States, where guys play for slave wages and free beer.

Not only are most junior players not good enough to reach

the American Hockey League, but a lot of them couldn't crack the best university teams in Canada.

Take the University of Alberta, for example, which won the Canadian university title in 2006 but wasn't an overly dominant squad by any means. The Golden Bears were made up entirely of players who'd come from major junior hockey. They had one former 40-goal scorer from the Western Hockey League, three 30-goal scorers and four who'd scored at least 20 in the WHL. There were three players on that team who'd been drafted by NHL teams. And five guys who had already played some level of pro hockey somewhere.

Now, you can't seriously believe that a team with that kind of pedigree and experience, a team of players in their early twenties, would lose to any junior club in Canada.

The difference in physical maturity alone between juniors and university players is immense. Most university players are between 19 and 25 years old, compared to juniors who are between 16 and 20.

You need only look at what happens to NHL prospects between the ages of 18 and 23 to understand how critical a development period this is for players. Things like size, speed and strength change immensely over these years. So the guy who played junior as a teenager is a completely different player by the time he's ready to graduate from university at age 23 or so.

About all university hockey lacks is the elite player, the super-talented guy the NHL scouts are drooling over because his skills jump out above all the rest. That player doesn't exist in the Canadian university ranks. Which is why the best American university teams generally beat those in Canada, since top NCAA schools combine the maturity of college-aged players with many of North America's elite pro prospects.

Fans aren't the only ones who need to be convinced of the quality of the Canadian university game. So do most players.

In fact, when most ex-juniors show up on campus, they think they've just joined the beer league. In their minds, the dream is over and no one is watching. They believe they are making, at best, a horizontal move, and certainly not a step up.

Juniors who are being recruited by university coaches often stare back in disbelief when it's suggested to them that they're moving to a more competitive level in the hockey world. And that complete lack of respect is a big part of why so many ex-juniors are embarrassed during their first month or so of university hockey. That's how long it takes them to realize they've woefully underestimated the competition and they'd better start taking the game more seriously.

It would be great if, at the end of every season, the Memorial Cup champion faced off against the Canadian university champion. But let's just say I'm not holding my breath waiting for that to happen.

69. When Evgeni Malkin fled his Russian club to join Pittsburgh during the summer of 2006, hockey fans in North America cheered. But Bob says the problem isn't the Russian ice hockey teams. It's the National Hockey League.

IMAGINE FOR A MOMENT that Canada is a desperate country with a broken economy.

Our hockey facilities are in poor shape and there simply isn't a minor hockey infrastructure that allows kids to play and develop in the game as they do today.

So, out of necessity, the National Hockey League teams in this country take over the development of players from the grass roots upward. They fund and operate the minor hockey system, provide the coaching and nurture players right from childhood to the pros.

And let's just say the Montreal Canadiens had done that with a player such as Sidney Crosby. Groomed him from boyhood all the way through becoming the best hockey prospect in the land.

Now, imagine how the Canadiens—and the rest of Canada—might feel if, around Crosby's 18th birthday, a team from Russia swept in and offered him a big, fat contract and suddenly he was gone. Just like that. And the Canadiens were left with no compensation whatsoever.

You can't imagine the outcry there would be in this country. Don Cherry would devote his life to the issue, and Canadians from coast to coast would be calling it a national crisis.

Sound ridiculous? Well, it's not if you're a hockey fan in Russia, because that's exactly what has been happening in that country as great young player after great young player is stolen away by the NHL.

I say "stolen" because the NHL hasn't paid one dime for such players as Alexander Ovechkin and Evgeni Malkin, or any of the other elite Russian players who've made their way to the NHL in the past few seasons. These are players whose development was paid for by the Russian clubs, who were nurtured and taught and trained by them. And the NHL comes along and says "thank you very much" without a hint of shame.

It's disgusting and it's downright disrespectful of Russian hockey and Russia itself.

Of course, the reason the Russians got nothing for these players is that they refused to sign the player transfer agreement that was negotiated between the NHL and the International Ice Hockey Federation in 2005. And when a new four-year agreement was being finalized in the spring of 2007, they refused again. Both agreements call for NHL teams to pay $200,000 for every player they sign from Europe.

Which is a pittance. I mean, just think of what Evgeni Malkin or Alexander Ovechkin is worth to the NHL and its teams. I don't blame Russian Ice Hockey Federation president Vladislav Tretiak for calling the NHL's offer nothing more than a "handout" while suggesting a more appropriate price for top players is a million dollars apiece.

The NHL is supposedly all about the free market and allowing players to pursue their careers wherever they'd like to. Which is fine. Except the NHL doesn't want to know anything about fair market value when it comes to compensating teams in Russia and elsewhere in Europe when they lose their best players.

And when you compare how the NHL operates in this regard to other leagues in professional sports, you get a sense of just how much the Russians are being screwed over.

When the Boston Red Sox decided they wanted to offer a contract to Japanese pitcher Daisuke Matsuzaka in December of 2006, they had to pay his former club a $51 million posting fee if they signed him. (Only players who have spent roughly a decade in Japanese baseball are able to sign with major league teams without compensation being paid to their former teams.) In baseball, teams seeking to sign prime players from Japan make sealed bids, and the highest bidder earns the right just to make an offer.

Fifty-one million! Now, Matsuzaka is a wonderful pitcher. But a guy in that sport with no major league experience is far less of a sure thing to succeed than is a hockey player such as Ovechkin or Malkin.

And look, if Matsuzaka never came to America, the Red Sox franchise would still be worth hundreds of millions of dollars and baseball would get along just fine.

But take Malkin and Ovechkin away from the NHL and you're talking about a serious loss in its superstar quotient.

The $51 million Boston paid Matsuzaka's Japanese team

was three times the amount that team spent on its payroll the previous season, enough to get the club out of debt and secure its finances for the foreseeable future.

In soccer, teams pay similar kinds of fees for the best young players. Consider that in 2005, Chelsea Football Club paid roughly $44 million to Olympique Lyonnais for star midfielder Michael Essien. And in May of 2007, Manchester United paid a 25 million euro transfer fee to Bayern Munich for the rights to Calgary-born midfielder Owen Hargreaves.

In basketball, teams build clauses into contracts that allow them to get a cut of what a player receives when he hits the National Basketball Association jackpot. In the cases of the best players, that figure can be in the $3 million range.

And yet the NHL thinks $200,000, less than half of the minimum salary you can pay a fourth-line grinder, is fair compensation for a superstar like Malkin? Never mind that in Moscow, one of the most expensive cities in the world, $200,000 is near meaningless.

And why is the IIHF not able to negotiate a better deal with the NHL for the transfer of players from Russia and elsewhere? It has no power. And the NHL has no more respect for the IIHF than it does for the Russian Super League. The NHL screws the teams in Europe because it can.

And that's part of the problem. The NHL has taken advantage of Russia and Europe for so long that the Russians don't trust it. The historically low transfer fees in hockey have jaded the Russians. The other European countries aren't any happier, it's just that they believe getting $200,000 is better than nothing.

The NHL needs to show Russian hockey some respect. It needs to reach out and understand what's going on in that country. The richest league in the world, with roughly $2 billion in annual revenue, should be sharing its resources in coaching and refereeing and player development. Then, once it's earned the trust of the Russians instead of their scorn, it should sit down and make a fair deal for their players—and for those in the rest of Europe.

Russia is a country that cherishes its natural resources, as it should. And it doesn't like seeing them raided, whether it's oil and gas or hockey players. I think this fight is as much about respect as it is about money. And respect, when it comes to the Russians, is where the NHL is bankrupt.

70. The mid-1990s were a sad time for hockey in Canada, with two National Hockey League teams moving to U.S. cities. Bob says you shouldn't hold your breath waiting for them to come back.

EVER SINCE THE Quebec Nordiques and Winnipeg Jets packed up and moved south during the mid-1990s, Canadians have been waiting for the National Hockey League to come back to those markets begging on its hands and knees.

And while returning to Quebec City or Winnipeg might once have seemed like a pipe dream, it's not nearly as far-fetched as it once was, at least in a practical sense. The problem is that practicality isn't the NHL's strong suit.

When the Jets and Nordiques departed, the NHL and its teams believed their league was quickly moving up the food chain in the United States. They believed that pro hockey was no longer a niche sport to Americans and was about to take its rightful place alongside the National Basketball Association, Major League Baseball and the National Football League.

Ice and snow, therefore, were supposedly no longer necessary to sell hockey. All you needed was a new arena and a market big enough to please network television in the United States.

And one more thing: it would certainly help if the NHL didn't have too many teams in places Americans had never heard of. Which is why, if the NHL had a secret list of 50 markets it wanted to be in—and I'm not so sure that list didn't exist—Quebec City and Winnipeg wouldn't have been on it. You can bet they'd rather have been in Boise, Idaho, than Winnipeg.

And I think that's still true today.

Which is why, despite the fact that you might be able to sell a lot more tickets in Quebec City or Winnipeg than a whole bunch of existing U.S. markets (where, exactly, would 15,000 paid admissions per night rank in the NHL these days?), it's never going to happen. Not even with a Canadian dollar above 90 cents (U.S.).

First of all, no American is ever going to move his team to Quebec City or Winnipeg. It's just too far, too cold and too foreign for anyone from the United States to consider, even if it made business sense. Which means the only way a team will ever get to Winnipeg or Quebec City is if someone local, someone with a lot of dough, is willing to buy an existing team and move it to one of those cities—*and* if the NHL governors decide not to block such a move.

The first thing you'd have to consider under that scenario is whether there are there are potential owners in either of those cities with the wherewithal to sustain teams through something like a dip in the Canadian dollar or a slowdown in the economy.

But even if there are, there's a much bigger roadblock to contend with. And that is that you can be absolutely sure that the reigning NHL administration will never approve an owner whose pledge is to take a team from the United States and move it to Canada. Not in a million years.

NHL commissioner Gary Bettman has done a nice job learning how to play to audiences in this country, so much so that he's received standing ovations on this side of the border. (Now, who'd have imagined that around the time the Jets and Nordiques were leaving?)

But Bettman remains wedded (to a fault, I would argue) to the notion that the NHL is one day going to be a valuable national property on American television, that the Stanley Cup final will grip the imagination of the American public from coast to coast and that his sport can hang its hat alongside baseball, basketball and football.

So tell me how that vision jibes with a team or teams packing up and leaving the United States for Canada? It doesn't.

Americans love to say they let the market dictate where business goes. But in this case, I believe Gary Bettman would only allow a team to move from the U.S. to Canada over his dead body. Because what says "the NHL is dead" in the United States like having a Phoenix or Carolina or Atlanta or Nashville or Anaheim suddenly move to Winnipeg?

You only need look at the experiences of Canadian businessman Jim Balsillie to know how determined the NHL is to make sure a team never moves to Canada. Balsillie would be a dream owner for the NHL, a guy with lots of bucks and a huge passion for hockey. The only problem is, he wants to own a team in Hamilton, Ontario.

That notion alone was enough for the NHL to chase him away from first the Pittsburgh Penguins and then the Nashville Predators. Balsillie would have been welcomed with open arms had he been pledging to move a team to Houston or Las Vegas or Kansas City or Oklahoma City or Cody, Wyoming, for God's sake. But Canada? Forget it.

I've always believed that the NHL's future is in markets where people *like* the sport of hockey. Which is why the NHL needs to retrench, forget about this notion of becoming a national property in the United States, get out of places where people are ambivalent about the game and concentrate on filling buildings with hockey fans.

Sounds novel, I know.

Not until the day that shift happens, and not a moment

before, can you start thinking about Quebec City and Winnipeg—and, maybe more likely, Southwestern Ontario, because I'm sure Mr. Balsillie's dream is still very much alive.

71.

The instigator rule in hockey is still the favourite target of those who subscribe to an old-style mentality about fighting. Bob says it's tired, it's stupid and it's time to bury this one. Not the rule . . . the argument.

ALMOST EVERY BARROOM conversation about hockey involves someone complaining that the instigator rule has ruined the game. That, somehow, giving additional penalties to players who start throwing punches wherever and whenever they see fit has made the game more dangerous.

Look, I could waste my time and energy explaining how completely idiotic that is. And how the logic that supports that argument is reasonable only to those who can't think outside of a hockey rink. And how to suggest today's game is more dangerous than the one we used to witness back in the 1970s, when enforcers ruled the NHL, is ridiculous.

But in order to do so, I'd have to believe that fighting is relevant to hockey, which is something I refuse to do.

So instead, I'll argue that arguing about the instigator rule is in itself a pointless waste of time. Which is why I won't do it.

72. It took a lockout and some strong arm-twisting to get the National Hockey League to introduce the changes it did in 2005–06. Here's what Bob would do if he had a magic wand to change anything else about the NHL.

IT IS WIDELY ACKNOWLEDGED that, were it not for the lost season of 2003–04, the National Hockey League would still be much like it was before the lockout. Without the break for self-reflection, there would likely have been no new interpretation of the rulebook, no stomach to remove the red line, and goaltenders would be as big as ever and as free as ever to handle the puck as they saw fit.

All of which means it will likely be a very long time before we again see a significant degree of changes in the game.

Of course, there are all kinds of changes we can only wish for. Things that would never receive enough support or would require the kind of forward thinking that isn't often found around a board of governors' table.

But it's fantasy time, so here's how, with no restrictions whatsoever, I would love to see the National Hockey League change.

1. Have a European division. It's ridiculous that the NHL continues to invest so much energy selling hockey in places where people aren't interested in pucks and ice. Especially when you've got a whole continent in Europe that loves the game. The NHL should try to become the first truly global professional sports league. Can you imagine the attraction of players such as Mats Sundin, Jaromir Jagr or Saku Koivu playing on home ice? And imagine the interest in the final. Perhaps not all of the European economies would be ready to host NHL franchises. But there'd have to be markets for teams in Sweden, Germany, Finland and Switzerland, at the very least.

2. Introduce a graduated minor penalty system. The NHL's penal system makes no sense when you consider that referees hand out the same penalties regardless of where infractions occur on the ice or what the circumstances are. Sure, there are double minor penalties and five-minute majors for serious infractions. But those penalties reflect the seriousness of the offence, not how it affects the game.

For instance, a penalty for gently tugging a player with a stick along the boards in the neutral zone shouldn't be of the same gravity as one for hauling a guy down as he sets up to shoot from the top of the slot. Or how about a guy who blatantly runs into the other team's goaltender versus a guy who accidently flips the puck into the crowd? Should those two guys get the same punishment? Soccer has different penalties for different sorts of situations, depending on how the infractions affect the game. So, too, does football, where holding, offside and pass interference all draw repercussions proportionate to how the game is affected. Hockey should introduce a three-minute minor penalty for infractions that directly nullify scoring chances, and leave the two-minute penalty for those that do not. Right now, there's still too much incentive to haul down an opposing player to prevent a scoring chance, and that's bad for the game.

3. Turn the Stanley Cup final into a one-game, winner-take-all affair. What's the biggest complaint fans have about the Stanley Cup playoffs? They last too long, and by the end everyone has hockey fatigue after two months of games every other night. And that's the view from the dedicated core of fans. Casual fans have bowed out by early May. The NHL is the only league in which playoff interest peaks during the first round and declines steadily because a lot of people just aren't willing to invest the time it takes to follow it all to the end. (Which is why I might suggest cutting the Eastern and Western Conference finals down to best-of-five as well.) So why not play the the Stanley Cup final as a one-game match in late May? Think about it: What are the two most popular sporting events on the North American calendar? How about the Super Bowl and the NCAA college basketball final. Why? Because teams play one game and it's over. Let the home team be determined by whichever one has the best regular-season record. Then, winning the Presidents' trophy would really mean something. Yes, hockey would take a hit at the gate by dumping the seven-game series format. But think of the value to television if you could promise one night when the Stanley Cup would be handed out. And if the final were one game only, that rather large portion of the American media that doesn't bother to cover the final might actually show up. Look, by the end of three rounds of playoffs, there are no flukes. So let the two best teams play 60 minutes (or more, if necessary) to decide it all.

4. Make the ice surface bigger. Here's an area where the NHL really blew it. Back in the early 1990s, the league was plotting an aggressive expansion strategy, and most of its existing teams had new arena designs in the blueprint stage. That would have been the perfect time to switch to the European-sized ice surface, which is 15 feet wider than the 200-by-85-foot rink the NHL uses. It's just simple logic that the more room players have to navigate, the more offence they can create. And similarly, the more territory a defenceman has to protect, the harder he's going to find it to do so. Over the past 34 years, the average NHL player has grown by two inches and 20.4 pounds. It only makes sense to give bigger players a bigger ice surface to play on.

5. Introduce a graduated points system for individuals. Getting a point on the stats sheet for inadvertently touching the puck before someone else puts it in the net is a gift. And there are all kinds of assists handed out that have nothing to do with making a play that leads up to a goal. So let's award three points in the stats column for scoring a goal, two for a first assist and one point for a second assist. Then you'd get a truer reflection of the most productive offensive players in the game.

73. **For most of the last century, hockey players were a poor lot, underpaid both by the standards of their true worth and in comparison to other professional athletes. But all that changed during the 1990s. Bob looks back on the most ridiculous contracts of hockey's inflationary era.**

NATIONAL HOCKEY LEAGUE players who toiled during the 1950s and '60s must have looked on in wonder with the salary explosion that began in the early 1990s.

It was almost as if the sport was playing catch-up by overpaying modern-day players to make up for all that money the owners had pocketed back in the good old days.

And in a sport where management has always held the upper hand—even before the arrival of the salary cap—it's remarkable how willing teams were to pay players beyond their worth.

Stupid contracts almost always fall into one of two categories. They're either served up to young hotshots on the basis of tremendous potential that may or may not be fulfilled. Or they're given to players who've had success by GMs who ignore the possibility that these players might already have peaked.

Look, there's nothing wrong with paying a superstar millions and millions of dollars if he's a proven commodity and one of best at what he does.

These contracts, however, still make my head spin and stand out as the very worst in recent NHL history.

5. Alexei Yashin, New York Islanders. If ever there was a player for whom a long-term contract should have been avoided, it was Yashin. Yet that didn't stop the New York Islanders from guaranteeing him $87.5 million (all figures U.S.) over 10 years during the summer of 2001. Yashin had scored at least 33 goals four times in his career before signing his Islander deal, but he never reached that total again. Meanwhile, with Yashin the Islanders went nowhere. Which is why in June, 2007 they opted to buy out the final four years of that ridiculous contract.

4. Rick DiPietro, New York Islanders. Signing the world's greatest goalie to the longest contract in NHL history would be a foolish thing to do. Doing it with a goalie yet to prove he belongs in the top third of the league is simply insane. Yet during the summer of 2006, the New York Islanders deemed Rick DiPietro worthy of a contract that guaranteed him $67.5 million over 15 years. The Islanders obviously believe that paying DiPietro $4.5 million a season represents a cost savings in goal compared to teams that spend upwards of $6 million on that position. But if he proves to be a mediocre player, DiPietro's contract could render the Islanders un–competitive for a long, long time. (DiPietro's season-ending concussion in March 2007 may not be a factor in his ability to perform in the future, and his risk of another concussion is not as high as it would be were he anything but a goaltender. If DiPietro can't play because of an injury, the Islanders will get cap relief. But if he's deemed healthy, yet for some reason never regains the form he showed in '06–07, the Islanders will be dragging an economic chain around.)

3. Paul Kariya, Anaheim Mighty Ducks. At the end of the 1996–97 season, Paul Kariya was finishing up a three-year, $6 million contract. When he next stepped on the ice the following December, his pay had jumped from $2 million per season to $8.5 million (the Ducks pro-rated his 1997–98 contract to account for the games he missed). This deal makes the list because it was a classic instance of an NHL team refusing to use the leverage granted to it in the collective bargaining agreement. Kariya had no arbitration rights, and the Ducks were required to give him no more than a 10 percent raise on his next contract. Instead, they caved and opted to give him *350* percent instead, thus bumping up salaries across the league. Kariya was coming off seasons of 50 and 44 goals, just three years into his NHL career. He never hit those heights again.

2. Chris Gratton, Philadelphia Flyers. One of the few players to switch teams as a restricted free agent under the collective bargaining agreement signed in 1995, Gratton got a five-year contract worth $16 million from the Philadelphia Flyers during the summer of 1997, which included $9 million just for signing his name. By the time the Flyers shipped him back to Tampa Bay in a trade 16 months later, he'd earned more than $10 million for contributing 23 goals to Philly's cause. Gratton's contract paid him roughly three times the league's average salary at the time the deal was signed. This for a player who had hit the 20-goal mark just once in his career and has been a bust ever since.

1. Alexandre Daigle, Ottawa Senators. The average National Hockey League salary was just over $450,000 when Alexandre Daigle was taken by Ottawa with the first pick of the 1993 entry draft. The same Senators organization that had spent its first NHL season nickel-and-diming its players to death graciously handed Daigle a five-year deal worth $12.5 million. That instantly made Daigle the sixth-highest-paid player in the NHL, behind only Mario Lemieux, Eric Lindros, Wayne Gretzky, Brett Hull and Mark Messier. The fact that the Senators needlessly signed Daigle before the draft was the first indication that they didn't exactly drive a hard bargain. As part of the arrangement, Ottawa retained marketing rights to Daigle's image and such. But if he bombed—which he did— what was that going to be worth? Nothing.

74.

You're the general manager of an average NHL team with enough money to buy one player at the league's maximum salary on the free agent market. Whom do you give it to: the superstar goal scorer (think Marian Hossa)? The playmaking forward (think Brad Richards)? The all-around blueline stud (think Chris Pronger)? Or the goaltender who's a sure bet (think Martin Brodeur)? Bob gives you his take on the most valuable position in hockey.

FOR THE PURPOSES of this argument, I've omitted once-in-a-generation players such as Bobby Orr, Wayne Gretzky and Sidney Crosby. We're talking about the value of a *type* of player, not the guys who are different from everyone else.

Watch the highlights on any night of the National Hockey League season and you're going to see the same things over and over: great saves, outstanding passes and spectacular goals.

What you will never—or, at least very rarely—see are the most important players on the ice doing what they do best. I'm talking about defencemen.

Sure, you'll see a defenceman make a big hit during a highlight reel every now and then. And, certainly, some of their assists make the cut for late-night replay. But the art of stopping a play from developing, of making the first pass out of the zone or of knowing exactly how and when to pinch inside the blue line, isn't the stuff that makes people fall out of their chairs in front of their television sets.

In fact, great defencemen in hockey are a little like offensive linemen in football: they often receive more attention for getting beaten or for taking a stupid penalty than for the many essential, if mostly unspectacular, plays they make routinely in a game.

And yet, elite defencemen—I'm talking about the very top rung at this position—are worth their weight in gold for contributing more to a hockey game than any other players on the ice.

Which is why, if I were a general manager with the money to buy one player in his prime, it would always be an elite defenceman.

Blueliners who can do it all are truly the rarest players in the game. Think about it. At any given point in hockey, there are lots of good goal scorers and playmakers. Even good goaltenders, relative to their numbers in the league, are plentiful.

But how many absolute studs are patrolling blue lines across the league at one time? Maybe, in a good year, four or five. In 2006–07, I think you could safely rate Nicklas Lidstrom, Chris Pronger, Zdeno Chara and Scott Niedermayer as a cut above all the rest in hockey. But that's it.

On the next tier you'd have players such as Ed Jovanovski, Brian Rafalski, Wade Redden, Dan Boyle, Dion Phaneuf and Tomas Kaberle, but as you move down the list from there, the drop-off is considerable.

Lots of defencemen are good at *some* elements of the game, but precious few can do it all. So when you find a guy who can be counted on to play a shutdown role, move the puck out of the zone flawlessly, kill penalties, play the point on the power play and contribute offensively, you grab him. Players like that, guys who play nearly 30 minutes a game, can transform the win-loss record of a team more than any other players, without even being noticed.

Consistency is another reason I'd always choose an elite defenceman. You only need to look at the repetition among the winners of and nominees for the Norris Trophy to see that the best in this class don't turn over very quickly. Which is why, over the past 24 seasons, there have been just 10 different winners of the Norris Trophy.

A lot of great goal scorers and playmakers have good years and not-so-good years. And goaltenders fluctuate from good seasons to below-average seasons all the time.

But great defencemen are steady, year in and year out. I mean, you just don't see a player such as Lidstrom suddenly have a crappy year. He's been nominated for the Norris Trophy eight times in nine seasons.

The same is true on a game-by-game basis, be it playoffs or regular season. Scorers go cold and goaltenders can lose their focus or struggle with technique here and there. But how often have you seen an elite defenceman looking lost on the ice for any length of time?

After the defenceman, I'd take the playmaker next. Players with vision on the ice, who can see which passes to make and which opportunities to pass over have skills that can't be taught or developed. They make power plays sharp and keep opponents guessing in all kinds of situations.

Good goaltending is essential in the National Hockey League. But even great goaltenders on average teams aren't going to take a team to the Cup. As important as goalies are, their impact will be limited if the team around them is full of flaws. Just ask Roberto Luongo about his days in Florida.

And lastly, I'd take the goal scorer. Guys who can bury the puck are great. But put it this way: nearly every team in the NHL has a gifted sniper. If you can't get the puck out of your own zone to begin with, if there's no one to set up the trigger men, or if every time the puck is turned over it ends up in the back of your net, goal scoring isn't worth much.

Except on the nightly highlight package.

75.

They were only hockey games, it's true. But short of participation in two world wars, Bob says nothing in Canadian history has been as culturally significant as the Summit Series of 1972.

THERE'S A SIMPLE way to recognize the most culturally significant events in any nation's history: ask the question, "Where were you when. . ?"

In America, most such events are, unfortunately, tragic— President Kennedy being assassinated; the space shuttle *Challenger* exploding moments after liftoff; Elvis dropping dead at age 42.

But in Canada, the most culturally significant single event in our history produced only tears of joy. When Paul Henderson scored for Canada with 34 seconds remaining to defeat the Russians in the eighth and final game of the 1972 Summit Series, it marked a moment unlike any before or since in this country.

Hockey will always have an important place in Canada's cultural psyche. But for a variety of reasons, the game will never mean as much to as many Canadians as it did during September of 1972, when circumstances both at home and in the hockey world aligned to create a unique experience.

First, let's look back on what kind of nation Canada was in 1972. Thirty-five years ago, this was a far more homogeneous country than it is today. We're talking about a nation of just 22 million people, mostly from European backgrounds, who'd grown up in a country where listening to or watching *Hockey Night in Canada* on Saturdays was a way of life.

I'm not sure how many Canadians have actually played hockey on a frozen pond, but in 1972 there was still a large portion of the population for whom that remained an ideal.

It was a country where you could still get people to rally around one thing. I mean, these days Canada is so diverse, with people of all sorts of different backgrounds and interests, a lot of whom didn't grow up with hockey and have never even put on skates.

Which is fine. But it's no longer possible to have our national identity completely wrapped up in one sport, never mind a single game.

Even among sports fans, you have so much more diversity than you did back in the early 1970s. Back then, if you were a fan of sport in Canada it was hard not to anchor your emotions in hockey.

While there was always the Canadian Football League, the NFL and NBA had virtually no Canadians within their ranks. And in baseball, beyond Ferguson Jenkins, the only Canadians were role players.

These days, we've had a Canadian win most valuable player in both the American and National leagues in baseball, we've a had a two-time MVP in the NBA and there are roughly a dozen Canadians in the NFL at any given time.

In the years leading up to and including 1972, Canada averaged about three medals per Olympic Games. At Torino in 2006, we won 24, and men's hockey wasn't one of them. However, Canada's success in other sports meant that there was remarkably little fretting about our version of the NHL all-star team going into the dumper at the Olympic tournament.

What all of this suggests is that we're no longer the one-sport nation we used to be back when the Summit Series was on.

Of course, not only were we a one-sport nation back then, but most Canadians thought of us as invincible in the sport we invented. Which is why the stakes and the emotions were so much higher back in '72 than they are when Canada plays international hockey these days.

Canada winning the gold medal in 2002 at Salt Lake was a terrific moment. But beating the Americans with our pros against theirs was hardly a culturally significant event for this country, even if it was our first gold medal in hockey in 50 years.

There's no mystique to our hockey rivalries anymore, no sense of playing for something more than just bragging rights, nothing that says our way of life is better than yours the way there was back in '72.

It's all just a game now.

So unless North Korea, or maybe Iran, comes up with a hockey team that might challenge our best, there's never again going to be that feeling of something so much larger being at stake.

The fact is that Canada–Russia '72 went from a hockey event to a nation-building moment. And through it we shared a bond that lasts to this day.

Try for a moment to think of any other event in Canadian history that created such a feeling. Then trying imagining what could possibly surpass it.

76. Canada versus Russia was, without a doubt, the greatest rivalry in international hockey. But it's passé. Bob says Canada's new international hockey rivalry is a one-way street.

CANADA VERSUS RUSSIA will always have a special place in hockey lore because it represents the first great international rivalry in the sport.

But it's had its day.

These days, a Canada–Russia matchup always leaves something to be desired, in part because it can't compare to what Canada–Russia used to mean.

In fact, it wasn't really Canada versus Russia, it was Canada versus the Soviet Union, and that is a fundamentally different thing.

In the good old days, losing to Russia seemed like a threat, not just to our hockey identity, but to our way of life. These were mysterious players whom we never saw aside from the international game. They hid behind the Iron Curtain. And every time you watched Canada and the Soviets, you could feel that they were as hungry for victory as our boys were.

The Russians of today are still great hockey players, but they've got no mystique. None.

Part of that is because they're all in the National Hockey League. But more importantly, I think they lack that passion to win for the mother country that their countrymen had a generation ago. These days, many of the best Russian hockey players don't even live in Russia during the off-season, and many have strained relationships with the Russian Hockey Federation. So you've got to wonder how fired up they are about defending the national honour on the ice.

Canada versus Russia these days is really no different than Canada versus Sweden or Finland or the Czech Republic. There's no more of a hate-on in this country for the Russians than there is for any other European hockey power.

The truth is that Canadians don't hate anyone in hockey nearly as much as they hate the Americans. Which is silly, perhaps, since we are cultural mirrors of one another. But for some reason, Canadians feel the need to hate *someone* in hockey. And so, since the Europeans all seem like good guys, why not the Americans?

But in order for there to be a true national sporting rivalry between countries, both of them have to be aware that it exists. And I don't think anyone in the United States—even hockey fans, such as they are—ever gets fired up about international hockey against Canada.

I mean, when the World Cup or World Junior Championship is on, you can't even find as much as a tiny item buried in most American newspaper sports sections.

Yet Canadian hockey fans these days have two priorities going into an international tournament. The first is to see Canada win gold. The second is to make sure the Americans don't.

77.

■ **Here's a different kind of fantasy argument. If you could pick any NHL brother combination from the past 40 years for your team, who would it be? But Bob has one rule—you've got to take all of them.**

YOU NEED ONLY look at the long list of brothers who've suited up in the NHL to know that genetics and environment go a long way towards making it in professional hockey.

There are dozens and dozens of sets of siblings who have played in the NHL. And yet the majority of them involve one brother who made it big and another who got just a taste of hockey's biggest stage.

Consider Mark Messier and his brother Paul, a third-round pick in 1978 who played just nine games in the NHL. Or Patrick Roy and brother Stephane, a centre who was drafted 51st overall in 1985 but played just 12 NHL games. Or Fedor Fedorov, whose selection at No. 66 by Vancouver in 2001 was actually eight spots higher than his brother Sergei had gone to Detroit in 1989.

There is a remarkably rich field to choose from when it comes to the greatest NHL siblings. But if I were a general manager who had to add one group or pair of siblings to my team, these would be my top choices from the past 40 years.

5. Gretzky: Wayne, Keith and Brent. You get the best forward in the history of hockey, but must also dress his two younger siblings, whose combined totals are one goal and three assists in 13 career NHL games. I don't care how bad Keith and Brent are. I'd still take the Gretzky trio on my team. Brent and Keith can play on the fourth line, kill penalties, whatever. Or stick them on a line with Wayne and tell them to go to the net and keep their sticks on the ice. See if he can ignite a little of the Brantford backyard magic in them. Any GM with a chance to draft Wayne Gretzky has to do it, even if it means being tied to his not-so-great siblings as well.

4. Sutter: Brent, Brian, Darryl, Duane, Rich and Ron. You've got to love being able to fill your top two forward lines with one family. The best thing about the Sutters is you get quality *and* quantity, because there are no weak links in this chain. The fewest NHL games played by any of them was Darryl's 406. And Duane's 139 goals was the lowest total among the six. These guys were great two-way players who could give a team toughness and skill at both ends of the ice. And they give you leadership, since four of them— Brian, Brent, Darryl and Ron—were captains of their NHL teams. Pick these guys and you might as well name your team The Sutters.

3. Hull: Bobby and Dennis. It's a no-brainer to select one of the top goal scorers in NHL history along with a brother who could put the puck in the net with the best of them. Dennis Hull spent most of his career in Bobby's shadow, but he had a shot that was at least as hard, if not harder, than Bobby's, and his offensive numbers during the prime of his career were enough to garner him respect beyond his famous last name: he scored at least 25 goals seven times in his career, with one 40-goal season in 1970–71. He was a member of Team Canada in 1972 and played in five all-star games. As for Bobby, the "Golden Jet" gets a bit of a raw deal because of the years he spent in the World Hockey Association. But it's remarkable just how dominant he was in the 1960s, when he led the NHL in scoring seven times. His 54 goals in 1965–66 was the highest total of the Original Six era, and of course he went on to score at a prolific pace with Winnipeg through a good part of the 1970s. Give me the Hulls and I'm not going to worry too much about how many goals my team is going to score.

2. Stastny: Peter, Anton and Marian. Peter and Anton Stastny arrived in Quebec together in the fall of 1980, and each scored 39 goals during their rookie NHL campaign together. A year later, Marian joined them. No brother trio can approach these guys in terms of goal production. And the most amazing thing is that they did it simultaneously and with the same team (until Marian moved to Toronto for the 1985–86 season). So you can actually get a pretty good sense of what your team would be like with the three Stastnys.

Here are their combined statistics for the five seasons from 1981–82 to 1985–86:

SEASON	GOALS	ASSISTS	POINTS
1981–82	107	193	300
1982–83	115	180	295
1983–84	91	142	233
1984–85	77	124	201
1985–86	95	154	249

Give me that trio anytime.

1. Esposito: Phil and Tony. The Espositos are the only brothers in hockey who each represented the very best at what they did. During the early and mid-1970s, Phil was the most prolific goal scorer in the NHL, notching at least 40 goals for seven seasons in a row, including five over 50. Tony, meanwhile, was at the very top of his profession until the mid-1970s, winning the both the Calder and Vezina trophies in 1969–70. With these two guys in the lineup, any team would be set in goal and have one of the all-time great finishers at the other end of the ice. And that's a pretty good foundation from which to build.

78.

Being a successful general manager in the National Hockey League these days is all about avoiding risk. So what's the riskiest thing any GM can do? Bob tells you the move that blows up in their faces more often than any.

THERE ARE NO GUARANTEES in life or in hockey.

Which is why every move that a general manager makes in the NHL's current economic environment involves calculating risk and assessing potential downside.

But there's no area where general managers get burned more often than goaltending. Teams are so eager to solve goaltending woes that they'll throw ridiculous amounts of money at players who look for a short time as if they can get the job done. And then they hope and pray.

But how many times have we seen a goaltender come along and have two or three good years, then sign the big contract and fade into oblivion? It happens all the time.

There are lots of reasons for this. For one, when a goaltender first enters the league, the team in front of him usually plays conservatively because they don't trust him to bail them out if they cough one up. Once goaltenders are established, however, that's no longer the case. And so often, when a guy is being counted on to cover up for mistakes, he can't do it.

There are also goaltenders who appear to be better than they are because they play behind solid defensive teams. But when that team changes personnel or coaches, or the goaltender moves to a team where he's not getting the same kind of protection, he can look completely different.

And then there is the mental factor. The psychology of sports is underrated in general. But I think it's particularly so in the case of hockey goaltenders. It's easy to be great when no one expects you to be. But some guys just can't handle the pressure when they get the big money and they're being counted on to handle the bulk of the workload.

Goaltenders bear the brunt of the pressure in hockey. Like starting pitchers in baseball or quarterbacks in football, they can't hide when they have a bad game.

Consider that, when you look at individual stats for goalies, as with pitchers and quarterbacks, you'll find columns for wins and losses. What does that tell you? Well, it says that we, as fans, are prepared to credit or blame them for the outcome of every game they play.

You can find all kinds of stats on Wayne Gretzky. But tell me what *his* won-lost record was? How about Jim Brown or Michael Jordan or Babe Ruth? Good luck looking up those numbers.

But find me a goalie with just one NHL game on his resume and I'll be able to tell you whether or not his team won the game. Now *that's* pressure. So it should come as no surprise that some goaltenders, while talented, can't hand the pressure night after night, season after season.

Which is why any general manager who signs a young goaltender to a big contract might want to say a few prayers before putting pen to ink.

Remember back in the early 1990s, when Maple Leaf fans were convinced that Felix Potvin was going to lead them to multiple Stanley Cups? He took the Leafs to the semifinals in 1993 against Los Angeles, posting a goals-against average of 2.50 in the regular season. He was 21 years old that spring. The Leafs then rewarded him with a three-year, $4 million contract that put him among the best-paid goalies in hockey. But he never had as good a season again. Potvin wasn't what you'd call a bust. But he certainly never lived up to his rookie season potential. Which is kind of what you could say about the Leafs' goaltender Andrew Raycroft, who looked like the real deal with the Bruins in 2003–04, when he was named NHL rookie of the year. But he hasn't looked as good since, and may never again.

Remember Jim Carey? His first two seasons with the Washington Capitals, 1994–95 and '95–96, were outstanding. But when he tailed off in his third year, the Caps dealt him to Boston, where his career went into the dumper almost immediately. Anybody remember who led the NHL in goals-against average during the 2002–03 season? How about Roman Cechmanek? Years from now, they'll say *who*? Which is about how memorable he was from that season onward.

Roman Turek put up great numbers playing behind Chris Pronger and Al MacInnis during two seasons with the St. Louis Blues. But when he moved north to Calgary to give the Flames a goaltending presence they could build on, he flopped after signing for $19 million over four years. When that contract was done in the NHL, so was Turek.

Which is probably the fate that awaits Martin Gerber, the Ottawa Senators' supposed goaltending saviour who inked a three-year, $11 million deal before the 2006–07 season—based on one good season with the Carolina Hurricanes. Or Ray Emery, who took his team to the 2007 Stanley Cup final, signed a three-year 9.5 million contract at age 25, and was terrible the next season.

But the king of the cheque-cashing goaltending flops has to be Jose Theodore. Theodore was a magician during the 2001–02 season when he won the Hart Trophy and led Montreal to a first-round upset of the Boston Bruins. And his godlike status in Montreal gave him tremendous leverage every time he was due for a new contract.

The Habs committed $16 million to Theodore over three years before the 2005–06 season, never considering that his best days might be behind him. It turned out they were. Which is why Montreal general manager Bob Gainey had to be delighted to be able to trade him and his contract to Colorado later that season.

The goaltenders who prove they can be great under any circumstances, year after year after year, are the exceptions. Far too many are teases who get very well compensated for what prove to be very short acts.

79. Hockey is a team game where the most important players don't always show up on the scoresheet. And others get lost in the shadows of the stars they play with. Bob gives you the players who've done the most, but draw the least attention.

THERE ARE ALL KINDS of reasons why some players get a disproportionate amount of attention over others.

Sometimes it's pure talent that shows up in statistics from year to year. And sometimes it's the personality of the player that acts like a magnet to the media and gets his face on television night after night. And sometimes it's a matter of style, a player's flair on the ice that that makes fans notice everything he does.

Then there are the guys who never get their due. Guys who consistently perform no matter what team they're playing for, no matter what they're asked to do.

Most times, their coaches and teammates know who they are. But sometimes teams are as blind as the fans, trading away players who go on to prove their value with other clubs.

So here is my list of hockey's most unappreciated players of the present and recent past.

5. Ray Ferraro. There's just something about beginning a career with the Hartford Whalers that ensures a player will never get the respect he deserves, and Ferraro is a great example. Here's a guy who played with six different teams in an 18-year career and never had a bad season. And he played on some stinkers, moving from Hartford to Long Island, the Rangers, Los Angeles and Atlanta before ending with a short stop in St. Louis. (The Whalers thought so much of him that they traded him to the Isles for defenceman Doug Crossman, who played just 41 games in Hartford before being bounced around the NHL.)

Buried during his first season on Long Island in 1991–92, he scored 40 goals the next year, playing as the second-line centre. In 1992–93, he led the Islanders in playoff scoring before they were knocked out in the Stanley Cup semifinals. He then went to the Rangers via free agency in 1995, but was sent to Los Angeles after just one season, in one of many brilliant New York personnel moves during the 1990s. Ferraro battled injuries in Los Angeles, but rebounded by scoring 48 goals during his first two seasons with the Atlanta Thrashers in 2000–01 and 2001–02. With different teams and better teammates, you can be sure Ferraro's 408 goals and 490 assists would have added up to more than one all-star game appearance.

4. Craig Ludwig. Being a defensive defenceman is never an easy way to earn respect, but Ludwig performed that role as well as anyone. He was a prolific shot blocker who turned that difficult skill into an art form. But he was best known for his punishing hits and ability to clear the front of the net. Ludwig helped anchor two Stanley Cup–winning defence units, one with Montreal in 1986 and another with Dallas 13 years later. He was strong and durable, playing 80 games in each of his last two seasons with the Stars. The one thing Ludwig didn't do was score goals, amassing two or fewer in 11 of his 17 seasons. But every team needs a dependable guy like him, even if he never gets much time on the publicity train. Too bad Montreal didn't know what it had when it traded him to the Islanders for Gerald Diduck, who played just 32 games in a Habs uniform.

3. Brian Rafalski. For a guy who's been a mainstay on the blue line with two Stanley Cup winners, a productive offensive player and a strong plus/minus player, you rarely hear Rafalski's name mentioned among the NHL's elite defencmen. Playing years on the same defence unit as Scott Stevens and Scott Niedermayer will do that to you. But here's a guy who wasn't even drafted coming out of college and had to ply his trade in Europe until age 26 before the New Jersey Devils signed him at the start of the 1999–00 season. Lacking the size to play the tough-guy role, Rafalski has been the perfect complement to the rugged defensive defencemen, allowing him to contribute his playmaking abilities from the back end. He doesn't take penalties and doesn't make many mistakes. And at 25 minutes or more of ice time each game, he's as valuable as almost any defenceman in the league.

2. Ron Francis. It was only during the latter stages of his career that Ron Francis started to get some of the respect due to him. Part of the problem was all those years in Hartford. Yet it was Francis's move to Pittsburgh late in the 1991 season that put the Penguins over the top to two consecutive Stanley Cups. Before that, Mario Lemieux's team had missed the playoffs in five out of six years and won just a single playoff round. When Francis arrived, it gave the Pens a second line that could be as potent as its first. Just stop and consider how much less attention Francis got than Mark Messier during his career, and then imagine how history might have been different had Francis been drafted by Edmonton and Messier by the Whalers. He didn't get the attention, and he never guaranteed a playoff win, but it's hard to ignore his standing on the all-time lists in terms of games played (third), goals (22nd), assists (second, behind Wayne Gretzky) and points (fourth). Not visible in those statistics are things such as his durability, ability in the face-off circle and the quiet example he set as a three-time winner of the Lady Byng Trophy.

1. Adam Oates. The guy played 22 NHL seasons and ranks 35th all-time in games played. And yet Adam Oates is an afterthought at best on any list of the all-time great players. Oates's problem was he wasn't a prolific goal scorer, notching 77 goals over two seasons in the early 1990s but never getting more than 25 in any other. His true greatness, however, was in the set-up, finding the open man and hitting him at the right time to produce a goal. Oates was the set-up man for three great scorers in Cam Neely with Boston, Brett Hull in St. Louis and Peter Bondra in Washington. He was already establishing that skill early in his career, with Detroit, before the trade to St. Louis, where he had an astounding 169 assists in his first two seasons playing with Hull. The Blues didn't appreciate his value, which led to his contract holdout and eventual trade to Boston, where he scored 254 points in his first two seasons with the Bruins. And as for longevity, Oates is one of the few forwards in league history who continued to play at a high level to age 40. He is the oldest player ever to lead the NHL in assists, at age 39 in 2001–02. A year later, he led Anaheim with 13 playoff points in its run to the Stanley Cup final. Oates wasn't given enough respect in his younger days, which is why the Red Wings traded him away in a deal they would live to regret. And now that his career is over, his accomplishments still aren't fully appreciated.

80. ■ Roger Neilson was eccentric, an original and one of the most successful coaches of his era. But he couldn't keep a job. Bob says one of hockey's best minds never got a fair deal.

TRACE THE COACHING CAREER of Roger Neilson, and a pattern emerges.

Neilson would get hired, improve the team he inherited and inevitably get fired.

It happened over and over and over again, from his days with the Toronto Maple Leafs in the 1970s right through to his final firing at the hands of Philadelphia Flyers general manager Bob Clarke in the spring of 2000, surely one of Clarke's least classy moves.

Here's a guy who coached 1,000 National Hockey League games with seven teams (eight if you count the two games he coached Ottawa at the end of the 2001–02 season to reach the 1,000-game mark for his career) over nearly a quarter century, with a winning percentage, excluding ties, of 55 percent along the way. And yet he never was allowed to hold a job for even four full seasons.

When Neilson took over the Leafs in 1977–78, the team improved by 11 points in the standings while cutting its goals against by 48. The Leafs that year reached the semifinals, their deepest playoff run since the Cup-winning year of 1967, and the second round the next season. When Neilson was fired after the 1978–79 season, Toronto went into a tailspin, failing to reach the third round of the playoffs again until 1993.

He went to Buffalo the next year, serving one season as an assistant to Scotty Bowman before taking over in 1980–81 and leading the Sabres to 99 points in the standings. Losing in the second round of the playoffs that spring, however, was a disappointment, and Neilson was fired. But the Sabres exceeded 99 points just once over the next 23 years. And it took 17 seasons for Buffalo to get closer to the Stanley Cup.

In 1981–82 Neilson took over a sub-.500 team in Vancouver with 10 games to go in the regular season and guided it all the way to the Stanley Cup final. Less than two years later he was gone, finishing the 1983–84 season mopping up behind the Los Angeles Kings' bench. The Canucks missed the playoffs in four of the seven seasons after Neilson left and were eliminated in round one in three others.

From there, Neilson went on to New York, where his third and final full season with the Rangers saw them achieve their highest point total (105) in 20 years before being eliminated in the second round. Yet the very next year, a 19–17–4 record was enough to get him fired in midseason. New York went on to finish that year 15–22–7 and miss the playoffs without him.

Under Neilson, the expansion Florida Panthers finished their charter season one game under .500, a far better first-year record than expansion teams in Anaheim, Ottawa, Tampa Bay, Columbus, Nashville, Minnesota, Atlanta or San Jose achieved. And yet, after a similarly respectable record of 20–22–6 in the lockout-shortened season of 1994–95, Neilson was shown the door. The Panthers reached the Stanley Cup final the next season, but it was Neilson who had laid the groundwork for that team's eventual success.

And then, of course, there was Philadelphia, which Neilson was forced to leave late in his third season (1999–2000) when his cancer struck, eventually being replaced by Craig Ramsay and told not to return.

Now, I think you could suggest that hockey coaches generally get fired for one of two reasons. It's either because their teams are woeful or because they fail to live up to expectations based on the talent they employ. And yet neither was ever the case for any significant length of time when Neilson was involved.

So why did Neilson have such a short shelf life? Why did a coach who was clearly one of the great hockey minds of his time keep getting passed on from team to team?

Part of it has to do with the fact that Neilson was a stubborn individual who was completely apolitical. He knew how to coach hockey, but had no appetite for trying to save his job by doing things designed solely to please his bosses. He was close to Darryl Sittler in Toronto, and Harold Ballard didn't like that. He butted heads with Scotty Bowman in Buffalo and paid a price for that. He was close to Eric Lindros in Philadelphia, and Bob Clarke hated that. And he refused to capitulate to the whims of über-captain Mark Messier in New York, and Messier eventually got him fired for that. He believed what he believed without regard for the negative personal consequences of his principles. And while his teams were usually the better for that, his career was not.

Neilson's eccentricities, whether his habit of bringing his dog to work or the endless hours he'd spend with a video machine, were endearing and cute when his teams were going well. But the minute things turned, they quickly became a reason to let him go.

Neilson's rugged individualism always provided lots of ammunition for a team that thought it might need a different kind of coach. Since there was only one Neilson, management could always be sure that changing coaches would mean real change.

The other thing that hurt Neilson was his timing. It wasn't until the New Jersey Devils won the Stanley Cup in 1995 that hockey came to accept fully that responsible, team-oriented, defensive hockey was a viable winning strategy. Dating back to the Montreal Canadiens of the early 1970s, the best teams had been offensive-minded, a trend that continued through the firewagon era of the 1980s to Mario Lemieux's back-to-back Cups in 1991 and 1992.

Yet throughout those years, Neilson continually put an emphasis on preventing goals, making players accountable and cutting down on mistakes. Owners complained it was boring hockey. And while they could stomach it at times when his teams were winning, they had precious little patience for

Neilson and his conservative strategies when the inevitable bumps in the road came along.

Which is a shame, because you can be certain that, had Neilson been allowed to finish the job in any one of his many stops along the way, he'd have achieved the one thing missing from his illustrious career: a Stanley Cup.

81. The Dallas Stars, Colorado Avalanche, Detroit Red Wings and New Jersey Devils captured every Stanley Cup over a period of nine seasons. Did they earn those prizes, or were they simply bought? Bob has the answer.

FROM THE MID-1990S onward, you could almost sense the anger among Canadian hockey fans watching the Stanley Cup being paraded down the main drag of another big American market year after year after year.

Colorado, Dallas, New Jersey and Detroit had it all when they combined to win nine Stanley Cups in a row from 1994–95 to 2002–03. As better teams with bigger budgets than most teams in Canada, it made them lightning rods for complaints about the state of the NHL.

And yet anyone paying attention would have to acknowledge that this was not a case of the New York Yankees' blueprint in action. That formula was, in fact, in the hands of the New York Rangers, and to a lesser degree the Toronto Maple Leafs and Philadelphia Flyers—teams that learned the hard way, or maybe didn't learn, that building a hockey team through free agency, especially under the old economic system, never works.

Hockey is, was and will always be a sport where success is built first and foremost through the draft. But fantastic trades were almost as important to the success of New Jersey, Dallas, Colorado and Detroit as amateur scouting and player development. Those teams were simply better at exchanging assets with their competition, consistently acquiring players of superior quality who became critical pieces of the Stanley Cup picture, often for little more than draft picks.

Free agency, the act of going out and buying the best available players on the open market, played almost no part in most of the Stanley Cups won from 1995 to 2003.

In fact, you could argue that a big part of the success of Colorado, Detroit, New Jersey and Dallas was that they all but ignored free agency during a period when other teams rushed to sign players on the open market each July. These teams recognized that paying top dollar for players already into their thirties, who were usually looking for long-term contracts, was not the way to go.

Instead, they used their financial resources to retain the assets they'd honed and developed or that they'd traded for. Consistency and familiarity, they seemed to understand, is a big part of success in hockey. So to suggest they simply went out and shopped for a Stanley Cup is absurd and downright disrespectful.

Here's a short case study on each of them.

COLORADO AVALANCHE
(Stanley Cups in 1996 and 2001)

The Avs are a perfect example of a team built through a combination of strong drafting and a few whoppers in the trade market.

Though Colorado benefited greatly from a series of high draft picks when the franchise was still in Quebec City, two trades put this franchise over the top.

The first occurred in 1992, bringing Peter Forsberg, Chris Simon and Mike Ricci to the Stanley Cup puzzle. Three years later, another blockbuster landed Mike Keane and Patrick Roy from Montreal.

Adding that kind of talent to a core of players acquired through the draft, a group that included Joe Sakic, Valeri Kamensky, Adam Deadmarsh, Adam Foote, Andrei Kovalenko, Alexei Gusarov, and Curtis Leschyshyn assured Colorado of being a Cup contender.

But it was other, smaller trades that also made a difference, landing such players as Scott Young, Sandis Ozolinsh, Warren Rychel, Dave Hannan, Claude Lemieux, Craig Wolanin and Uwe Krupp.

The scouting department continued to produce after the franchise's relocation to Denver, with Chris Drury, Milan Hejduk, Dan Hinote, Ville Nieminen, Alex Tanguay and Martin Skoula all contributing to the 2001 Stanley Cup campaign. Aside from Tanguay and Skoula, none of those players were selected within the first 70 picks of any draft year.

The Avs also added depth to the 2001 team through trades, adding Ray Bourque, Greg de Vries, Chris Dingman, Rob Blake, Shjon Podein and Nolan Pratt.

And what about free agents? Well, the 1996 Stanley Cup champions had just two: Jon Klemm, who wasn't drafted, and Troy Murray, who joined the Avs after scoring just 13 goals in 132 games the previous four seasons.

Same thing in 2001 where, besides Klemm, only Eric Messier—who was also undrafted and out of hockey at one point—and Dave Reid were signed off the open market.

DETROIT RED WINGS
(Stanley Cups in 1997, 1998 and 2002)

For their first two Cups in 1997 and 1998, near-flawless scouting and trades that initially seemed insignificant proved the recipe for success.

I don't believe any team in hockey can match Detroit's drafting record over the past 25 years, a list of players that includes Steve Yzerman, Sergei Fedorov, Nicklas Lidstrom, Darren McCarty, Slava Kozlov, Vladimir Konstantinov, Martin Lapointe, Matthieu Dandenault, Jamie Pushor and Chris Osgood.

But the 1997 and 1998 teams also had their share of trade additions, including Brendan Shanahan, Larry Murphy, Tomas Sandstrom, Slava Fetisov, Greg Johnson, Kris Draper, Aaron Ward, Igor Larionov, Kirk Maltby, Mike Vernon, Jamie Macoun and Dimitri Mironov.

Unlike the Colorado example, there were no real block-busters among the wheeling and dealing. But consider that to get Draper, Ward, Maltby, Fetisov and Murphy, Detroit gave up only Paul Ysebaert, Dan McGillis, a third-round pick and future considerations.

As for free agents on the 1997 and 1998 teams, there were five in total: Tim Taylor, Bob Rouse, Doug Brown, Brent Gilchrist and Kevin Hodson—none of whom will be remembered for bringing a Cup to Hockeytown USA.

It wasn't until the 2001–02 Cup run that Detroit made significant use of the free-agent market, signing Brett Hull, Luc Robitaille, Boyd Devereaux, Steve Duchesne, Manny Legace and Fredrik Olausson.

It was a luxury most teams couldn't afford, to be sure. And those players might have helped tip the scales in Detroit's favour at playoff time. But this was still a team that was built, not bought.

NEW JERSEY DEVILS
(Stanley Cups in 1995, 2000 and 2003)

The Devils are another example of an organization that won multiple Stanley Cups while ignoring free agents almost completely. In fact, New Jersey signed and used more undrafted free agents than it did free agents from other NHL teams—the two most notable being Brian Rafalski and John Madden.

The 1995 team was built through the draft, with a core that included John MacLean, Bill Guerin, Scott Niedermayer, Brian Rolston, Sergei Brylin, Mike Peluso, Jim Dowd, Valeri Zelepukin, Ken Daneyko, Chris McAlpine, Martin Brodeur, Kevin Dean, Chris Terreri and Bruce Driver.

Trades also contributed to that team, adding Tom Chorske, Claude Lemieux, Neal Broten, Shawn Chambers, Bobby Holik, Stephane Richer, Tommy Albelin and Danton Cole. Two other players were acquired through free-agent compensation—Scott Stevens and Randy McKay. The one and only free agent on that team was Bobby Carpenter.

By 2000, the Devils had added to their core through the draft with such players as Jay Pandolfo, Krysztof Oliwa, Patrick Elias, Petr Sykora, Colin White and Scott Gomez. Trades brought Jason Arnott, Chris Terreri (who'd been dealt to San Jose after the '95 Cup), Sergei Nemchinov, Steve Kelly, Claude Lemieux, Vladimir Malakhov, Lyle Odelein and Alexander Mogilny. But there were no new free agents on that team.

By 2003, further trades had brought Jamie Langenbrunner and Joe Nieuwendyk from Dallas, as well as Jeff Friesen, Grant Marshall, Turner Stevenson, Pascal Rheaume, Richard Smehlik and Oleg Tverdovsky.

The draft had added Brian Gionta, Jiri Bicek, Corey Schwab, Christian Berglund and Michael Rupp.

Free agents? One: Jim McKenzie.

DALLAS STARS
(Stanley Cup in 1999)

The Stars built less of their team through the draft than most Stanley Cup champions, although Modano, Derian Hatcher, Jamie Langenbrunner and Jere Lehtinen represented the heart and soul of that team.

The Stars were built largely through trades, some of which were talent-for-talent trades, while others dealt young prospects for established players. Guy Carbonneau came cheaply in a trade with St. Louis for Paul Broten, while Joe Nieuwendyk came from Calgary because the Stars were bright enough to have drafted Jarome Iginla. Darryl Sydor and Sergei Zubov came in trades with Los Angeles and Pittsburgh in deals both those teams would like to have back. Mike Keane and Brian Skrudland came in a deal with the New York Rangers.

There were seven free agents on the Stars, although only two were significant: Brett Hull and Ed Belfour. A top-notch scorer and first-rate goaltender are key ingredients to a Stanley Cup. But they would have meant little without the shrewd management that built that team.

So there you have it. Did money help Detroit, Dallas, Colorado and New Jersey? Sure. But it was nowhere near the most important ingredient that went into those teams.

That didn't stop clubs such as the Calgary Flames from trying to convince people that the big American teams were wielding their economic clout unfairly. During those nine seasons that Colorado, Detroit, New Jersey and Dallas shared the Cup, the Flames missed the playoffs seven times and suffered two first-round knockouts. Naturally, all this was someone else's fault.

Of course, the Flames' woes couldn't have been due to the fact that, of the 24 players selected among Calgary's first two picks between 1992 and 2003, 13 combined to play a total of 31 NHL games, including nine who didn't or haven't played at all. It couldn't have been because, of those picks, exactly one—Cory Stillman—has hit the 50-point mark in any single season.

And it wasn't because the trades Calgary pulled off during that span included sending Doug Gilmour, Kent Manderville, Ric Nattress, Rick Wamsley and Jamie Macoun to the Leafs for

Gary Leeman and spare parts. Or that they traded Michael Nylander to Tampa Bay for Andrei Nazarov, the Russian goon.

Or that they sent Jean-Sebastien Giguere to Anaheim for a second-round draft pick in 2000. Or that they opted not to re-sign Martin St. Louis.

Money didn't win Stanley Cups in the years leading up to the lockout. Brains and good management did. Even if that's a little hard for some folks to swallow.

82. Mike Milbury was good at one thing when he was general manager of the New York Islanders: keeping his job. Bob says Milbury's teams might have won multiple Stanley Cups during his reign, if he'd just left well enough alone.

IT'S WELL DOCUMENTED that great teams are built primarily through the entry draft. Which is why a perusal of the 1990s selections of the New York Islanders certainly leads one to believe that this team should have been challenging for the Stanley Cup each year by the end of the decade.

The Islanders, like all teams, had their share of misses. But this team can't blame its scouting staff for its on-ice woes. The quality of players selected by Long Island during the 1990s is impressive, a list that includes Scott Lachance, Zigmund Palffy, Darius Kasparaitis, Todd Bertuzzi, Bryan McCabe, Tommy Salo, Brad Lukowich, Wade Redden, J.P. Dumont, Zdeno Chara, Roberto Luongo, Eric Brewer, Tim Connolly and Taylor Pyatt, right up to Rick DiPietro and Raffi Torres, who were taken in 2000.

With those 16 players, you'd have the makings of a damn fine hockey team today. And yet, from 1993–94 to 2003–04, the years during which the Islanders should have been reaping the benefits from this crop of draftees, they missed the playoffs seven times and were eliminated in the first round four others.

How in the world can that be? Well, the answer comes in the actions of the most self-destructive trader in National Hockey League history, former Islander general manager Mike Milbury.

Had Milbury simply stayed out of the kitchen and worried about managing his assets instead of looking to upgrade them, the Islanders might have been the best team in hockey. And I would argue that they would have been perennial Stanley Cup contenders by the turn of the century. But Milbury, king of the hustle, always had a deal cooking, his eyes on some other prize.

He traded at the start of seasons, throughout the campaign and right up to the deadline. Then he'd start all over again at the draft so that the churn of good players out of Long Island became like a revolving door.

Milbury was so infatuated with players on other teams that he somehow managed to tear to shreds what should have been an NHL powerhouse—and eventually, in a move long, long overdue, do himself out of the GM job at the end of the 2005–06 season.

Consider that at the start of the 2006–07 season, exactly one of those 16 quality players I mentioned was wearing a New York Islander uniform. And that player, Rick DiPietro, is going to be wearing one for a very long time, since Milbury's successor, Garth Snow, signed him to the longest (and craziest) contract in NHL history, a 15-year deal worth $67.5 million.

So where did it all go wrong for poor Mike? Well, let's go through the list and explore the fascinating journey of how Mike Milbury managed to scatter the Islanders' Fab 15 to the wind.

January 23, 1996: Milbury trades goaltender Damian Rhodes and defenceman **Wade Redden** to Ottawa for goaltender Don Beaupre, forward Martin Straka and defenceman Bryan Berard. Not a bad deal for Mike, except that he couldn't stop there. Berard was traded to Toronto for Felix Potvin in what amounted to the exchange of an elite defenceman for an average goaltender. Straka was claimed off waivers two months later by Florida after playing just 22 games for the Islanders. Whoops.

November 17, 1996: Islanders trade **Darius Kasparaitis** and Andreas Johansson to the Penguins for Bryan Smolinski. Kasparaitis was the best player in the deal. Mike loses again.

February 6, 1998: Milbury trades defenceman **Bryan McCabe,** centre **Todd Bertuzzi** and a third-round draft pick to Vancouver for centre Trevor Linden. Linden spent less than two years on Long Island and never had 20 goals in a season again in his career. Meanwhile, McCabe and Bertuzzi quickly evolved into stars.

May 30, 1998: Milbury trades forward **Jean-Pierre Dumont** to the Chicago Blackhawks for centre Dmitri Nabokov. Awful. Nabokov played 55 career NHL games.

March 9, 1999: Milbury trades defenceman **Scott Lachance** to Montreal for a third-round choice in the 1999 entry draft (forward Mattias Weinhandl). Weinhandl had a six-goal season for the Isles and was eventually put on waivers.

March 21, 1999: Milbury trades goaltender **Tommy Salo** to Edmonton for forward Mats Lindgren and an eighth-round pick (Radek Martinek) in 1999. Salo was the Oilers' starting goaltender for five full seasons. Lindgren's best with New York was a nine-goal season.

June 21, 1999: Milbury trades forward **Zigmund Palffy**, forward Bryan Smolinski and goalie Marcel Cousineau to the Los Angeles Kings for centre Olli Jokinen, forward Josh Green, defenceman Mathieu Biron and the Kings' first pick (Taylor Pyatt) in the 1999 entry draft. Not a bad deal, but Jokinen,

Green, Biron and Pyatt were all gone from Long Island by the start of the 2001–02 season.

June 24, 2000: Milbury trades defenceman **Eric Brewer**, forward Josh Green and a second-round selection (Brad Winchester) in 2000 to the Edmonton Oilers for Roman Hamrlik. Hamrlik for Brewer would have been a push.

June 24, 2000: Islanders trade goaltender **Roberto Luongo** and forward Olli Jokinen to the Florida Panthers for forwards Oleg Kvasha and Mark Parrish. Getting one of those guys would have been a steal for Florida. But both?

June 23, 2001: Milbury trades defenceman **Zdeno Chara**, forward Bill Muckalt and the second-overall pick in the 2001 draft (Jason Spezza) for Alexei Yashin. The mother of all bad Milbury trades.

June 24, 2001: Milbury trades forwards **Tim Connolly** and **Taylor Pyatt** to Buffalo for Michael Peca. A decent deal, but he still overpaid, considering that the Sabres had to trade Peca, who was in a contract holdout.

March 11, 2003: Milbury trades forward Brad Isbister and forward prospect **Raffi Torres** to the Edmonton Oilers for defenceman Janne Niinimaa and a 2003 second-round pick (Evgeni Tunik). Torres was the best player in the deal by far.

March 9, 2006: Milbury trades defenceman **Brad Lukowich** to New Jersey for a third-round pick in 2006. The destruction was complete: 13 trades that got rid of 15 quality NHL players.

Not only were the Islanders made worse off by these trades in totality, but all but one or two of them made them worse immediately. And the few deals that you could argue were good for the Islanders at the time were later undone by future trades.

It's a reign of error unlike any in NHL history. And the kind of thing that should make Islander fans sit and wonder what might have been. Because during years when their team was missing the playoffs, it should have been hoisting the Stanley Cup.

83.

The International Ice Hockey Federation says too many European players are being lured to North America before they're ready or able to compete in the NHL. Bob says they're right, and the NHL needs to stop being so greedy.

DURING THE FALL of 2006, the International Ice Hockey Federation came out with a scathing report on the manner in which the National Hockey League has been abusing its rights to sign players from Europe.

The IIHF claims the NHL signs European players prematurely, before they are NHL-ready, and that European players are better off when they are allowed to develop in their own leagues than the minors in North America. And it insists that the NHL's gluttony is diminishing the European leagues and the quality of players within them.

In short, it claimed that, rather than treating Europe as a place from which teams can look to upgrade the talent available to them in North America, NHL teams thoughtlessly pick from Europe at their whim. Which really shouldn't come as a surprise to anyone, since NHL teams are in a competitive business. And so they're happy to get their hands on any player from Europe who might have a shot at helping them, no matter how small a role that might be or how remote that player's chances might actually be of making it to the NHL. It's cheap, and there's no reason not to do it.

Okay, so here's the problem. As long as the NHL has such a sweetheart deal with the IIHF, one that allows it to bring over players on the cheap, there's no incentive for NHL clubs to be choosy.

By negotiating such a discount deal with the IIHF, the NHL has conditioned its teams to pluck whatever European players they want without regard for cost or the good of leagues in Europe.

In other sports, teams go overseas only to recruit players they think will have an impact, usually an immediate one. Baseball's minor leagues aren't full of marginal prospects from Japan. And in the NBA, the vast majority of international players have achieved a considerable level of success overseas before they come to North America.

Yet in the NHL you see all kinds of European players playing nominal minutes on the third and fourth lines when they could be starring in their home countries. Even worse, you've got lots of them in the minor leagues, sweating it out in obscurity, where they're of no real value to anyone.

And why would teams rather have their European prospects in North America than in Europe? Well, one reason is that they don't have to pay them much. And another is the belief that European prospects need time to adjust to the game as it's played here, from the physical contact to the officiating to the different size of ice surface.

Which would be fine if there was any real evidence that players can't be successful coming directly from Europe to the NHL. But what about Alexander Ovechkin, or Teemu Selanne or Peter Stastny or Nicklas Lidstrom or any of the dozens of other European players who've had immediate success in the NHL?

As upset as the IIHF is about the current situation, it believes things are about to get worse. In the past, NHL teams were able to draft European players and hold onto their rights forever, theoretically allowing them to play in Europe until they were good enough to sign an NHL contract. However, the new NHL collective bargaining agreement signed in 2005 changed that. So now European players, like North Americans, must be signed within two years of being drafted or they can re-enter the draft.

The NHL Players' Association didn't like the double standard, whereby its North American members enjoyed the leverage that comes with the two-year limit while the rights to European players were owned in perpetuity.

Now the IIHF is convinced many, many more players will be leaving Europe prematurely for the back ends of NHL rosters or the minor leagues.

There's an easy way to solve this, but it's not one the NHL is going to like. The IIHF needs to broker a bigger fee from NHL teams for the players they take from Europe. It needs to be high enough to prevent a team from taking flyers on players and induce them to wait until players are ready to contribute in the NHL. That won't be easy, because the IIHF has virtually no bargaining leverage over the NHL. And without a transfer agreement at all, NHL teams would just do as they have done with Russia—take players for free.

With a higher fee for players, the NHL would still have access to the best players in the world, but it would end the conspicuous consumption from Europe of those who aren't ready and might never be.

84. The National Hockey League's decision to shut down the season in 2004–05 was supposedly all about the players receiving too big a share of the pie. But Bob says the early post-lockout evidence suggests it was about much more than that.

DURING THE 2003-04 SEASON, the 30 National Hockey League teams collectively spent $1.34 billion (U.S.) on player salaries. That much we know.

The rest of the league's economics are a guessing game, because teams don't open their books and league revenues remain private.

Few would have taken issue with the notion that player salaries had spun well beyond a reasonable limit leading into the lockout, having hit an average of $1.8 million. Even the NHL Players' Association, under former leader Bob Goodenow, seemed to accept that premise when it offered up a 24 percent rollback across the board in December of 2004 in an attempt to end the lockout.

But none of that explains how, two seasons into the post-lockout world, the NHL's overall payroll was at $1.242 billion, not even $100 million less than the pre-lockout figure that supposedly had the game on the brink of disaster. Or how the league could afford to raise the salary cap for 2007–08 to $50.3 million, a 14 percent increase over the figure for 2006–07.

This is a league that claimed losses of $274 million in 2002–03, according to an NHL-sponsored report prepared by former U.S. Securities and Exchange Commission chairman Arthur Levitt. (Interestingly, *Forbes* magazine pegged the NHL's overall annual loss at $123 million, $151 million less than the Levitt figure, and one much more consistent with where the league's economics are today.) Salaries were supposedly a matter of life and death that left the NHL with no choice but to take the most drastic, unprecedented and risky labour strategy in the history of professional sports. And yet, three years later, salaries are already back to where they were.

The new NHL's numbers don't add up. Within about a year of the lockout ending, three-quarters of the 24 percent rollback the players granted had been returned to them by the same owners who'd shut down the game.

This, despite the fact that hockey would seem to have sustained considerable damage by shutting itself down for a year—fallout it must have foreseen going into the lockout.

Obviously, the lockout wasn't about reducing the players' overall share of revenue. It was about creating a system where the richest of the rich teams—Toronto, Dallas, Detroit, Philadelphia, Colorado and the New York Rangers—get a huge windfall by lopping tens of millions of dollars off their payrolls.

That is, a team like the Leafs, which finished the 2003–04 season with a payroll of $72 million on the books, gets to cut $32 million without having to apologize to its fans for making itself less competitive.

Now, in exchange for such magnificent savings, the richest of the rich teams in turn agreed to put some of their huge windfall into revenue sharing. That goes to prop up teams in places where there shouldn't be National Hockey League franchises, such as Florida, Nashville and Atlanta, which were all part of Commissioner Gary Bettman's grandiose vision.

In effect, that money is being used to cover up mistakes the league made during its unsuccessful rush to gain a national footprint that would entice and drive national television in the United States.

And we all know how that turned out.

The fact is the NHL lockout was more about the *redistribution* of payrolls than a reduction. In other words, the fans in strong markets are subsidizing owners in weak markets. The league can say it did that in the name of competitive balance, but we all know that's a crock, if only because competitive balance has never been a problem for the NHL.

This was all about a league that had huge disparity in team-by-team revenues and in which the big boys weren't willing to share without getting a huge payoff first.

Is the NHL's economic model today better than the one it had prior to the lockout? Sure it is, given the corner the league had backed itself into.

But was it really necessary to shut the game down for a year to accomplish what amounts to nothing more than a redistribution of salaries throughout the league? You're telling me that the NHL couldn't have achieved that with a revenue-sharing and luxury-tax model, which the players were agreeable to long before things got ugly? No way.

Of course, the NHL also suggested the lockout was partly about making the game more affordable for fans, that somehow the paying public would get a break at the ticket and concession windows by having the players take the fall. How's that going?

85. In most sports, getting penalized is a bad thing. But in hockey, penalty stats are considered good for a player's resume. Bob explores the backwards world of NHL hockey and the positive reinforcement of penalties.

HOW OFTEN HAVE YOU heard a discussion of a hockey player's abilities touch on the number of minutes he spends in the penalty box?

All the time, you hear fans say things like, "Hey, this guy had 15 goals and 26 assists—but wait, don't forget about the 141 penalty minutes."

Stop now for moment and consider what a penalty does to a hockey team. It forces the team to play shorthanded for two minutes—as in four players against five. Now, how in the world is that a good thing?

To some observers, penalty minutes indicate toughness or the willingness to get dirty in the corners. But there's no real correlation between a player who can intimidate, who can physically punish opposing players with big hits, and a guy who takes lots of penalties.

Don't believe me? Scott Stevens was one of the toughest hockey players I've ever seen. He was an unforgiving body-checker who struck the fear of God into players every time they crossed his blue line. But Stevens was never much of a fighter. In fact, in only three of his 22 NHL seasons did he ever have more than two fights.

He spent at least 150 minutes in the penalty box for each of his first nine seasons, which he played in Washington and St. Louis. But Stevens' best years in the NHL came later, with the New Jersey Devils, when he was perhaps the most intimidating player in hockey and helped lead them to three Stanley Cups. And yet Stevens' penalty minutes declined significantly during those years, including seven seasons when he spent 80 or fewer minutes in the penalty box (not counting the lock-out-shortened season of 1994–95, when he had 56) and two full seasons when he had fewer than 50. And in 153 career playoff games with the Devils, the toughest man in hockey took just 186 penalty minutes, or the equivalent of a little more than one minor penalty every two games.

How about Chris Pronger? Is there a tougher defenceman to play against than this guy, a player who's on the ice for roughly half of every game, consistently facing the best players on the opposing team? And yet in recent years he has consistently drawn fewer than 100 penalty minutes. On the 2005–06 Edmonton Oilers he was tied for seventh, with 74. Would Chris Pronger be worth more if he were spending 150 minutes every season in the box?

But the best example might be New Jersey's John Madden. Here's a guy who is a ferocious checking centre, one of the toughest guys in the league for scorers to match up against. In 2006–07 he had 14 minutes in penalties! And that isn't even the lowest single-season total of his career. Part of why Madden is so valuable is that he never hurts his team by forcing it to play shorthanded. And yet he plays like a warrior.

Can you think of any other sport where accumulating penalties is an asset? There's plenty of intimidation in football. But you don't hear people say a defensive lineman is more valuable because he was called 15 times in a season for roughing the passer. In fact, penalties for holding or interference in football are considered signs of weakness—that the player is a liability.

Yet in hockey, you almost never hear a player criticized for taking too many penalties. Occasionally, players will get heat for taking a dumb penalty at a critical juncture. But when's the last time you heard someone say a team had to get rid of a player because he spends too much time in the box?

Instead, guys are praised for the numbers of penalties they take. The Ottawa Senators, for example, have a plaque on their wall that honours Chris Neil for being the franchise's all-time leader in career penalty minutes—right beside the ones that honour the team's all-time leaders in goals, assists and shutouts. Again, can you imagine a football locker room where the all-time leader in holding penalties is honoured?

Since the NHL is so bent on keeping statistics, here's one I'd love to see on every player's bio: goals scored against his team while he was serving a penalty.

Putting a premium on players who take penalties is especially crazy given the way hockey is being officiated these days, since the majority of penalties are for hooking, interference, holding or other similar infractions. Fighting has become such an insignificant part of the game that it rarely accounts for a significant percentage of a player's penalty minutes (and since fighting is irrelevant to the outcome of hockey games, penalty minutes for fighting are irrelevant as well).

So, when I see a player with 200 penalty minutes on his statistical line, what it tells me is that this guy can't defend without resorting to the old clutch-and-grab tactics, that in most instances he's likely to get burned by an opposing player or end up in the box. And neither of those things is good for a hockey team. It's no coincidence that of the 11 teams that gave up the fewest power plays during the 2006–07 season, 10 made the playoffs. Anaheim was known as a tough team unafraid to take penalties. Yet the Ducks actually ranked 16th in number of power plays surrendered.

There are all kinds of reasons why Lou Lamoriello's New Jersey Devils won three Stanley Cups from 1995 to 2003 and are in the hunt every year. But one of the most important is that New Jersey is consistently among the least penalized teams in the league.

They spend far more time with the man advantage than playing shorthanded. And as shocking as that may be to some folks, that's a very good thing.

86. He is the first and only commissioner in the history of the National Hockey League. So, what do we make of Gary Bettman? Bob gets out his scorecard.

ON FEBRUARY 1, 1993, Gary Bettman took over a small but profitable professional sports league that had a dream of becoming part of the American mainstream culture.

The National Hockey League had a strong regional base in the United States and eight markets in Canada where teams were wildly popular. But there was this sense that the business of hockey had underachieved, that with more exposure and a better plan, the NHL could be so much more than it was.

It was into that setting that Gary Bettman stepped—the former assistant general counsel of the National Basketball Association, hired with a mandate to do three things:

1. Bring the NHL the same kind of popularity as the National Basketball Association
2. Broker agreements with the NHL Players' Association that would keep costs under control
3. Expand television exposure.

"I'm looking forward to a tremendous challenge," said Bettman when he was hired.

So now, with a decade and a half in the books, it seems fair to judge how Gary Bettman has done in pursuing the lofty goals set for him back in 1993.

To be fair, Bettman is employed by the owners, who continue to live out this fantasy that hockey is going to be a mainstream, big-time television sport in the United States. So we can't fault the commissioner for all of the NHL's shortcomings. They weren't all his ideas. But based strictly on the mandate under which he was hired, here's my evaluation of Gary Bettman's term thus far as NHL commissioner.

POPULARITY

Let's be clear that the popularity of the NHL in Canada has never been, and never will be, an issue. So, when we take stock of Bettman's ability to popularize the game, we're talking about the United States. Now, how do we measure the popularity of a sport? That's not easy, because of regional differences and the difficulty of judging perception versus reality. But here's a basis I think is fair. I believe you can get a pretty good sense of how popular a sport or individual athlete is in America by studying the number of times that sport or that athlete appears on the cover of *Sports Illustrated*. For more than half a century, *SI* has accurately depicted with its covers the things Americans are most interested in. *SI*'s market is absolute mainstream America, not a niche. And its goal every week is to sell as many magazines as possible by featuring the most popular sports in America. So, using this criterion, let's take a look at the popularity of Gary Bettman's NHL today.

February 1, 2007, marked Gary Bettman's 14-year anniversary as commissioner in the National Hockey League. During that time, hockey was featured on the cover of *Sports Illustrated* a total of 13 times. More significant is the fact that seven of those covers appeared during Bettman's first five years on the job. The magazine hadn't had a hockey cover in almost five years when the Hansons from *Slapshot* appeared on its July, 2007 "Where Are They Now?" issue. The magazine's last previous hockey cover had been dated October 14, 2002, when the Detroit Red Wings were featured in an NHL preview. The last hockey cover before that was about Brittanie Cecil, the girl who was killed by a puck at a Columbus Blue Jackets game. Despite the fact *SI* employs a fabulous hockey writer in Michael Farber, it seems that the sport doesn't enjoy enough popularity in the U.S. to appear on its cover. Yet in the 14 years leading up to Bettman's appointment as commissioner, hockey was featured on 22 covers, including 11 during 1987, 1988 and 1989 alone. Okay, so a lot of those pre-Bettman covers featured Wayne Gretzky in his prime. But let's back up another 14 years. From February 1, 1965 to February 1, 1979, there were 32 *SI* hockey covers. So, if anything, hockey seems to be moving away from the consciousness of American sports fans. Here's another fair barometer of hockey's popularity: sports talk radio. And the NHL, at least on national sports radio networks such as Fox and ESPN, is dead, dead, dead. I mean, these guys would rather talk about the 200th-ranked American college basketball team. The only time hockey is mentioned on national sports radio in the U.S. is as a punch line or when some player clubs another over the head with his stick. I can't remember a time when hockey was less relevant on a national scale in America. Gary Bettman's leadership in making the NHL more popular there has been an abysmal failure.　　　　　　　　　　GRADE: F

CONTROLLING PLAYER COSTS

When Bettman took over as NHL commissioner, the average NHL salary was $467,000. In 1994, Bettman and the owners led hockey into its first prolonged labour stoppage in pursuit of a hard salary cap that would control player salaries. The lockout wiped out roughly half a season, but Bettman came out of it with a deal that he and the owners believed would curb salary escalation. They were wrong.

In part because demand for players was fuelled by their own expansion plan and in part because teams refused to use the leverage afforded to them in the collective agreement, player salaries soared to an average of $1.83 million in 2003–04, the final season before Bettman and the owners shut down the game again to achieve their hard salary cap.

It's tough to lay all the blame at Bettman's feet, because he didn't control the way teams spent. But the fact is that former NHL Players' Association head Bob Goodenow did a much better job of teaching his charges how to use the agreement to their advantage than Bettman did with the teams. The combination of the disparity in revenues between teams, the overall lack of revenue sharing in hockey, and a salary arbitration system that meant one bad signing would have a domino effect across the league allowed players to drive salaries to new heights. It wasn't all Gary's fault. But he negotiated the deal, extended it twice—and *then* tried to blame all of hockey's ills on it. The new agreement negotiated during the summer of 2005 will control costs for some teams in a more effective way. But it also came with a tremendous cost to the game. It was, in effect, merely Bettman's attempt at cleaning up a mess for which he bears a great deal of responsibility.　　　GRADE: D

EXPANDING TELEVISION EXPOSURE

In television it's all about potential, at least for a while. Networks will stick with a property if they believe they can grow it. Which is exactly what ESPN believed when it signed a five-year, $80 million contract in the fall of 1992 that also included the airing of some games on ABC.

Three years later, new commissioner Gary Bettman added to the ESPN deal with a five-year full-season package on the Fox Network, worth $155 million over five years, which at the time was considered a coup.

Ratings weren't bad. Fox averaged a 1.9 rating for regular-season games in 1996–97 and a 4.0 rating during the Cup final. (Each Nielsen ratings point represents one percent of the U.S. households with a TV set.) And though those ratings were trending downward when the Fox deal ended in 1999, ESPN and ABC still saw enough potential to sign a five-year, $600 million deal, giving the league both value and exposure. (By comparison, the 1997 NBA Finals averaged a 16.8 rating on NBC.)

At some point during the term of that contract, however, Gary Bettman's NHL lost its appeal both to viewers and television networks. Whether it was the aesthetics of the game, the growing number of teams or competition from other forms of televised entertainment, fewer and fewer Americans were watching hockey.

In 1999–2000, ABC averaged a 1.3 rating for its regular-season games and a 3.3 for the Cup final. By the final year of that deal in 2003–04, the rating had slumped to 1.1 for the regular season and 2.6 for the Stanley Cup final.

But the bad news for the NHL was about to get worse. First, the NHL was forced to sell its over-the-air rights to NBC in a deal without up-front money. In the first year of that "profit-sharing" arrangement, NHL regular-season games drew an average rating of 1.1 during the 2005–06 season, about the same pitiful viewership ABC attracted two years earlier. Ratings in 2006–07 on NBC were much the same, with Game 3 of the Stanley Cup final tying a historic low for prime-time network broadcasting.

And we learned just how much NBC values hockey in May of 2007, when it pulled away from overtime of Game 5 of the Eastern Conference final between Ottawa and Buffalo to show pre-race coverage of the Preakness. Instead of seeing Daniel Alfredsson score the goal to put Ottawa in the Stanley Cup final for the first time in 80 years, viewers got shots of barns and stables. What a colossal embarrassment for a league that keeps telling us it's thriving in the United States. I mean, can you imagine any other sports property having an overtime game cut off like that? But NBC doesn't care about a sport in which the deciding game of a conference final drew a 1.2 rating.

The NBC horror is a happy story compared to Bettman's management of the NHL's cable property in the U.S. Coming out of the lockout, the NHL opted to sell its American cable rights to Versus Network, which at the time was known as the Outdoor Life Network. OLN offered a two-year commitment of $65 million and $70 million, with a $72.5 million option for the third year and three more beyond that.

ESPN, given the choice of matching that offer, politely declined, thus ending its long relationship with the NHL.

On Versus, a station available to 70 million U.S. homes— about 20 million fewer than ESPN—the NHL's average rating through 2005–06 and the early part of 2006–07 was a 0.2— yes, zero point two—or less than half of what it used to get on ESPN2.

For comparison, consider this: in January 2007, the University of Cincinnati and Western Michigan University played in the inaugural International Bowl college football game at Toronto's Rogers Centre. The game drew a 1.3 rating on ESPN2. That's right: a meaningless college football game played in Canada between two no-name schools clobbers

NHL games on Versus. That's partly because it's football, but it's also partly indicative of the power of ESPN.

By moving off of ESPN, the NHL lost not only a superb carrier for its games, but credibility and daily visibility on the most important sports network in America. As anyone can understand, networks that air games of a particular league are far more likely to feature that league during its highlight shows. Since the NHL left ESPN, hockey has been banished to the bottom rung of ESPN's *SportsCenter* broadcasts, the feeding ground for sports fans across America. There's no way to put a price on that. But Bettman's failure to recognize its importance is a colossal failure in judgment, and one from which the league may not recover.   GRADE: D MINUS

I'm not suggesting Gary Bettman has an easy job. I'm not saying the owners are fun to work for or that making the NHL popular with fans in the United States and on American television is something Superman could do. But that's what Bettman was hired to do. That's the job he accepted. And it is the job upon which he should be judged. He took the job. Not me.

87. Their names don't appear among any of the NHL's all-time leaders in statistical categories. But Bob says there have been some great hockey players who've come and gone too fast. He tells you which ones did the most in the shortest spans of time.

LONGEVITY IS A BIG part of greatness in hockey. It defines players such as Gordie Howe and Chris Chelios. And it's why some players, while not true superstars for any length of time, are afforded a great deal of respect and admiration.

Go over the all-time leaders in any category and it's a mix of all-time talent and those who managed to play consistently for a remarkable length of time.

Most high-quality NHL players play at least 10 full seasons, which is the equivalent of about 800 games. But some never do, leaving us to wonder just where they might rank among the all-time greats if their health and stamina had been better or if they'd had a stronger desire to continue their careers.

Here's my take on the NHL players who got the biggest bang out of short careers.

6. Hakan Loob. How's this for a six-year NHL career: one 50-goal season, three 30-goal seasons, a 100-point season and a Stanley Cup victory to end it on. Loob was one of those smaller players who might not have stood up well to the rough-and-tumble NHL over the long haul. But his desire to return home and raise his family in Sweden was enough to make him turn his back on the NHL at age 29, in his prime and at the height of his popularity, missing out on the salary explosion that was about to come.

5. Kent Nilsson. Nilsson was like a hurricane who blew into the NHL, scored a tonne of goals and was gone in flash. After two seasons with Winnipeg in the World Hockey Association, Nilsson scored at least 40 goals in three of his first four NHL seasons and at least 30 in five of his first six. In his final NHL season of 1986–87 he was traded from Minnesota to the Edmonton Oilers late in the year, and he scored 19 points in the playoffs while helping Edmonton to its third Stanley Cup at age 31. And then he was gone, back to Europe, where he played several more seasons before making a brief appearance with the 1994–95 Oilers. Eight NHL seasons, 686 points and then out of sight.

4. Cam Neely. Neely played just five NHL seasons in which he was on the ice for at least 70 games. The rest of his career was patched together between injuries that limited him to fewer than 50 games in five others, on his way to a total of just 726. During his final 10 NHL seasons, all spent with Boston, Neely averaged .655 goals per game, a figure better than the career average of all modern-era NHL players except Mario Lemieux (.754) and Mike Bossy (.762). In 1993–94, the final 50-goal season of his career, he played just 49 games.

3. Mike Bossy. Bossy got nearly 10 full NHL seasons under his belt, playing 752 games in a career in which he achieved incredible personal and team success as a member of the New York Islanders. He hit the 50-goal mark in his rookie year, then did it eight more times before "slipping" to 38 during his final NHL season at age 30. For those keeping score, Bossy's streak of nine consecutive 50-goal seasons is one better than Wayne Gretzky's eight. His 53-goal rookie season was an NHL record, and he later became the first player since Maurice Richard to get 50 goals in as many games. He might have made it 10 consecutive 50-goal seasons had he not been limited by injuries to 63 games during his swan song in 1986–87. It's just a guess, but a healthy 20-year career from Mike Bossy might have given Gretzky a run for his money in the all-time goal-scoring race. And then, of course, there were those four Stanley Cups.

2. Bobby Orr. Bobby Orr played 80 games in an NHL season just once. He hit the 70-game plateau four times and the 60-game mark in three others. And for just how many of his 657 career games Orr was truly healthy, we'll never know, but you can guess it might have been about half. All of which makes his six 100-point seasons in the NHL—as a defenceman—all the more remarkable. As a point of comparison, consider that the following players all rank among the top 25 in all-time NHL points, yet never made it to the 100-point mark in six different NHL seasons: Brett Hull (4), Ron Francis (3), Joe Sakic (5), Doug Gilmour (3), Stan

Mikita (0), Denis Savard (5), Luc Robitaille (4), Mike Gartner (1). So, just where might Bobby Orr rank had he not played his last full NHL season at age 27?

1. Ken Dryden. It's strange to look back and recall that Ken Dryden played only seven full seasons in the NHL, plus the one remarkable playoff season that preceded his rookie campaign. Dryden's accomplishments are stunning. Besides being part of six Stanley Cup champions with Montreal, he won the Vezina Trophy five times. He won a Calder Trophy as the league's top rookie one year *after* he led Montreal to the Stanley Cup in the spring of 1971, when he captured the Conn Smythe Trophy as the most valuable player in the playoffs. Sure, he was fortunate to play for one of the greatest dynasties of all time. But that much individual and team success in such a short span of time is remarkable. During his seven full seasons in the NHL, Dryden won 252 games. That's 57 more than Patrick Roy did during his first seven NHL campaigns, en route to becoming the all-time leader with 551. Most remarkable might be that Dryden's career shutout total of 46 is only marginally lower than the 57 games he lost during his career. As a former college player, he started his NHL career late at nearly age 25, and then retired at 32. In terms of greatness, Orr was the best of all time. But no one accomplished more team and individual success in such a short career than Ken Dryden.

88. Young hockey players learn all kinds of skills when they're growing up—shooting, stickhandling, checking and passing, to name a few. But Bob says the most underrated skill in today's game is not only remarkably effective, it also hurts.

THE WILLINGNESS TO SACRIFICE one's body in the pursuit of victory is a staple of professional sports. No matter what game we're talking about, there are instances when athletes must choose between protecting their health and taking one for the team.

And yet I'm not sure there's a sport that requires its players to do anything quite like diving in front of a 100-mile-per-hour slap shot. Baseball players are certainly not asked to step in front of a fastball to get on base. But hockey players do the equivalent more and more these days.

The art of shot blocking didn't use to be much of an art. It was something players did mostly out of instinct, and they reserved it for the playoffs or the late stages of critical games. With a game or a season on the line, players would risk limb, and certainly a great deal of pain, to throw themselves in front of a shooter to stop a puck from reaching the net.

These days, however, they do that in *every* game. There's even a technique to it. I mean, in the first period of a game in mid-October, there are guys willing to stand there and take a puck to who-knows-where in the name of preventing a goal.

Of course, this may not be entirely by choice. Coaches around the National Hockey League have grasped how effective shot blocking can be and that the teams that were among the best at it in the first year of post-lockout hockey—Edmonton, Carolina and Buffalo come to mind—had tremendous success.

Since players are no longer able to hook and hold like they once did, blocking shots has become a necessity for every team, especially during the penalty kill. With a slightly deeper offensive zone to operate in, point men have more room to move around and fire the puck. So the best response for the defending team is to collapse around the goal and fill the shooting lanes in preparation to make a block.

You hear coaches today talking about blocking shots in hockey almost the same way they do in the NBA. You never used to hear a head coach suggest, as did former Boston Bruin coach Dave Lewis, that, "The value of scoring a goal and blocking a shot should be equal."

It's no coincidence that we're seeing far more players injured when blocking shots than ever before—the most noteworthy being Anaheim's Chris Pronger, who had his foot cracked midway through the 2006–07 season.

So, if you're trying to guess what the next innovation in hockey equipment might be, think about skates with added protection. I know the NHL is all aflutter about introducing new jersey designs for the 2007–08 season, but maybe finding a way to keep multimillion-dollar athletes from breaking their feet should be more of a priority right now.

The fact is that the league's best shot blockers are worth their weight in gold. They're brave, they're tough and they frustrate the heck out of teams gearing up for that big shot from the point that's supposed to find its way through the crowd to the net.

Anyone who does that for a living, in my mind, is more than earning his keep.

89 ■ It's the best debate of the post-lockout era: if you were building a National Hockey League team today, whom would you take: Alexander Ovechkin or Sidney Crosby? Bob tells you which one will pay off more.

FOR AS LONG AS THEY are both playing in the National Hockey League, Alexander Ovechkin and Sidney Crosby will be forever linked. In a league that was starving for offence, these two players entered the post-lockout NHL and took it by storm. And thus the debate began.

While Crosby dominated media attention in North America during the 2005–06 season, it was Ovechkin who skated away with rookie-of-the-year honours. Yet by their second season in the NHL there was little to choose between the two when it came to their performance on a night-to-night basis.

The 2007–08 season saw Ovechkin take a huge step forward, leading the NHL in both goals and assists, while because of injury Crosby missed 29 games in an otherwise stellar year.

Both have incredible style and skills, and represent the kinds of players whose mere presence can make everyone around them feel more confident. And statistically, you can make the case either way. Ovechkin is the best pure scorer in hockey, as his 163 tallies in 245 games suggests. That's .66 goals per game, a pace significantly better than that of Crosby who has averaged .46 goals per game in his 213 career games. But in terms of points, it's Crosby who holds the edge, averaging 1.38 per game versus 1.26 for Ovechkin.

And in terms of the impact each has had on his respective team, they're nearly identical. Through the first two seasons of their careers, they'd each participated in about the same percentage of their respective teams' goals—42.6 per cent for Crosby versus 41.9 per cent for Ovechkin. And had Crosby been healthy throughout the 2007–08 season, their percentages would have remained neck-and-neck again, with Ovechkin involved in 46.2 per cent of Washington's goals while Crosby's numbers from 53 games extrapolate to being involved in 45.3 per cent of Pittsburgh's goals for a full season.

So when you consider that Crosby is 23 months younger than Ovechkin, a player who seems physically mature beyond his years, it seems to me that Crosby is the one with more untapped potential at this stage of his career.

Which is just one of the reasons I'd take him over Ovechkin right now.

Crosby, not unlike Wayne Gretzky, is a playmaker. He's got tremendous vision and the ability to see possibilities on the ice that others do not. He's a terrific passer, can dig for pucks along the boards and is an acrobatic wonder. And his balance, which makes him almost impossible to separate from the puck, is unparalleled in the game.

But the best thing about Crosby is the way he makes everyone around him better. That's the biggest difference between great playmakers such as Crosby and great finishers like Ovechkin. And any time you have choice between those two types of players I'd always take the guy who can make the play over the pure goal scorer.

In a skills competition, I'd probably take Ovechkin. And with a minute to play in a game where my team needs a goal to tie things up, he'd probably be the guy I'd want going over the boards.

But over the long term, when you're talking about building a team around one player, it would have to be Crosby, especially when you factor in potential longevity.

While in today's NHL there's no guarantee of owning a player past age 25, I'm going to assume that the Penguins and Capitals are going to pull out all the stops to get Crosby and Ovechkin signed to longterm contracts. Which raises the question of which player is more likely to still be tearing it up when he's in his late 20s or early 30s?

Both players play with a remarkable aggressive and potentially risky edge to their games. But you've got to think that Ovechkin's pure power and speed game is less likely to sustain itself long-term than Crosby's game of playmaking and passes.

The player most often cited as comparable to Ovechkin is Pavel Bure. Bure wasn't as big as Ovehckin but he had that same goal-scoring instinct, fearlessness and ability to drive past defenders to the net with blazing speed and power. Bure paid for that style dearly with a series of knee injuries that hampered him during his final few years in the NHL and ended his career at age 32.

Wendel Clark was a completely different player than Ovechkin. But I think there are some parallels between the way Clark recklessly threw his body around when he was young and the way Ovechkin does right now.

I'm not saying what happened to Clark and Bure is necessarily going to happen to Ovechkin. But I'd say there's a better chance of his body being worn out by his style of play than there is of that happening to Crosby, even though he can be reckless in his own way.

At this early stage of his career, Crosby seems to see the ice better than anyone. In Gretzky's case, that skill prevented him from sustaining the kinds of direct hits that can break a player down. I think the same is true of Crosby, and although he's considerably more reckless than Gretzky was, he's also built like a fire hydrant.

There's one other reason I'd want Crosby on my team that has nothing to do with the kind of hockey player he is. And that's marketing. If my team was in Canada it wouldn't be such a big deal, because Canadians don't much care if someone is from Europe as long as he can play hockey. But in the United States, I don't care how good a European hockey player is, you're never going to get as much marketing bang out of him as you can from a North American. Even though Ovechkin seems to have the more engaging personality of the two, it doesn't matter.

Stop for a moment and try to name the most successfully marketed European hockey player ever in America? Hmmm. Still thinking? Me too.

Give me Crosby—both on and off the ice.

90.
There's nothing hockey fans enjoy more than sitting back and rehashing the exploits of some of the National Hockey League's all-time great teams. But how about the other extreme? Bob gives you his take on the worst teams of all time.

THE NATIONAL HOCKEY LEAGUE'S expansion from six to 30 teams brought a lot of things to the game. And one of those was a chance to watch some really, really awful hockey teams endure some painful seasons. The 1992–93 Ottawa Senators, 1974–75 Washington Capitals and 1972–73 New York Islanders come to mind as just some of the woeful expansion teams that rarely won a period, much less a game.

But what about the teams that couldn't use expansion as an excuse for futility? The ones that mismanaged themselves right into the toilet for no other reason than crappy coaching, crappy players, crappy management or all of the above?

Here are my picks for the worst NHL teams of the post-expansion era that had no business being this bad.

5. 1995–96 OTTAWA SENATORS
(82 games, 18-59-5, 41 points, 191 GF, 291 GA)
By its fourth year of existence, no team can still blame expansion for a last-place finish. And yet the Ottawa Senators in 1995–96 managed to make it four years running as the worst team in hockey. That season was actually Ottawa's best to date. The young Senators teased their fans into thinking things would be better, beating Hartford by a 5–0 score on November 2 to move to 6–5 on the season. And with a new arena about to open up, there was actual optimism in Ottawa for a change. But after that victory they went 2–32–1 over their next 35 games, including losses in their first four home dates at the new Palladium.

The only bright spot was rookie Daniel Alfredsson, who won the Calder Trophy with a team-leading 26 goals, providing a glimpse of better days ahead for the Senators.

4. 1983-84 PITTSBURGH PENGUINS
(80 games, 16-58-6, 38 points, 254 GF, 390 GA)

The 1983–84 Penguins may not have accomplished much in the standings, but they did more to advance the cause of the franchise than any other edition of this team.

By finishing last overall, these Penguins made Pittsburgh a big winner for years to come by earning (few would disagree) the top pick in the 1984 draft and the right to select Mario Lemieux.

Among the few positives for this team was Mike Bullard's 51-goal season. The drop-off from there, however, was steep on a club that included an aging Rick Kehoe and a young Marty McSorley.

The Penguins somehow dressed 48 players during that woeful season, more than two teams' worth, but nothing worked. Of those 48, only three—Bob Errey, Phil Bourque and Troy Loney—were around for the Stanley Cup years.

3. 1973-74 CALIFORNIA GOLDEN SEALS
(78 games, 13-55-10, 36 points, 195 GF, 342 GA)

Craig Patrick is a member of one of hockey's royal families, and he has enjoyed more than his share of success over the years as an executive with the 1980 U.S. Olympic team and the Pittsburgh Penguins during their Cup years.

But his playing days with the 1973–74 California Golden Seals stand somewhat apart.

Of all the terrible teams the ill-fated franchise iced in its brief history in northern California, the 1973–74 edition hit rock bottom. Budding star Reggie Leach had 22 goals and 24 assists before being shipped to Philadelphia and winning a

Stanley Cup the following season. Poor Gilles Meloche carried the lion's share of the work in goal, enduring a 9–33–5 record in 47 games and posting a 4.24 goals-against average while backstopping one of hockey's most porous defence units. How great was the gap between best and worst teams in hockey that season? Consider that the Philadelphia Flyers and Chicago Blackhawks each allowed 164 goals; the Seals let in 342. That's a difference of better than 2 goals a game. The Seals won two games after February 6 that season, suffering through 10 games from that point forward in which they allowed at least six goals.

When head coach Fred Glover resigned, Marshall Johnston retired as a player and went behind the bench for the final 21 games, going 2–16–3 in his coaching debut.

2. 1983-84 NEW JERSEY DEVILS
(80 games, 17-56-7, 41 points, 231 GF, 350 GA)

The New Jersey Devils finished three points higher than Pittsburgh in the standings, thus missing out on the chance to draft Mario Lemieux, but it's hard to describe this team as truly better than the Penguins. They just weren't as good at being bad, and therefore ended up with Kirk Muller as the No. 2 pick the next spring.

Defenceman Ken Daneyko, who made his NHL debut that season, could be excused if he failed to foresee the three Stanley Cups he would eventually win with New Jersey. Mel Bridgman led the Devils in goals that season with 23 (Pittsburgh, by comparison that same season, had three players with more goals than Bridgman). Aging veterans Chico Resch and Ron Low split the goaltending, combining for 95 appearances in an 80-game schedule, meaning there were 15 instances where one replaced the other in mid-game.

The Devils were looking good in the race to the bottom of the standings and the right to draft Lemieux, until they blew it by going 5–4–1 during a stretch of games from February 14 to March 6. Over the same span, the Penguins went 2–8–1, thus moving ahead in the Alphonse-and-Gaston sweepstakes for good. Although the Devils won just one game after March 6, it was a case of too little, too late to earn the prize.

Were the Devils and Penguins really in a battle to get Lemieux? Consider that after March 6, the two teams combined to go 3–21–1 to season's end. You decide. The Penguins may have finished last, but I think the Devils were worse.

1. 1989-90 QUEBEC NORDIQUES
(80 games, 12-61-7, 31 points, 240 GF, 407 GA)

Guy Lafleur left New York for his home province to join Peter Stastny, Michel Goulet and sophomore Joe Sakic with the Nordiques. What could go wrong? Everything.

The 1989–90 Quebec Nordiques are unquestionably the hands-down winners among post-expansion non-expansion losers. This was a team full of underachievers, whose best players were either years past their prime or years away from reaching it.

Ron Tugnutt, Greg Millen and Stephane Fiset were among the seven goalies the Nordiques used that season as they allowed 407 goals, 48 more than the next-worst total in the league that season. Sergei Mylnikov, Mario Brunetta, Scott Gordon and John Tanner all found their ways into games on a team whose goals-against average was 5.09.

After scoring 62 points in 62 games, Stastny was mercifully traded to New Jersey late in the season, while Goulet was shipped to Chicago. That only weakened an absolutely dreadful team and contributed to Quebec closing the season by winning just one of its final 17 games.

Joe Sakic somehow managed his first 100-point season, finishing with 39 goals and 63 assists. Lafleur, at age 38, played just 39 games but still finished fifth in team scoring with 12 goals and 22 assists.

The Nords proved that a team full of high draft picks doesn't assure greatness. Quebec had 11 players who had been taken higher in their respective draft years than Sakic (who went 15th overall in 1987): Michel Petit, Lafleur, Joe Cirella, Lucien DeBlois, Bryan Fogarty, Brian Lawton, Craig Wolanin, Everett Sanipass, Curtis Leschyshyn, Daniel Dore and Robert Picard. That many top picks on such a horrid team is just one more thing that made the Nords one of a kind.

91. The National Hockey League has some terrible hockey markets and some great ones. The best are places where everyone knows the game, knows the league and follows hockey at all levels. Well, hockey may be Canada's game, but Bob says the best all-around fans in hockey aren't found north of the border.

IT HAS ALWAYS been assumed that if you want to find the best hockey fans in the world, you should look somewhere in Canada. After all, Canada invented the game. Canadians love it. And in many parts of the country they eat, breathe and sleep hockey.

All of which is true.

But the best hockey fans in the world aren't found anywhere in Canada. They're in Minnesota. That's right, the State of Hockey.

You see, being a hockey fan means more than just the willingness to line up like a bunch of sheep for NHL games at exorbitant ticket prices. If that was the criterion, the debate would start and end with the blind loyalty of Toronto hockey fans.

But true hockey fans are those who celebrate and appreciate the game at all levels, not just professional hockey. They're those who truly love the sport and aren't just there because it's the thing to do or the place to be seen. They're the fans who support their NHL team, win or lose, but who still love the game when the glitz and glare isn't there.

Well, sorry, Canada, but this one isn't even close.

The NHL's expansion map of the past 15 years depicts a wasteland of half-filled buildings and places where the sport is buried behind every other form of entertainment. But one thing the league got right was in going back to Minnesota, where the Wild have tapped into the hockey madness that runs through and around the Twin Cities area.

Here's a team that, through its first six seasons, reached the playoffs just twice, but has sold out every home game in club history—regular season, playoffs *and* preseason. The Wild has 16,500 season-ticket holders and more than 7,500 in the Wild Warming House, the waiting list for season-ticket holders.

Of course, waiting lists aren't uncommon in Minnesota. They have them for college and high school hockey, too.

Of the five Division I NCAA hockey programs in Minnesota, four of them consistently rank among the top 20 in attendance, including the University of Minnesota Golden Gophers, who play to more than 10,000 a game with waiting lists for those who can't get in.

But where you really get a sense of how people in the Minneapolis–St. Paul area feel about hockey is the attendance for high school games. Here's a place where it's not unusual to see a couple of thousand fans turn out for a high school game, especially when one of those tradition-steeped rivalries is being contested.

And when the annual state high school championship is played each year in St. Paul at the Xcel Energy Center, they put more than 125,000 people through that building in four days.

In fact, if you want to attend the high school championship weekend, you can start by putting your name on the waiting list.

Minnesotans know, love and support their hockey unlike any fans in the United States. And the passion, energy and enthusiasm for the sport at each level dwarfs anything you'd find north of the border.

They even have their own answer to the CBC's beloved *Hockey Day in Canada*. Except that instead of televising three National Hockey League games, as in *Hockey Day*, the Minnesota version on the local Fox Sports station features a marquee high school matchup, a college game, and finally, a Minnesota Wild game.

And here's something else to consider about the loyalty and passion of Minnesota hockey fans. Unlike Canada, where, aside from Toronto, none of the Canadian NHL teams has competition from the National Basketball Association, Major League Baseball or the National Football League, Minnesotans have access to them all.

And so it's not as if their passion for hockey is rooted in the fact it's simply the biggest thing in town. Because it's not. But Canadians could sure learn a few things about supporting their game from a market that didn't even have an NHL team a decade ago.

The best of the rest:

2. Ottawa. The Senators sell out virtually every game, while the junior Ottawa 67's and Gatineau Olympiques also thrive.

3. Detroit. One of the few American cities where people know the history of the game and you can feel the presence of hockey. And the Red Wings have actually been the most popular team in town at times. Junior hockey in suburban Plymouth and college hockey in Ann Arbor (40 miles west) are well supported.

4. Calgary. Flames attendance dipped during the lean years, but its fans have consistently made junior hockey's Hitmen one of the country's top draws.

5. Vancouver. Canucks fans have stayed loyal through years of disappointment and have rallied around junior hockey as well.

WHAT? NO TORONTO OR MONTREAL?

They may represent the most storied hockey rivalry in Canada, but fans in Toronto and Montreal refuse to acknowledge hockey outside of the NHL. The university teams in both places are ignored, playing before puny crowds all season long. And efforts to drum up support for junior hockey have either failed or struggled.

The Montreal Rocket franchise in the Quebec Major Junior Hockey League lasted four seasons before packing up and moving to Prince Edward Island for the 2003–04 season. In Toronto, only the suburban Oshawa Generals have a decent following. Attendance for the area's other three teams—Brampton, Mississauga and Toronto St. Michael's—has been lousy. Even the baby Leafs, the Marlies, haven't drawn flies since relocating to downtown Toronto from Newfoundland for the 2005–06 season, placing near the bottom of the American Hockey League in attendance, behind or near such hockey hotbeds as San Antonio and Norfolk.

People may line up for the right to pay hundreds of dollars to watch the Leafs or Habs. But just try getting anyone in Toronto or Montreal to pay for any other brand of hockey. Which is why there's no way either of these cities make my list.

OR EDMONTON?

They're still in love with the glory days and can't stop coming up with excuses for why they haven't won a Cup since 1990. And any city in Canada where Gary Bettman gets a standing ovation can't convince me it's home to the best fans in hockey.

92. Hockey is a game with endless possibilities and very few boundaries for what can occur. But Bob says there are some events and achievements

that have become part of hockey history, never to be seen again.

ONE OF THE best ways to understand where a sport is today is to look at its history.

Reflect on some of the remarkable accomplishments in the National Hockey League's past and you'll surely come across a few things that would be hard to imagine today.

Sometimes it's because the game or the business has changed. And sometimes it's because no player or team has come along since that can compare in any way.

"Never again" are words that should be thrown around carefully in the sports world. But there are some things in hockey I'm quite sure we will never see again. I mentioned during my chapter on the greatest dynasties that that phenomenon is long gone in the NHL. Here are my arguments for other things hockey fans shouldn't hold their breath waiting to witness once more.

A player playing until age 52. During the 1979–80 season, Gordie Howe suited up for 80 games with the Hartford Whalers, scoring 15 goals and adding 26 assists.

Howe's illustrious NHL career began in 1946. Which is astounding when you consider that he was able to play professionally in the best league in the world 35 years later.

But Gordie Howe was one of kind, both as an athlete and in terms of the hockey world in which he lived.

Howe played six of his final seven pro seasons in the World Hockey Association, which was a step down from the NHL. And his final NHL season was the first after four former WHA teams merged with the NHL to form a 21-team league. That season was probably the lowest point in terms of the dilution of NHL talent. In a little over a decade, the league had grown to three and a half times its previous size, and the influx of American and European players hadn't really begun yet.

I don't believe for a minute that Gordie Howe would be able to earn a job at age 52 in today's NHL. It's just too fast and competitive, and the players are all in unbelievable physical condition. None of which takes away from what Howe managed, no matter when he did it. But it does make it highly unlikely we'll see it happen again.

Teams with astounding numbers of penalty minutes. In 1991–92, the Buffalo Sabres had not one, not two, but three players who eclipsed 300 minutes in penalties, en route to an NHL team record of 2,713.

The only way a team could amass that number of penalty minutes is if a large percentage of them happened to be acquired through offsetting fighting or roughing penalties, or misconducts that don't cause teams to play shorthanded.

But in the modern NHL, players who specialize in fighting don't often get enough ice time to rack up the numbers of fighting majors that guys like Rob Ray and Gord Donelly used to. The modern goon is likely to see only five or six minutes of ice time per night—on his best nights. And no team is going to have two or three guys like that taking regular or semi-regular shifts. Goons also tend to take their share of slashing, hooking and cross-checking penalties, which would be a killer these days because of the way power plays dominate the game.

In 2005–06 there were only three players in the entire league who topped 200 minutes: Sean Avery (257), Brendan Witt (209) and Chris Neil (204). And Avery scored 15 goals, including three on the penalty kill. In 2006–07, only Ben Eager of Philadelphia hit that plateau, with 233.

Playing like the '91–92 Sabres today would simply be a recipe for disaster.

Astounding unbeaten streaks. In 1979–80, the Philadelphia Flyers went 35 games without a loss. In 1977–78, the Montreal Canadiens went 28 games without a loss. The Habs of 1976–77 went 34 games without losing at home.

And in 1974–75, they went 23 games on the road without dropping one.

All of these sorts of records are safe for eternity because of overtime and the shootout. For instance, during Philadelphia's streak in 1979–80, the Flyers managed 10 tie games. You've got to think that with overtime and shootouts, the Flyers probably weren't going to end up on the right side of every one of those contests. Add in the fact that parity has levelled the playing field to get rid of superteams, and it's even less likely we'll ever see the kinds of unbeaten streaks that used to tantalize the imagination.

A goaltender playing 502 consecutive games. Glenn Hall was one of the greatest goaltenders in hockey history, with a career that spanned from the mid-1950s through the expansion era, ending after the 1970–71 season. Most remarkable, however, was his streak of playing every minute of every regular-season game for 502 consecutive contests (552 including playoffs), a string that spanned eight seasons. There are workhorse goaltenders in the game today, but even a guy like Martin Brodeur takes a night off now and then—his career high is 78 out of 82 games. Of course, back when Hall set his mark, a season was only 70 games long, there was a lot less travel, and in his early days teams didn't even dress backups. These days, beyond the more intense travel schedule, teams simply don't want to risk pushing a guy too hard and causing an injury. The best goaltenders in the NHL represent huge economic investments for their teams. Which is why even the best guys are told to take a seat about once every 10 games or so.

A skater playing 964 consecutive games. Doug Jarvis accomplished this feat over a 12-year span with three different teams, ending in October of 1987. But no one has come close in years. Steve Larmer got to 883 games, but that ended back in 1993. And Mark Recchi got to 570 nearly a decade ago. The game today is played with bigger players, travelling at higher speeds, which makes it nearly impossible not to get dinged in some way over the course of a couple of seasons. With longer travel and an 82-game season, it only makes sense for guys to sit out every now and then when they don't feel quite right. In the old days, going under the knife meant kissing the rest of the season goodbye, so players would often try to play through the pain until the off-season. Now, medical technology allows players the option of taking a month off for minor surgery and being back on the ice without missing a beat. Hockey's still a sport where playing hurt is part of the call of duty. But not to the extent it used to be.

93. Some have gone to jail. Others we've hardly known. And more than you can count have acted only with self-interest in mind. Bob ranks the worst owners in recent National Hockey League history.

THERE'S NO TOPIC quite so rich as that of ownership in the National Hockey League.

The business of hockey, particularly during the past quarter century, has been the business of selling teams, either through the hatching of expansion franchises or by owners looking to cash in on the notion that NHL hockey is about to become a national phenomenon in the United States.

There have been kooks, crooks, liars, misers and guys who have spent like there was no tomorrow.

The worst of them have ruined hockey in some cities where there actually was a significant following for the sport. Then there are the nut cases, the guys who were in and out of the sport just long enough to have done something so bizarre that they leave behind their own little legacy.

With those criteria in mind, here are my nominations for the worst owners in the NHL's post-expansion era.

10. Charlie Finley. Most people remember him for his baseball days, but Finley also made a brief foray into hockey. He bought the struggling California Golden Seals and decided, having outfitted his Oakland A's baseball team in white shoes, that white skates would looky dandy, too. They didn't. But they were hardly the worst thing about the Seals. It was all enough to make Finley sour on hockey by his fourth season, and he sold the last-place team back to the league midway through the 1973–74 campaign.

9. Art Williams. Williams had a short but memorable time in hockey, owning the Tampa Bay Lightning from 1998 to 1999. The former high school football coach and one-time owner of the Canadian Football League's Birmingham Barracudas had a thick southern drawl that made him seem even more of an outsider to hockey than he already was. Williams brought his football mentality to hockey, taking every loss as if it was the end of the world and trying to fire up his troops with inspirational speeches that went over like lead balloons. But he'll best be remembered for draft day 1998, when he referred to first-overall pick Vincent Lecavalier as the "Michael Jordan of hockey." A year later, he sold the team, after absorbing too much in the way of losses and heartache.

8. Charles Wang. There's not much worse than a hockey owner who thinks he knows the game but doesn't have a clue. How else could one explain Charles Wang's consistent backing of general manager Mike Milbury, from the time he bought the New York Islanders in 2000 through the end of the 2005–06 season. Once Milbury moved aside to another front-office position, Wang hired Neil Smith, who lasted all of 40 days before being replaced with the team's backup goalie, Garth Snow. Goalies seem to be a favourite of Wang's. He once wanted to employ a sumo wrestler to play goal. Then he opted for Rick DiPietro and his 15-year, $67.5 million contract.

7. Howard Baldwin. Baldwin gets my vote because he's the opposite of all those tightwad owners: a guy who spent and spent and spent on players until he had run his team straight into the ground. Baldwin paid out a $48 million contract to Jaromir Jagr in 1997 and then filed for bankruptcy a year later. A *year* later! If you want to know why the Pittsburgh Penguins were in such disarray during the early part of this decade, just go back to the owner who won a pair of Stanley Cups in the early 1990s and kept the bankroll going trying to make it happen again.

6. Norm Green. There's got to be a special place on this list for anyone who couldn't make NHL hockey work in Minnesota. Green bought the North Stars in 1990, calling Minnesota a "hockey entrepreneur's dream," then claimed to be losing millions before departing for a sweetheart deal in Dallas. Hatred towards Green spawned an industry of T-shirt production denouncing the Canadian real estate developer who became known as "Norm Greed." Green's attempts at charm also got him into trouble in Minnesota. As part of a harassment lawsuit settled out of court, Green admitted to giving unsolicited kisses to female employees and commenting on their makeup, diets and appearance. He claimed he didn't know the behaviour was inappropriate because he was Canadian. Green may have been a bad owner and a poor ambassador for Canadian office etiquette, but he was no dummy. Five years after buying the Minnesota North Stars for $31 million in 1990, he flipped them, as the Dallas Stars, to Tom Hicks for $84 million.

5. Bruce Firestone. He's a folk hero in Ottawa for leading the bid that landed the Senators without actually having the money to pay the NHL's $50 million franchise fee. Though he lasted just one season as owner, Firestone achieved notoriety when he was penalized for openly suggesting that his team was throwing a game to ensure the first pick of the draft and the privilege of selecting Alexandre Daigle. Now, intentionally losing the 82nd game of the schedule during a season in which you've won only 10 contests ain't quite like the Black Sox scandal. (And, really, since the prize was Daigle, no harm, no foul.) But it gets him on my list.

4. Peter Pocklington. It's fair to say that nothing Peter Pocklington did before The Trade matters. By selling Wayne Gretzky, the game's greatest player, as part of a deal in which he collected $15 million in cash, he entered the class of one of the great lowlife sports owners. Pocklington claimed to have consistently lost money on the Oilers, but fans always believed it was a cash cow used to offset losses from his other businesses. Nor was he shy about putting the gun to the head of local officials every time he wanted something, threatening on various occasions to yank his team out of town. Had Pocklington had his way, the Oilers would have moved to Houston after he sold the team to a Texas buyer in 1997 in a deal that fell through only because of a binding relocation agreement. As for the Gretzky deal, even Pocklington couldn't deny he'd screwed the fans. "As a business deal, a hockey deal, [trading Gretzky] was good for Wayne, good for his family, good for everyone other than the fans in Edmonton," Pocklington told *The Globe and Mail*'s Allan Maki in 2003. "I understand how they feel, but life goes on."

3. Jeremy Jacobs. Turning a good hockey market into a backwater is quite an accomplishment, but Jacobs has managed to do it. Since Jacobs bought the Boston Bruins in 1975, it's been all downhill, with the owner always taking an active hand in what's done—or, more importantly, not done. Charging top dollar for your product while refusing to spend top dollar on talent is a sure way to earn the scorn of your fans. During the lockout, Jacobs was among those insisting the work stoppage was about rolling back ticket prices. Then he jacked Bruins ticket prices up, some as high as 50 percent, within a year of the lockout's ending. He has trotted former general manager and president Harry Sinden out to take his bullets for three decades. Then he addressed the 73-year-old's stepping down in 2006 this way in comment to the Boston *Globe*: "Statistics tell me that men over 70 don't live as long as men over 40 . . . I'm not looking for him to go anywhere, but he's looking at the clock, same as everyone. He can tell time, like everyone."

These days, his son Charles runs the team. This guy was a toddler when the Bruins last won a Cup. Not exactly an inspiration to the market, or to the players.

2. Harold Ballard. If it had been possible to kill interest in the Toronto Maple Leafs, Harold Ballard would have found a way to do it. But it isn't, and Ballard knew it, which is why he was happy to alienate everyone associated with the club—players, coaches, fans—and still count his nickels from one full house after another. Ballard was cheap when it came to putting together his hockey staff, refused to embrace the club's history, including former players, and grew resentful of whatever current players drew the fans' affection, including Darryl Sittler, Tiger Williams and Dave Keon. Ballard was a misogynist and a tyrant who ran the Leafs based on whims. He couldn't even fire a coach properly, dismissing Roger Neilson in midseason and then having to hire him back when he couldn't find a replacement. Neilson refused to go for Ballard's idea of taking the bench after his firing with a bag over his head. Of course, there were plenty of bags over heads at Maple Leaf Gardens during Ballard's reign, one of the sorriest in hockey history.

1. Bill Wirtz. How bad of an owner do you have to be to virtually kill one of the great hockey markets of the Original Six era? By dint of that accomplishment alone, the late Chicago Blackhawks owner Bill Wirtz gets my nod as hockey's worst owner of all time. This was a guy who once fired coach Billy Reay by having a note slipped under his door on Christmas Eve. This was a guy who ran a front office that changed coaches and GMs so often that no one was sure who was running the team. This was a guy who couldn't find a way to get his team into the playoffs at a time when most other big-market teams were taking advantage of soaring payrolls to stay competitive. Wirtz became owner of the Chicago Blackhawks in the early 1950s, and carried on living in the 50s until his death in 2007. In an age that is all about competing for exposure and using the media to your advantage, Wirtz steadfastly refused to air Blackhawk home games on television, agreeing to five local telecasts for the first time during the 2006–07 season. That, combined with Wirtz's renowned reluctance for investing in players or adequate hockey staff, turned his team into a laughingstock.

How bad were things in Chicago under Wirtz? Heck, the National Lacrosse League and WNBA teams often got more attention than this once-proud franchise. All of which is why, when *ESPN The Magazine* rated the worst owners in all of professional sports in 2004, Wirtz was the runaway winner.

This is the city that has consistently supported the Cubs and White Sox, even though those teams have had just one World Series win between them in the past 90 years. And yet those same fans couldn't put up with Wirtz, whose legacy is turning one of the NHL's once-proud markets into just another American one where the NHL struggles to get noticed.

94.

August 9, 1988, is a day that will never be forgotten in Canada. But on the day Wayne Gretzky was traded to Los Angeles, Canadian hockey fans comforted themselves by suggesting it was at least good for hockey. Bob disagrees.

THERE'S A WHOLE LOT about the National Hockey League today that doesn't make any sense at all.

Here is a league that is bloated to 30 teams, has no national presence in the United States and has half its teams shovelling money to those in places where teams can't sell tickets.

The league's performance in the Sun Belt is an embarrassment, one for which the NHL is constantly making up excuses and was willing to shut down the game in 2004–05 to preserve.

So, who do we blame? Well, how about Wayne Gretzky? Or if not Gretzky himself, then the men who engineered the trade that moved him to Los Angeles in August of 1988 and set off a series of events the NHL is still trying to sort out.

In the late 1980s, little was wrong with the NHL except that, as a business, it was stagnant. The great expansion wave had come and gone, leaving the business of hockey largely unchanged despite spreading its wings into 21 markets. But the NHL hadn't added a team since the four former World Hockey Association clubs joined before the 1979–80 season, and three of those were in Canada. In fact, by adding Hartford and subtracting Atlanta when the Flames moved to Calgary for the 1980–81 season, the NHL's American presence had remained the same since Washington and the New York Islanders were added for 1972–73.

All that changed the day Gretzky was traded and became the catalyst for everything that followed.

The game's greatest player had been a superstar his entire career. But as long as he was winning Cups in someplace called Edmonton, the NHL could only leverage his star power so far.

But get him to Los Angeles, and the potential would be unlimited.

Gretzky arrived with the aura of the game's one true superstar, an athlete considered the equivalent of Michael Jordan in basketball or Pele in soccer. And while Americans still might not have been able to understand the concept of offside, they understood greatness and what it meant to be in the glow of stardom.

A sport that had always been marginalized in Los Angeles was suddenly a marquee attraction, playing before sellout crowds. Gretzky's friends included the rich and the famous, with movie stars dotting the seats around the lower bowl each night.

Out of that spectacle grew a vision of the NHL as the big-time attraction that could stand alongside any other form of entertainment. But it was all a mirage.

What was really a celebration of one guy was mistaken for a love affair with hockey in general. People thought they saw something that wasn't really there. But, for the moment, it was powerful and it was real. And the NHL was able to harness its power, sell a vision, and change the landscape dramatically.

Just consider how much the NHL changed within the decade after Gretzky's trade to Los Angeles. At the time of the deal, the league had no penetration into the Sun Belt beyond Los Angeles. Yet by 1998 there were teams in San Jose, Anaheim, Tampa Bay, Miami, Raleigh and Nashville, with Atlanta soon to follow. Disney and Blockbuster came to play, while the business grew beyond the means of such places as Quebec City and Winnipeg.

Franchise values soared, as did salaries, ticket prices and everything else associated with the NHL. American network television became interested, and hockey actually started to surface in American popular culture like never before.

Everyone, it seemed, was scrambling to find a way to harness or keep up with the unprecedented growth in the game.

All of which set the NHL on course to what became its primary business during the 1990s: selling franchises to Americans. There was no shortage of buyers, all of whom were riding the momentum set off by Gretzky in L.A. In Number 99, the NHL finally had a name to hang its identity on.

Gretzky made $2.8 million his first year in L.A. But Kings owner McNall rewarded his most prized possession with a new deal worth $25.5 million over three years, making him the highest-paid player in all of professional sport. The result of such a staggering leap in the game's top salary gave leverage to every other NHL player and fuelled the salary boom that ratcheted the cost of labour upward until the lockout.

And through it all, the NHL couldn't stop itself. It kept expanding and expanding, hatching team after team cobbled together from the league's scrap heap of players, pocketing expansion fees that were immediately ploughed back into player salaries.

The new teams were short on talent and therefore turned to clutch-and-grab hockey in order to stay competitive night after night. And the league was loath to crack down—in part because it wanted its newest teams to succeed and keep the momentum building.

It all happened so fast that no one had a grip on the steering wheel. Even when the owners shut down the game during the 1994–95 season, it was their resolve to keep the party rolling that ultimately led them to sign a somewhat flawed agreement.

The only problem was that Gretzky couldn't play forever. And so, by the mid-1990s, with his skills in decline and his prime benefactor, Bruce McNall, on his way to jail, all of the momentum created by the Gretzky trade began to subside.

The business of sports is one where growth has to be sustainable. And when it's not, the process of receding, of getting smaller, is ugly.

So much of the NHL's hope and promise was predicated on one player that what was to come was inevitable. Gretzky faded, the game faded and every vital sign in the United States started to slip. The momentum was reversing.

In Gretzky's wake the game returned to what it had always been, only now it was overextended in all areas. The Sun Belt teams have become Wayne Gretzky's welfare children, each with its hand out, begging for survival through revenue sharing from those in actual hockey markets.

By the time the game shut itself down prior to the start of the 2004–05 season, nearly every problem hockey faced could be traced to the Gretzky trade. From the clutch-and-grab style that stifled the game, to the salary inflation that had some teams on the brink, to the massive disparity in revenues between teams in good hockey markets and those where the NHL never should have been in the first place, it could all be traced back to August 9, 1988.

So, how would the NHL look today if Wayne Gretzky had finished his career as an Edmonton Oiler? Well, perhaps very much as it did the day of that infamous trade: a smaller league, with seven or eight teams in Canada and others confined to places where people actually like hockey. In other words, it would be much, much better than what we have today.

95. Shootouts are apparently here to stay. If that's so, says Bob, let's at least find a way to appropriately reward the way the game is supposed to be won.

HOCKEY IS A 60-MINUTE GAME. It's not a 65-minute game and it's not a skills competition.

Yet the way the NHL hands out points these days almost encourages teams to play for overtime. It doesn't reward teams that get the job done in regulation time. More and more, you see teams merely playing to get to overtime where they can be assured of taking at least one point home.

And while that's bad enough, the notion of allowing the game to go beyond overtime to a shootout and then awarding the winning team the same two points in the standings as for a win in regulation time drives me crazy.

If the shootout is here to stay, then the NHL needs at least to diminish its impact on the standings. Right now, teams can make the playoffs by virtue of their success in an event that involves a huge amount of luck and bears no resemblance to the game itself. And that's blatantly stupid.

The NHL needs to put some value back in a 60-minute win and reward teams that win games the way they were meant to be won.

Under what I call the 4–3–2–1 system (ingeniously named, don't you think?), the NHL would award four points to any team that wins a game within regulation time, three points if it wins a game during the five-minute overtime period and two points if it wins in a shootout. The team that loses in overtime or a shootout would still get its one point in the standings for achieving a tie in regulation time. But this system would diminish the value of that point in the standings and recognize that games are supposed to be won in regulation time.

This system acknowledges every way there is to win a hockey game and assigns an appropriate value to each. It also protects the heritage of hockey, since teams have always been awarded the single point for a regulation tie.

It's true that, under this system, a team could still theoretically lose all 82 games in overtime and end up with 82 points (just as it could now.)

But with the reward for losing in overtime or the shootout just one quarter of that for winning a game within three periods—instead of one half, as is currently the case—the impact of all those shootout or overtime losses is much, much less.

This method protects the integrity of the 60-minute game by giving teams the incentive to push for victory within three periods. Would it change strategies? Probably. And you could be sure it would during the final few weeks of the regular season, when teams are pushing for that four-point win to catch or stay ahead of those teams they're battling in the standings.

Just imagine how the standings would shake out on a night when some teams come away with four points, others come away with nothing and others come away with two or three.

But best of all, the 4–3–2–1 system all but eliminates the chance for teams to ride up the standings because of the shoot-out, despite having fewer wins in regulation time than others.

Here's a look at how the 4–3–2–1 system would have changed the final 2005–06 standings.

EASTERN CONFERENCE

ACTUAL		4–3–2–1 SYSTEM	
Ottawa	113	Ottawa	211
Carolina	112	Carolina	196
New Jersey	101	Philadelphia	176
Buffalo	110	Buffalo	198
Philadelphia	101	New Jersey	171
NY Rangers	100	NY Rangers	170
Montreal	93	Montreal	166
Tampa Bay	92	Tampa Bay	160
Toronto	90	Toronto	159
Atlanta	90	Atlanta	157
Florida	85	Florida	143
NY Islanders	78	NY Islanders	132
Boston	74	Boston	124
Washington	70	Washington	112
Pittsburgh	58	Pittsburgh	96

WESTERN CONFERENCE

ACTUAL		4-3-2-1 SYSTEM	
Detroit	124	Detroit	257
Dallas	112	Dallas	191
Calgary	103	Calgary	189
Nashville	106	Nashville	189
San Jose	99	San Jose	167
Anaheim	98	Anaheim	175
Colorado	95	Colorado	170
Edmonton	95	Vancouver	164
Vancouver	92	Edmonton	157
Los Angeles	92	Los Angeles	157
Minnesota	84	Minnesota	149
Phoenix	81	Phoenix	143
Columbus	74	Columbus	122
Chicago	65	Chicago	106
St. Louis	57	St. Louis	88

Here's how the 4–3–2–1 system would have changed the final 2006–07 standings.

EASTERN CONFERENCE

ACTUAL		4–3–2–1 SYSTEM	
Buffalo	113	Ottawa	195
New Jersey	107	New Jersey	182
Atlanta	97	Carolina	162
Ottawa	105	Buffalo	194
Pittsburgh	105	Pittsburgh	173
NY Rangers	94	Atlanta	162
Tampa Bay	93	Montreal	160
NY Islanders	92	Toronto	159
Toronto	91	NY Rangers	157
Montreal	90	Tampa Bay	156
Carolina	88	NY Islanders	154
Florida	86	Florida	149
Boston	76	Boston	124
Washington	70	Washington	120
Philadelphia	56	Philadelphia	95

WESTERN CONFERENCE

ACTUAL		4-3-2-1 SYSTEM	
Detroit	113	Detroit	206
Anaheim	110	San Jose	204
Vancouver	105	Vancouver	181
Nashville	110	Nashville	197
San Jose	107	Anaheim	193
Dallas	107	Dallas	183
Minnesota	104	Calgary	174
Calgary	96	Minnesota	173
Colorado	95	Colorado	170
St. Louis	81	St. Louis	133
Columbus	73	Edmonton	132
Edmonton	71	Columbus	125
Chicago	71	Chicago	118
Los Angeles	68	Phoenix	117
Phoenix	67	Los Angeles	112

In both seasons since the lockout, the 4–3–2–1 system would have rewarded teams for winning in regulation time and taken away from those that were inappropriately rewarded for success in shootouts. For example, the Edmonton Oilers got into the playoffs in 2005–06 by winning six games in overtime and seven via the shootout. Yes, the Oilers were a great story in the spring of 2006, coming within a game of winning it all. But this notion that they were somehow the product of the NHL's new economic system is bunk. They were a product of the shootout. If you had the same salary cap system but no shootout, the Oilers would have been golfing during the playoffs.

Which would have been fine with me. Because if you can't earn your way into the playoffs by winning during regulation time, or at least overtime, I'm not sure you deserve to be there.

The same thing is true of the 2006–07 standings, where the 4–3–2–1 system would have produced two different division winners and three different playoff teams in the Eastern Conference. The Montreal Canadiens and Toronto Maple Leafs, for example, had 34 and 32 wins, respectively, in regulation time during the regular season. But they both failed to make the playoffs, finishing behind the New York Rangers and Islanders, each with 30 regulation-time wins, and Tampa Bay with 29.

Worse than the Leafs and Canadiens not getting in during was that Carolina—which, like the Leafs, had 34 regulation-time wins—also did not. But unlike Toronto, Carolina doesn't just squeak in under the 4–3–2–1 system. The Hurricanes would go from the outside looking in to the number three seed in the playoffs as the Southeast Division winner.

Carolina won 40 games in either regulation time or overtime during the regular season. And yet, because they never won a shootout, they didn't get a chance to defend their Stanley Cup?

That's crazy. And just one more reason why hockey has to recognize that not all wins are created equal.

96.

Hockey fans love to refer to the days of the Original Six as the golden age of hockey, when every team was loaded with talent. Bob says none of those teams would stand a chance in today's National Hockey League.

WHEN THE TORONTO MAPLE LEAFS won the final Stanley Cup of the Original Six era, they did so with a team that included seven players over the age of 35. It was an era in which players didn't work out year-round, an era in which fitness coaches didn't exist. It was a time when the science of bringing hockey players to their physical peaks was unheard of.

Which are but a few reasons why those Leafs, and any other teams from the Original Six era, would get clobbered in today's NHL, despite the league being five times as big. If those players were transported forward in time to today's NHL, none but the very best and fittest of them would be able to cut it.

This notion that today's NHL is talent-poor compared to the days of the Original Six is simply not true.

Let's start with size. During the 1972–73 season, the average NHL player was 5-foot-11 and weighed 184.5 pounds. That's more than 20 pounds lighter and two inches shorter than the average player on the ice today.

When you combine that advantage in size with the speed of today's players and the shape they are in, there's no comparison at all. I mean, today you have a guy like Zdeno Chara who's 6-foot-9, with a wingspan that covers half the ice, who can also skate and handle the puck. Sure, he's a freak. But there are lots of freaks in today's game, players who combine speed, size, strength and balance like nothing players of 40 years ago ever saw.

There's also a tremendous difference in conditioning. Today's players show up to training camp already in shape. Back in the day, they used training camp to play themselves into shape in the hope that they'd be in peak form by Christmas. But now, after a couple of weeks off at the end of the season, they're back at it with their personal trainers throughout the summer, ready to be graded for fitness levels when training camp opens. Needless to say, they're not smoking cigarettes in the dressing room, either.

Then there are the differences in the way the game is played. In the 1950s and '60s, it was normal for players to take two-minute shifts. These days, most players are out for about 45 seconds. It's an all-out sprint at a much higher tempo than the way the game was once played, when it was a matter of pacing oneself to last the full two minutes. So now let's imagine a player from the 1960s at the end of a two-minute shift competing against a modern-day guy who's been built to go hard for 45 seconds. Imagine the outcome when the smaller and less fit player, out of breath, goes to the boards to battle for the puck against the modern player. No contest.

Then you have the equipment. Hockey sticks didn't even have curved blades until the late 1960s. And there was nothing like the flexibility of today's sticks, which are so light you can barely feel them in your hands. The same thing is true of the skates players wear today, which have undergone a high-tech revolution over the past several decades.

But the biggest improvement in the game might be the area of goaltending. When it comes to equipment, where do you begin? We're talking about guys without masks compared to those decked out in overinflated pads from head to toe.

And 40 years ago there was no science of goaltending. Teams just left goalies alone to figure things out for themselves. Not only does every team these days have a goaltending coach, but the goalies are in better shape today than the forwards were in the 1960s.

The NHL today draws from a far bigger pool of players than it once did. The league in the Original Six era was made up almost exclusively of players from Canada. Today, Canadians make up about half of the NHL, with 17 percent coming from the United States and roughly a third from Europe.

Back in the 1960s, you had a small handful of elite junior teams for development, each of which was the property of an NHL franchise. And while players sometimes stepped into the NHL from other amateur leagues, there were far fewer opportunities for players to develop their skills under the best coaches and against the best competition.

Today, the Ontario, Western and Quebec Major Junior Hockey Leagues consist of 60 teams from coast to coast, all of which are staffed like mini-NHL teams.

Players these days receive far better coaching, from a younger age, than any generation before them. There weren't hockey camps for young players in the 1950s and '60s. They didn't retain agents at age 15 to ensure they got all the help and advice they needed to make it to the next level.

All of those things should be obvious to anyone who has followed hockey over the past four decades. But here's the best proof that today's players are far better than those of the pre-expansion era. It's often argued that the lack of goal scoring in today's NHL demonstrates there's not as much talent in the game as there used to be. That's completely wrong. In fact, historically, goal-scoring goes up when there is a dilution of talent in hockey. It was that way when the NHL first doubled in size from six to 12 teams in 1967. And it was that way again when the league absorbed four World Hockey Association franchises in 1979.

Goal-scoring today is, in fact, about where it was during the end of the Original Six era. Which speaks overwhelmingly to the talent of today's offensive players, who face far better goaltending and much, much tougher defensive play, both in terms of the strategies teams use to defend and the individual defensive skills possessed by players. Yet they're able to produce the same number of goals per game as players did 40 years ago.

Reminisce all you want about the Original Six days, when every team was supposedly loaded with eye-popping talent. It's a myth. Today's NHL has its share of challenges. But a lack of talent for a 30-team league isn't one of them.

97. Canada's greatest hockey province? That's easy. Bob says you need only look to the province that consistently produces NHL players but has never been home to an NHL team.

TAKE A LOOK DOWN the roster of most any National Hockey League team and chances are you'll find at least one player from Saskatchewan.

Then go back through NHL history and start listing off the all-time greats. The delegation from Saskatchewan is headlined by Gordie Howe and includes Max Bentley, Bryan Trottier, Glenn Hall, Eddie Shore and Clark Gillies, to name just a few.

Which is something when you consider that Saskatchewan has the smallest population of any of the six Canadian provinces that regularly produce NHL players.

Examine the population of those provinces next to the numbers of NHL players they produce, and it becomes obvious which one outdoes them all when it comes to turning out players for the top hockey league in the world.

	NUMBER OF NHL PLAYERS*	POPULATION (2006 CENSUS)
Ontario	146	12,160,282
Alberta	67	3,290,350
Quebec	55	7,546,131
British Columbia	40	4,113,487
Saskatchewan	34	968,157
Manitoba	17	1,148,401

* start of 2005–06 season

Let's put it another way. Here's how many NHL players you get for every resident of the province:

Saskatchewan	one NHL player for every 28,475
Alberta	one NHL player for every 49,109
Manitoba	one NHL player for every 67,553
Ontario	one NHL player for every 83,290
British Columbia	one NHL player for every 102,837
Quebec	one NHL player for every 137,202

That is, Saskatchewan turns out 72 percent more NHL players per capita—nearly twice the rate of the next best province and nearly five times as efficiently as the population in Quebec.

And it doesn't end there.

Of the six best NHL-producing provinces, Saskatchewan

has the smallest population, yet has more hockey arenas than any province besides Ontario and Quebec. And with roughly 28,000 registered hockey players, the percentage of the overall population in Saskatchewan that plays organized hockey is significantly higher than that of the other five:

Saskatchewan	2.83 percent
Ontario	2.03 percent
Manitoba	1.99 percent
Alberta	1.79 percent
Quebec	1.17 percent
British Columbia	1.02 percent

Even in girls' and women's hockey, participation rates are highest in Saskatchewan. Here's the percentage of the female population that plays organized hockey in those same six provinces:

Saskatchewan	.78 percent
Ontario	.57 percent
Alberta	.40 percent
British Columbia	.29 percent
Quebec	.14 percent
Manitoba	.09 percent

And when you measure the ratio of NHL players to registered male hockey players in each province, Saskatchewan comes out on top again:

Saskatchewan	1 NHL player for every 710 players
Alberta	1 NHL player for every 782 players
British Columbia	1 NHL player for every 943 players
Manitoba	1 NHL player for every 1,173 players
Ontario	1 NHL player for every 1,502 players
Quebec	1 NHL player for every 1,513 players

So, how does an often economically challenged region of Canada lead the country in hockey participation rates for males and females, as well as efficiency at producing pro players for a sport in which costs are traditionally very high? It's simple.

In much of this country, hockey is a minivan sport. Which means that in order for a youngster to play it, Mom and Dad have to be willing to get up at obscene hours for practices, give up their weekends and invest huge sums of money to keep their kids on skates. Ice time is hard to come by in most major cities, and the costs associated with that ice time—and everything else, for that matter—are extraordinary.

And as for kids being able to get extra time on an outdoor rink or pond, global warming has taken care of that tradition quite nicely in much of this country. It's pretty much over.

But in Saskatchewan, kids are still raised in an environment where hockey is both affordable and accessible, with far more rinks per person than any of the provinces listed above.

That's right: there are still towns in this province where getting ice time isn't a matter of paying for it or booking it weeks in advance. Kids can go down and knock on the door of the guy who's got the keys to the local arena and just go play.

Try that sometime in Toronto or Vancouver.

In much of Saskatchewan, the barriers to playing the game that exist in so much of this country simply aren't there. And in a province where winter sets in around Halloween some years, there are always outdoor options to play the game as well.

Kids who grow up in that part of the country aren't too spoiled to wear hand-me-down equipment. They don't require the best of everything to show off to their friends. These are kids who come from hard-working backgrounds, where you earn everything you keep. And they take that attitude with them every day to the rink.

It's interesting that, during times when some of Canada's NHL teams have come knocking for government support, they've suggested that without a local NHL team, kids might not be so inspired to play the game. I think the example of Saskatchewan puts the lie to that notion once and for all.

As for fan support of hockey in Saskatchewan, the province supports 11 teams in the Saskatchewan Junior Hockey League. And Saskatchewan is the only province that supports five Western Hockey League teams, including Moose Jaw (population 32,000), Prince Albert (34,000) and Swift Current (14,800)—the latter being the smallest market in all of major junior hockey.

It's true that the best players from Saskatchewan aren't always the most naturally gifted players in the game. But I think that's symptomatic of guys who've reached the NHL mostly on guts, just like the player who might just be the most popular Toronto Maple Leaf of all time.

Wendel Clark was right off the farm in Kelvington, Saskatchewan. This is a guy who gave you the sense that he would crawl across broken glass to play the game. He was tough, unspoiled and overcame whatever deficiencies were in his game with pure determination and fearlessness.

Wendel Clark embodied everything that is great about hockey players from Saskatchewan.

The fans loved him. I admired him. And he's just one small part of why, in my mind, there's no doubt where the heart of hockey in this country lies.

98. Every once in a while, someone in hockey will pipe up and suggest that the National Hockey League needs to expand its playoff pool. Bob says there's not a dumber idea out there.

NOT EVERYTHING ABOUT the National Hockey League's expansion to 30 teams has been positive. That is, I know, an understatement.

But the very best thing about the league's growth over the past 15 years is the fact that it hasn't expanded its playoff pool at the same time. And by not doing so, it's managed to put some teeth back into a regular season that used to be meaningless.

Look, nothing was more ridiculous about the NHL during the 1980s than the notion of playing 80 games to eliminate five out of 21 teams. I mean where's the drama in that? Was anyone really going to get themselves worked up over whether the Hartford Whalers were going to make the playoffs? Hockey became not about paying attention to who might finish first. It was all about watching to see who would finish *last*, because that was all that mattered.

And for me, and I suspect a lot of others, that took a lot of the excitement out of the game. Think about it: you'd turn on your television set in January and see that the Oilers were about to play the Flames, and then realize the game was absolutely meaningless because both teams had clinched play-off spots around Halloween.

It was almost as if the NHL played an 80-game exhibition schedule before it got down to business in April.

Now, however, with 16 out of 30 making the playoffs, even some very good teams don't clinch spots until mid-March. And some, like the Vancouver Canucks of 2005–06, don't make the playoffs at all. And that means no more first-round patsies, no more teams that have been sleepwalking through the season being invited to compete for the Stanley Cup.

No more teams like the 1988 Toronto Maple Leafs, who made the playoffs with a record of 21–49–10. Now, predictably, the Leafs bowed out in the first round to Detroit that season. But what if, somehow, they'd managed to get the Cup final? Wouldn't that have completely undermined the entire 80-game exercise the NHL was selling to its fans from October to April?

Yet now that we've finally got some teeth in the regular season, there are calls to open the playoffs up to more teams. I assume that must be so we can hold the Stanley Cup final in July.

Beyond that, it must be so that more fans get a chance to experience playoff excitement. The first problem I have with this idea is that rewarding mediocrity is never good for any sport.

And secondly, the way things are right now, the final month of the season is like playoffs already for teams that are chasing those last few spots. I mean, has there been much in hockey of late that was more exciting than watching the New York Islanders, New York Rangers, Tampa Bay Lightning, Montreal Canadiens, Toronto Maple Leafs and Carolina Hurricanes battle for the final three playoff spots in the Eastern Conference during the final 20 games of the 2006–07 season? This was a race that played out every night for more than a month and wasn't decided until the final game of the year.

And now some people want to destroy that by letting 20 or 24 teams in and having some sort of mini three-game play-in tournament to get down to 16 teams. What a completely stupid idea.

If a team can't make the playoffs in 82 games, there's no need to stretch things out three more games to let them try again.

Look, I'm not convinced it was any stroke of genius that got the NHL to its current playoff situation. But the league shouldn't screw with one of the few positive things to come out of its otherwise ill-conceived expansion.

99. There's nothing more infuriating to fans than a selfish hockey player. You know, the guy who signs his contract and then goes to sleep while his team goes into the tank. Bob wonders what the ultimate team sport would look like if you paid the players based on team play.

HOCKEY PLAYERS LOVE to give credit to their teammates whenever they have success.

Ask any hockey player about the season he's having, why he's scoring more goals—or, in the case of a goalie, why he's winning more games—and it's always about his teammates, the guys in the room.

Until, that is, he gets to salary arbitration or it's time to negotiate a contract, and then it's all about him.

But if hockey players really believe their game is all about playing for each other, about playing as a team and overcoming adversity together, then why aren't they compensated that way?

That's right: the best and fairest economic model for the ultimate team sport would be to base a significant portion of each player's pay on team success. How many nights do you think Alexei Kovalev would take off under this system? I can tell you: none.

And neither would any of the other players known to cruise through some of those midwinter, midweek classics.

It wouldn't cost the owners a dime more in player expenditures than the current system. And the highest-paid players in the game would be decided based on a combination of individual past performance and current team success.

Let me explain.

During 2006–07, NHL owners committed roughly $1.24 billion to player payrolls. In other words, the average NHL team that season spent $41.3 million on players. Under my economic model, every team would have a pre-season salary cap of $20 million. That cap would then rise as the team wins more games. That's because, with every win, the team would be allowed to dip into a league pool and divide the proceeds among the players. At the beginning of the season, there would be $639 million in the kitty—that's the aforementioned $1.24 billion, less $20 million per team.

When it came time for a player to negotiate his contract, players wouldn't be offered a dollar figure; instead, they'd get a percentage of their team's overall player payroll. And the eventual size of that payroll would depend on how the team does during the regular season.

Let's use Tampa Bay's Vincent Lecavalier as an example of how this would work.

During the 2006–07 season, Lecavalier was paid $7.17 million of Tampa Bay's $43.5 million budget. In other words, he earned 16.5 percent of the team's overall player payroll.

Under my system, Lecavalier's contract would state that he is due 16.5 percent of all Tampa Bay Lightning player compensation.

Under a $20 million salary cap, Lecavalier would be guaranteed $3.3 million if the Lightning somehow didn't win a single game during the entire season. However, Lecavalier's salary, and that of every other Lightning player, would grow with each game the team wins during the regular season. Under my system, the winners of each of the 1,230 NHL games in a season would receive $406,504.06 to divide up among themselves, based on the percentages each player negotiated with the team. In other words, based on his being due 16.5 percent of all Lightning player compensation, Lecavalier would earn $67,073.17 for each regular-season game his team wins.

The total pool for regular-season games would amount to $500 million, with another $139 million being awarded to teams that make the playoffs and advance through each round. Playoff compensation would be delivered as follows:

- Each team that makes the playoffs receives an additional $2 million.
- Each team that wins a first-round series receives an additional $4 million.
- Each team that wins a second-round series receives an additional $8 million.
- Each team that wins their conference final receives an additional $10 million.
- And the Stanley Cup winner receives an additional $23 million.

So, to use Vincent Lecavalier as an example, based on his salary negotiated at 16.5 percent:

- Compensation if the Lightning win 30 games and miss the playoffs: $5.31 million
- If the Lightning win 40 games and miss the playoffs: $5.98 million
- If the Lightning win 50 games and lose in the first round: $6.98 million

- If the Lightning win 50 games and lose in the second round: $7.64 million
- If the Lightning win 50 games and lose in the third round: $8.96 million
- If the Lightning win 50 games and lose in the Stanley Cup final: $10.61 million.
- If the Lightning win 50 games and win the Stanley Cup: $14.4 million.

Okay, I know there are all kinds of forces in hockey—starting with the NHL Players' Association—that would fight such a system to the death. But if you wanted to see players try hard every night, if you wanted the money in the sport go to the very best players on the very best teams, which seems fair, then I'm saying that making payrolls dependent on team performance would be the solution.

100. The National Hockey League has been handing out suspensions to deal with player violence for as long as it's been around. Is there any way to make hockey discipline more effective? Bob says it would take just one small change.

IT'S INEVITABLE. Several times during each National Hockey League season, a player does something remarkably stupid to another player.

Sometimes it's an incident that garners attention beyond the hockey world, like Todd Bertuzzi's attack on Steve Moore in March of 2004, or Chris Simon's stick to the face of Ryan Hollweg in March of 2007. Other times it's something less blatant that the league has to deal with. But there's always something.

I've got to say that on the whole, the NHL has made great strides since Colin Campbell became its chief disciplinarian as senior vice-president and director of hockey operations prior to the 1998–99 season.

Under Campbell, the NHL has toughened up its approach to dealing with players who commit ugly acts of violence, handing out four of its longest suspensions to Simon (25 games, 2007), Marty McSorley (23 games, 2000), Bertuzzi (20 games, 2004) and Gordie Dwyer (23 games, 2000).

So while there was a time when it seemed the NHL was completely complicit in the perpetuation of violence on ice, that's no longer the case. Suspending hockey's worst offenders for 20 or 25 games when they've done something stupid is real progress for the NHL. No doubt about it.

But since most of the players who receive long suspensions are marginal anyway (Todd Bertuzzi being the exception), there's no real consequence to the teams.

Suspending goons is not going to get rid of the problem. So, what to do?

The most common suggestion is to make the offenders sit out for as long as the player they injure is off the roster. But that kind of thing is nonsensical—there's just no direct correlation between the degree of violence used by a player and the resulting injury. Sometimes the intended victim dodges a bullet, and other times a player is hurt unintentionally, or on a clean play. The crime is not defined by how badly a guy is hurt.

There is, however, an easy solution if the NHL wants to get serious about ending gratuitous hockey violence—and, more importantly, getting rid of the kinds of players who tend to commit this stuff.

It needs to focus on coaches.

Now, I'm not talking about making coaches subject to league discipline when one of their players slashes somebody too hard and draws a one- or two-game suspension.

I'm talking about the worst stuff, the things that have no business being in the game, and which always seem to be committed by the same types of players over and over again. Coaches need to bear some responsibility when these things happen. Because coaches can prevent them.

That is, if a coach wants to have a Tie Domi or a Dale Purinton or a Brad May on his team, or on the ice at a particular moment, he's got to be accountable for what his protege does when he goes over the boards.

I mean, how in the world do you not suspend or fine former Vancouver coach Marc Crawford for what Todd Bertuzzi did to Steve Moore? Just like Pat Quinn should have been fined or suspended when Tie Domi ambushed Scott Niedermayer with an indefensibly dirty hit during the 2001 playoffs. Just like former Washington coach Terry Murray should have had to take his lumps when Dale Hunter ran Pierre Turgeon into the boards after he'd scored for the New York Islanders during a playoff game in 1993. These were incidents the coaches could have headed off. And if they could have, they *should* have.

In just about any other field, if you're in charge, you take the blame when something goes wrong. NHL coaches shouldn't be let off the hook.

The league got it right when it fined Calgary coach Jim Playfair $25,000 for "a variety of actions" after his team got out of control at the end of a playoff game against Detroit in the first round of 2007.

But why shouldn't Anaheim coach Randy Carlyle have been subject to discipline when one of his guys, Brad May, sucker-punched Minnesota's Kim Johnsson right out of the playoffs the same year?

Coaches need to be more accountable for what their players do on the ice at all times, not just when all hell breaks loose.

The coaches are the only ones with the power to get rid of violence in hockey, because they are the ones who choose the players for their teams, award ice time and control the way players play. So until the league focuses on coaches, the problems associated with violence in hockey are never going to go away.

Players feel as if they're accountable only to themselves and their teammates. And thus, thanks to hockey's ridiculous code of retribution, players occasionally do violent and dangerous things in the name of standing up for their teammates. And the coaches, frankly, are often only too happy to see it happen.

But if coaches were subject to league discipline when one of their players commits an act that clearly has nothing to do with either scoring goals or trying to prevent them, players would become directly accountable to the very people who put them out on the ice in the first place.

Let's put it this way: What kind of leash do you think a player is going to be on once he's cost his coach a suspension or a fine? Hotheads and goons would be stapled to the bench at the first sign of trouble.

And the effect would go much deeper than that. The possibility of league discipline would force coaches to reconsider the value—and potential downside—of having players whose only role is to fight and intimidate. Because, as we all know, those are the players who get in the most trouble.

People are wringing their hands all the time, wondering how to get these guys out of the sport. Well, it's simple. Tie their behaviour to the people who control when and how they play.

This one change wouldn't just reduce the numbers of ugly incidents. It would remove the kinds of players who most often commit them from the game.

It wouldn't mean the extinction of true tough guys, the ones who strike fear into their opponents with bone-crushing hits. It just means that tough guys in hockey would be forced to play the game the way it's meant to be played. I know that's a not a concept the hockey traditionalists will swallow easily.

But is it really that radical? Only in hockey, I suppose.

101. The NHL is so delighted by the success of outdoor games that it's talking about holding one every season. But are they really good for the game? Only at the cash register, says Bob.

I'LL ADMIT I was curious when the National Hockey League played its first open-air game of the modern era in November 2003 between the Montreal Canadiens and Edmonton Oilers. I even watched a bit of it. I'm guessing there were lots of viewers like me who took in five or ten minutes and then decided it was just another hockey game before moving on to something else.

Besides, I couldn't take any more of hearing how only in Canada could such a magical event take place. Especially since the first large-scale outdoor hockey game took place two years earlier at Spartan Stadium in East Lansing, Michigan, when Michigan State hosted the University of Michigan.

And I was back, checking it out a little over four years later when the Pittsburgh Penguins and Buffalo Sabres played at Ralph Wilson Stadium in Buffalo. Same thing. Five minutes here, five minutes there. And with that, I've got to say I've seen enough outdoor hockey to last me the rest of my life. But the folks who run the National Hockey League feel quite differently when it comes to outdoor games. They want more of them, lots more. Like maybe even one a year.

Why? Well of course because this is bringing hockey back to its roots, back to where we all grew up skating on frozen ponds. In fact, you can't watch a minute of one of these outdoor games without hearing some reference to boyhood and dreams and that kind of stuff. So this must be what it's all about, right? Well, unless your childhood hockey involved playing in front of thousands of drunken fans who'd been tailgating hours before the game, I'd say: not exactly.

The real reason the NHL wants to play these games is because they make an awful lot of money. For an owner who's looking at selling out a 60,000 seat stadium, it's like having three or four extra home games without having to pay the players extra. And since the demand to attend these games is so strong, it's not like you've got to scale back ticket prices at all to sell that many. Now, I have no problem with any of this, really. But let's all be clear that this is why these games are being played—they're cash cows.

It's when I hear people saying that these games are going to jumpstart interest in the NHL—especially on American television—that I feel like I want to puke, because the notion that these games are in any way a springboard to something else is totally absurd. If hockey fans like these things then great, have more of them. But don't tell me this is the catalyst that will lead hockey to bigger and better things.

But wait! Didn't the Pittsburgh–Buffalo game on New Year's Day draw the biggest hockey audience on American television since Gretzky's retirement? Yes it did. Which proves my point exactly. When a novelty game, something that is nothing more than the dressing-up of an ordinary mid-season contest, is your biggest television draw in a decade, you've got a problem. I mean what other sport would be boasting that a novelty event outdraws its championship by a mile?

These games are a blip on television and a meaningless one at that. What effect did that Pittsburgh–Buffalo showcase have on ratings later that season on NBC? Virtually none. Because none of the people who'd tuned in to see what a game played in a snowstorm looks like were watching the rest of the season.

Of course the other problem with outdoor games is that they're courting disaster in terms of a possible injury to a star player who is forced to skate on crappy ice. Yes, as the game in Buffalo proved, you can still play a game even in less-than-ideal conditions. But don't you think there were people relieved at the sight of Sidney Crosby skating off under his own power at the end of the game, and not taken from the ice on a stretcher after his blade got stuck in some groove in the ice?

The other question I have is: at what point does this idea tip and stop being a novelty? Is once every four years enough to keep it fresh? How about once every two? Or can they really get away with doing one a year? The NHL had better decide and get it right. Because once the novelty wears off, these outdoor games become just one more ordinary hockey game on TV. And U.S. television audiences have proven time and time again they aren't much interested in those.

102. NHL teams are always in a quandary whenever a successful head coach decides he's had enough and wants to step down. The most obvious thing to do is simply promote an assistant coach to the big job. But Bob says that's the worst idea there is.

WHEN THE MOST successful season in Ottawa Senators history ended in the spring of 2007, Bryan Murray decided he no longer wanted to be a head coach.

And so, despite the fact he seemed well-suited to a team he'd led through two very successful seasons—the second of which ended with Ottawa's first berth in the Stanley Cup final—Murray moved on to the general manager's job. And in hiring a new coach, Murray repeated a mistake that gets made by general managers all the time in hockey. He hired one of his assistant coaches, John Paddock. Now, I know what Murray was thinking. He was figuring that the Senators had been pretty successful with him in control and so the best succession plan was to find someone who coached just like him, thought just like him and shared his ideas about how the game should be played.

What a dumb idea. Dumb because the surest way to ensure failure for any NHL team that's on a good roll is to bump an assistant coach into the top job thinking that the result will be a seamless transition and continued success. So when Paddock was fired in February 2008, forcing Murray to return behind the bench, it was merely the continuation of a pattern seen so many times before where assistant coaches are simply unable to command the respect of their charges once they move into the top job.

It didn't work in Detroit when the Red Wings replaced the legendary Scotty Bowman with assistant Dave Lewis. It didn't work in Calgary when Darryl Sutter stepped aside and handed a very talented Flames squad over to assistant Jim Playfair. And it didn't work in Philadelphia where Bill Barber lasted one season after moving up from assistant coach in 2001–02, or when Tony Granato made the same transition in Colorado or when Mike Kitchen tried it in St.Louis.

The reason is simple. Assistant coaches are generally the good cops on a hockey staff. They work more closely with the players individually than the head coaches do. They're not the ones in charge of overall team discipline and players usually feel they can confide in them more openly. In many ways, they become the players' friends. Which means that, while players may like them, they don't necessarily respect them in a way that players need to respect a head coach.

We've all seen examples in other walks of life where people who were subservient or not your direct boss rise to a position of power. And it's awfully tough for that kind of person to be seen in a different light by those with whom they've worked for years. And in sports, where so much of success is tied to players being willing to follow directions and respond to those in charge it's very tough indeed.

When Murray was looking to replace himself in the summer of 2007 he interviewed the players, of all people, and asked them who they thought the new coach should be. Is it any surprise that the players came out overwhelmingly in favour of Paddock? I mean come on. When you were a kid and your parents asked who you wanted as a babysitter, did you say the one who made you go to bed on time or the one who let you stay up, eat popcorn and watch TV?

No surprise then that Paddock lost his dressing room when goaltender Ray Emery was able to walk all over a coach he didn't respect one bit. That was the beginning of the end for Paddock, who met the same fate as most assistant coaches who take on the big job without changing teams.

Now, there are a few exceptions to this rule but there's also a reasonable explanation for them. At of the end of the 2007–08 NHL season, there were four NHL head coaches who'd been promoted from assistant positions with the same club—Edmonton's Craig McTavish, Chicago's Denis Savard, Philadelphia's John Stevens and Tampa Bay's John Tortorella. Three of those four took over crappy teams and one—McTavish—took over one that was coming off a slightly better than .500 season. And I would argue that it's easier for an assistant coach to move up and take over a crappy team than a good one because at least then he has the freedom to change things up and do things his way to earn some respect. When an assistant takes over from a successful head coach, he's almost beholden to the ideas and methods of that coach and can't really build his own identity. Which is one more reason he doesn't get any respect. It should also be noted that Tortorella and Stevens were assistants for less than one season when they took over, so it wasn't like the players had seen them in a subservient role over a long period of years.

The failure of assistant coaches who take over good hockey teams is one of those hockey truths that just isn't fair. Long-serving, faithful assistant coaches deserve their shot coaching a top team after showing years of loyalty, hard work and devotion. Particularly since they're usually a big part of why a team has been successful in the first place.

But it's much better for everyone involved if they pack a suitcase and get their chance somewhere else.

103.

At the outset of the 2007–08 National Hockey League, the NHL sent a message that it was finally getting tough with players who commit dangerous acts of violence on the ice. But Bob reckons the NHL's sense of justice is still as twisted as ever.

WHEN PHILADELPHIA'S Steve Downie took a vicious run at Ottawa Senator Dean McAmmond during an exhibition game in September 2007, it was like a batting practice fastball for NHL discipline chief Colin Campbell. In Downie, he had a rookie player who wasn't expected to play a big role with Flyers in 07–08, and one who'd arrived in the NHL with a well-earned reputation as a wild man. And so it was easy for Campbell to throw the book at Downie, knowing he would be applauded for doing so. Was Downie's hit among the worst in NHL history? Far from it. But Campbell was supposedly signaling a new era by handing Downie a 20-game suspension, which tied for the fifth-longest in NHL history.

A few weeks later, Campbell got another fat pitch down the middle of the plate when Philadelphia's Jesse Boulerice delivered a cross-check to the face of Vancouver's Ryan Kesler. Boulerice was another marginal player. Easy. Twenty-five games. And then, as if Campbell had ordered it up, along comes Chris Simon, who gets nailed for trying to use his skate blade to injure Pittsburgh's Jarkko Ruutu during a game in December. Again, easy as pie, 30 games, the longest suspension in NHL history.

But I couldn't help but wonder, as I watched these incidents play out, what was going happen when someone who isn't just a fringe player commits an act worthy of severe punishment. Would the standard change? Had the NHL not only decided to deliver harsher suspensions but also committed to giving players equal treatment under its penal code? Of course not.

We all learned that a few months later when Anaheim defenceman Chris Pronger got an eight-game suspension for committing roughly the same act that Simon did a few months earlier. How could this be? Well, surely it must have had to do with Simon being an eight-time offender when in came to NHL suspensions, since repeat offenders normally pay a higher price in all systems of justice. Well, guess what? Pronger was an eight-time offender too. Which is why this was the perfect test case to illustrate that the NHL still refuses to grant equality before the law to its players, the very same right that is fundamental to any fair system of justice. Justice is supposed to be blind but in the NHL who you are seems to matter far more than what you did or how many times you've done it before.

The NHL just can't get past the fact that Pronger was far more valuable to the Ducks than Simon was to the Islanders. But suspensions aren't supposed to be aimed at the team, they're aimed at the player. And yes, Pronger paid a much bigger financial penalty by missing eight games than Simon did by missing 30 games—but so what? Since when is wealth and status supposed to matter in a judicial system? If you steal a car, the judge doesn't go lighter on you just because you happen to be a valuable employee.

What the NHL needs is some strict sentencing guidelines for suspensions and an overhaul of the system that applies them. It needs to take the discipline process out of the hands of Colin Campbell and put it into those of an independent arbitrator, someone whose job it will be to answer two very simple questions: what did you do and have you done it before? There would be no discussion of how much the player will lose in wages or whether he's a good guy in the sport. And there'd be no need to have his team representatives there to lobby for the suspension to be minimized. You'd simply have an arbitrator make a fair decision based on sentencing guidelines prescribed for different acts of violence, each with a range depending on the severity of what occurred. Which, as drastic as all that sounds, is the way our justice system works in the real world. In society, judges are given sentencing guidelines for those who break the law, allowing them to dole out punishment based on the seriousness of the act and the history of the perpetrator.

So who would oppose this? Not the players. I had Paul Kelly, the new director of the NHL Players Association, on my program after the Pronger suspension. I asked him whether suspension guidelines should be the same for all players regardless of who they are—and he said yes, he absolutely endorses that position. So if the union has no problem with it, why would the league refuse to follow through? It's simple. The owners know that getting suspended is a part of the culture of hockey. They believe that violence sells and they encourage it. And they know that every once in a while some player they count on to score goals or prevent them—like Pronger—is going to do something stupid. And they want to make sure that when he does there's a Get Out Of Jail Free card there to be played.

I've written earlier in this book about how holding coaches accountable by suspending them for what players do on the ice would curb violence in the sport tremendously. And while some scoffed at that notion when this book was first published, many people—including NHL commissioner Gary Bettman himself—were considering just that type of thing when the Flyers had three players suspended during the first few months of the 2007–08 season. But I'm convinced now that the NHL also needs a standardized code of crime and punishment and some actual deterrent. The league needs to be able to say "If you do this, you'll get this. And if you do it again, you'll get this. And if you keep doing it and don't get the message then you're going to be gone from the game forever." Because the perception right now is that getting suspended is a part of playing hockey. It's the price you pay to play a certain style and it's worth it because there's value in doing it. Players with a history of suspensions bring fear and danger to the ice and those two things are absolutely central to the culture of hockey.

What if we said that when you're suspended for a second time, the number of games you sit out doubles? And for a third time it triples? And if you happen to find yourself suspended for a fourth time, you are no longer able to seek employment in the NHL? I mean you really have to ask yourself why we have players who've been suspended four and five or eight times. It can only be because the punishment is not a deterrent. I defy anyone to cite the case of a team that got rid of a player because he'd received too many suspensions. You can't. In fact, in the case of Simon, it works the exact opposite way. He's only employable because he's got a reputation for being dangerous thanks to all those suspensions.

What may sound radical isn't really at all. But anything less wouldn't change the culture where injuring someone with a vicious act and then serving your time—dependent on who you are—is all part of the job in the NHL.

104.

Politicians usually have no business sticking their nose into sports matters. But Bob says Quebec Premier Jean Charest had it right when he called for an all-out ban on fighting in junior hockey after the much publicized Jonathan Roy goalie punch-up in March 2008.

MY POSITION on fighting in hockey couldn't be clearer.

Fighting is stupid. It's irrelevant. It's insulting to the players who play the game properly and the fans who pay to see it played that way. And it's dangerous. And while I've usually directed my attack on fighting at the professional ranks of hockey, I believe it's worth examining a little more closely the phenomenon of fighting in junior hockey and why it's so much more destructive than what goes on in the NHL.

First of all, junior hockey is a sport played by kids. Some junior hockey players are as young as 15 years old. So in theory, if you've got a 15 year-old out on the ice with a 19 or 20-year-old, you can have a fight between a minor and someone who's been an adult for nearly three years. On the street that would be assault of a minor. But in junior hockey somehow that doesn't bother people.

The amazing part of this to me is that the Canadian Hockey League, the umbrella for Canada's three major junior leagues, falls under the jurisdiction of Hockey Canada. And those would be the same folks at Hockey Canada who are always telling us how they're making the game safer for our kids to play. I mean if fighting is part of junior hockey because it makes the game safer (as many suggest) why not bring it in at the novice level? Let's see the nine-year-olds dropping the gloves? The one and only reason that junior hockey allows fighting is that the NHL needs a place to cultivate its next generation of goons. And since NHL teams pay junior clubs for developing players, the junior teams are only too happy to do whatever they're told.

And yet I'm dumbfounded that people flinch so little at the notion of teenagers bare-knuckle fighting before paid audiences in this country. Canadians like to think of themselves as a fairly civilized lot. We're supposedly more polite than most people on Earth and our rates of things such as violent crime are a mere fraction compared to those of our southern neighbours. And yet can you think of another country where this kind of thing would be tolerated? I can't.

Think back for a second to the outrage during the summer of 2007 when it was learned that Michael Vick was involved in a dog-fighting ring. People were made sick by the fact that this lowlife was participating in something as awful as putting two helpless dogs together to do battle for sport. There were protests every time he appeared in court. So okay, you tell me what's worse: people who profit from dogs fighting each other or people who profit from teenagers fighting each other? Think about that for a second.

The fact that junior hockey is marketed at families and young fans just makes this all the more abhorrent. I mean junior hockey players make school visits all the time and their images are actually on some of the publically funded materials handed out at schools. And so when a young fan goes to a junior hockey game and sees one player knock the snot out of another because of the way he looked at his captain, what's a kid supposed to think? How in the world do you turn around and suspend that kid the next week when he goes and does the same thing in the schoolyard? I mean aren't bullying, intimidation and violence the things we're trying to get out of schools? And yet they're all on display at the local junior hockey rink, perpetuated by the very players who are held up as role models to school kids.

The other thing that makes junior hockey fighting so loathsome is the constant peer pressure for players to drop the gloves, whether they want to or not. Fighting in pro hockey has evolved into a specialist's role, where the same two or three guys do most of the fighting. And in the NHL there are plenty of players who never fight at all. But in junior hockey there's peer pressure—and pressure from the scouts—to drop the gloves and mix it up. Even if a kid has no aspiration to be a fighter in the pros, he's got to drop the gloves in junior or he's going to be considered soft. And so the option of just playing hockey simply doesn't exist for all but the most highly-skilled kids.

Look, I'm glad the reaction to the Jonathan Roy incident in March 2008 was as loud as it was. I'm glad people were outraged that the great Patrick Roy had to be suspended for supposedly encouraging his son to skate the length of the ice to pound out his unwilling counterpart. Had this incident involved any other player, or any other coach, it would have passed as just one more fight night in junior hockey, which is actually what it was.

And if this incident does eventually result in junior hockey banning fights once and for all, then that—ironically—may be Patrick Roy's greatest contribution to hockey.

105. Every January, the CBC brings us *Hockey Day in Canada*, a full day of features and interviews about the goodness of hockey sandwiched in around three NHL games involving all six of Canada's teams. But are all those stories of small-town rinks and smiling faces a realistic portrait of hockey in Canada? No way, says Bob.

THE ONE THING I can't stand about most hockey fans is the way they romanticize their sport into some metaphor for life in Canada. You'd think we were all born in frozen outposts where all we did was play hockey and dream of making it to the NHL.

And nothing perpetuates this myth more than the phenomenon known as *Hockey Day in Canada*, a CBC invention that tries to blur the line between the American-based entertainment business known as the National Hockey League and all those kiddies who supposedly play the sport for the love of the game. The problem is, I don't believe what I see on *Hockey Day in Canada*. More specifically, I think the picture presented of Canadian hockey as this world of happy, well-balanced kids and adults all getting along famously is pure fantasy.

First of all, the vast majority of Canadians live in big urban centres where the costs associated with kids playing hockey are soaring. And yet you sure wouldn't know this the way Hockey Day jumps around from one tiny town to another, as if that's all there is that dots this great land.

But what really gets to me about *Hockey Day* is that it's billed as a celebration of all things good in hockey when in fact there's a whole lot of stuff that's wrong with hockey. So I want to know: where is *that* show? Where's *Hockey Sucks Day in Canada*—that's the day I'm interested in. The day when non-hockey people are engaged in serious and deliberate debate on the issues that really envelope this game.

I'm just not that interested in the story of another 12-year-old who grew up on the wrong side of the tracks and eats, breaths, and sleeps hockey. Or the town that has a rink with a roof that is falling apart and some benefactor comes through with $50,000 for a new one. Or the NHL player who sends used and smelly equipment to some place in Northern Saskatchewan so a bunch of kids can play. All that stuff is fine, I guess. But what about all the issues *Hockey Day* excludes—the ones no one wants to talk about. Let's have a day when we have eight hours of programming about brawls and concussions and lost eyes. Let's talk about coaches who abuse their players. Let's talk about paedophilia and how it's perpetuated in hockey. Junior hockey conducted a commission on that but now no one wants to talk about it.

Let's talk about Mike Danton and examine just how he became estranged from his family and taken in under the watchful eye of his minor hockey coach and later agent David Frost, whom he subsequently tried to have killed. Let's talk about Stu Hyman, that guy who at one time controlled something like 90 teams in the Greater Toronto Hockey League. Let's talk about why we feel the need to have levels of hockey where kids are on the ice five nights a week, and being driven for two or three hours to get to and from games. Let's talk about whether there are enough arenas and how we pay for them. Let's talk about how many kids play hockey and, more importantly, how many don't. And then let's talk about how many leave the game at 13 or 14 and why there's no such thing as midget hockey in much of this country. Let's talk about the thousands of dollars it costs to have your kid play for a pee wee triple-A team. Let's talk about why we feel the need for there to be bodychecking in minor hockey, so bigger kids can crush smaller ones.

This notion that we all play hockey and love the grand old game is ridiculous because if that's true, then why are kids quitting? Where are those stories? Let's talk about all the unsavory stuff that no one wants to talk about. *Hockey Day in Canada* doesn't deal with any of these things. That's why I'd love to see *Anti-Hockey Day in Canada*, a day of reality and scepticism when the question can be asked: "is this the game you really want?"

ACKNOWLEDGEMENTS

David Naylor:
Thanks first of all to the staff at Doubleday Canada for all their work, especially editor Nick Massey-Garrison who was a great sounding board throughout and was the rudder of this project from start to finish.

Special acknowledgement goes to Sean Farrell of Montreal who took time out from his work for the Associated Press to do research, and Dan Moscoe of Toronto whose insight and attention to detail were invaluable in putting together the manuscript.

I have to mention my good friend Alec Milne of Ottawa, who's way too smart to be a sportswriter but was handy to have around for tips and feedback as the work came together.

I'm always telling people the best thing about sports writing is the conversations you have after the games are done, when the colleagues from your own and rival papers gather to re-hash a night's events and unlock the problems of the sports world. To that end I'd like to give thanks for those great conversations that give birth to new ideas in places such as Hurley's Irish Pub in Montreal, where just down the road from the Bell Centre I've been able to share many a late-night debate with friends such as Matt Sekeres, Chris Stevenson and Stephen Brunt, way past all of our bed times. I learn more from guys like them—and many others in the sports writing fraternity—than anyone.

I'd also like to thank Bob McCown, who probably doesn't recall our first conversation in about 1980 when he was hosting *Talking of Sports* on CKFH in Toronto and I was a nervous 12-year-old on the other end of the phone. I listened to Bob religiously in those days, and he was as much an idol of mine as any athlete of the time. Back when I answered a trivia question on his show to win a free car wash, the notion of one day working alongside him on a book would have seemed pure fantasy.

And finally, I'd like to thank my wife, Kimberly, and my children, Kevin and Mary Madison, who put up with nearly a year of me saying goodnight to them at the dinner table before walking down the hall to my home office and burying myself in hockey arguments for the rest of the night. Thanks for everything.

Bob McCown:

Everyone—at least, everyone I know—believes they have a book in them waiting to get out. I suppose I was the same, except that this wasn't the book.

More than a year ago, the phone rang and at the other end was Nick Garrison from Doubleday. "Are you interested in doing a book?" he asked. "No," I responded, although I really didn't mean no. What I meant was yes, I was interested, but I'd been asked before and there were always more reasons to say no than yes. Like, lots of work for not much money.

But Nick didn't want to do just any book, he wanted to do a book about hockey and could we meet to discuss it. This was a trap and I realized immediately that if I took the meeting it was going to be very difficult to turn him down, face to face, which is why I agreed. (I have no self-control.)

Now had I compiled a list of topics I might consider for

my first offering as an author, hockey would not have been at the top. Hell, it wouldn't even have been on the list. I figured: What we certainly do not need in this country is another book about hockey!

But Nick and the Doubleday folks didn't want another ode to the great game, rather they were presenting me with an opportunity to slag the crap out of it . . . if I so chose. One hundred chapters . . . one hundred opinions . . . one hundred arguments. Yummy! "I can say anything?" I asked. "Yes." "Then I'm in."

But now came the reality that I might actually have to do some work. Having spent 32 years in radio and television, "work," by the purest definition, was not something with which I was intimately familiar. So, since I had little, if any, experience in the field of work, the Doubleday people suggested a co-author. "How does this work? I asked. "Well, the co-author will talk to you and then put your words on paper." "So I talk and he writes?" "More or less." This was getting better and better.

Turned out, choosing the collaborator was easy. They had two suggestions and one was David Naylor of *The Globe and Mail* who I knew and whose work I respected. Naylor was in. And so it began.

Over the next six months, David would call me with a topic or two and we'd talk about them. If I didn't like the topic or didn't have a strong opinion on it, we'd throw it out. But I'd say nine out of ten are in the book. All of the ideas and opinions are mine, but all of the background information and statistics are Naylor's. David did an unbelievable amount of work to provide statistical or anecdotal support for my opinions. I think it's all true—but damned if I know.

While we were working on the book, it seemed to me that Naylor and Garrison were deliberately keeping me out of the loop. When I talked to Nick, it seemed he had always just gotten off the phone with David and vice versa. Nick kept telling me how much he enjoyed a particular chapter that David had e-mailed him. "Great," I'd say, "Glad you liked it. I especially liked that one too!" But most of time I had no idea what freaking chapter he was talking about. Paranoia prevailed. Were they trying to squeeze me out of my own book?

And, in the end, that really is the point.

This isn't *my* book. It's *our* book. David's, Nick's . . . and mine. Without the two of them, there isn't a blue line's chance in hell you would be reading this right now. And without me? Hmmm. Paranoia again.

So thanks, David. Thanks, Nick. Thanks, Doubleday folks.

But mostly, thanks to the morons and boneheads who run hockey, especially the NHL, 'cause without your incompetence, writing this might not have been possible, and it certainly wouldn't have been nearly as much fun.